Formational Leadership

Formational Leadership

Developing Spiritual and Emotional
Maturity in Toxic Leaders

MARCUS K. KILIAN

WIPF & STOCK · Eugene, Oregon

FORMATIONAL LEADERSHIP
Developing Spiritual and Emotional Maturity in Toxic Leaders

Copyright © 2018 Marcus K. Kilian. All rights reserved. Except for brief quotations in critical publications or reviews, no part of this book may be reproduced in any manner without prior written permission from the publisher. Write: Permissions, Wipf and Stock Publishers, 199 W. 8th Ave., Suite 3, Eugene, OR 97401.

Wipf & Stock
An Imprint of Wipf and Stock Publishers
199 W. 8th Ave., Suite 3
Eugene, OR 97401

www.wipfandstock.com

PAPERBACK ISBN: 978-1-5326-3418-5
HARDCOVER ISBN: 978-1-5326-3420-8
EBOOK ISBN: 978-1-5326-3419-2

Manufactured in the U.S.A.

The Asbury Journal granted permission to quote from Randy L. Maddox, "John Wesley and Eastern Orthodoxy: Influences, Convergences, and Differences" (*Asbury Theological Journal* 45/2 [1990] 29–53). HarperCollins Publishers granted permission to quote from N. T. Wright, *After You Believe: Why Christian Character Matters* (New York: HarperCollins, 2010).

Contents

List of Figures | vii
List of Tables | viii
Preface | ix
Acknowledgements | xiii

Chapter 1: Introduction | 1

Chapter 2: Toxic Secular and Christian Leadership | 13
    Abuse of Power in Secular and Christian Organizations | 14
        Secular Contexts | 14
        Christian Contexts | 24
    Development of Personality Disorders | 30
        Model of Four Personality Styles and Leader Types | 32
        Narcissism and Perfectionism | 35
    Conclusion | 41

Chapter 3: Wesleyan Spirituality | 43
    The Historical and Social Context | 43
    Wesley's Influences and Formation | 45
    Theological Foundations: Anthropology, Hamartiology, and
        Soteriology | 50
    Conclusion | 56

Chapter 4: *Orthokardia*: **Spiritual and Emotional Maturity** | 58
    Christian Perfection: Love for God, Others, and Self | 59
    Healthy Emotional Development | 66
        Attachment Theory | 66
        Bowen's Family Systems Theory | 71
    Implications for Leadership Development | 78
    Conclusion | 84

Chapter 5: *Orthodynamis*: Right Power Motives and Christian Affections | 86
    Virtue Ethics: The Contributions of Aristotle and Biblical Ethics | 87
    Religious/ Christian Affections | 93
        Three Key Christian Affections: Humility, Gratitude, and Compassion | 97
    Power and Influence and Leadership | 104
    Means of Grace | 111
    Implications for Leadership Development | 117
    Conclusion | 123

Chapter 6: *Orthopraxis*: Right and Just Leadership Practices | 126
    Wesleyan Spirituality and Postmodern Thought and Culture | 127
    Wesley's Social Ethics and Justice | 130
    Organizational Cultures Based on Social Holiness and Justice | 138
    Implications for Leadership Development | 145
    Conclusion | 148

Chapter 7: Summary and Final Conclusion | 152

Appendix
    Leader Personality Style Questionnaire | 159
    Formational Leadership Culture Questionnaire | 162
Bibliography | 165

Figures

Figure 1	Relationships between Orthokardia, Orthodynamis, and Orthopraxis	8
Figure 2	Relationship between Leadership Effectiveness and Emotional and Spiritual Maturity	9
Figure 3	Four Personality Styles / Leader Types	33
Figure 4	Orbitofrontal Cortex (OFC)	69
Figure 5	Personality Styles and Attachment Styles	79
Figure 6	Relationships between Humility, Gratitude, and Compassion	111
Figure 7	Personality Styles, Power Motives, and Christian Affections	122
Figure 8	Relationships between Orthokardia, Orthodynamis, and Orthopraxis	150

Tables

Table 1   Power Sources, Power Types, and Influence Processes | 105

Table 2   Power Motives and Christian Power Stages | 108

Table 3   Power Sources, Power Types, Influence Processes, and Leadership Styles | 110

Preface

I WAS BORN AND grew up in Germany and enculturated in a context that was critical of toxic charismatic leadership in the light of Adolf Hitler's negative legacy and the resulting atrocities of the Holocaust. During the 1970s and 80s, while I was in primary and secondary school, I witnessed that many Germans had been very suspicious of nationalism and patriotism. In addition, German people became very wary about abusive power after World War II.[1] Unfortunately, I have also witnessed toxic leadership in Christian contexts at times, which was very disappointing for me. Leadership in general and Christian leadership in particular needs to embody Christian virtues, which necessitates self-awareness and humility to receive feedback from others, including followers. Having lived in and having been acculturated to the United States of America for twenty-plus years, I now see the benefits of transformational leadership approaches as long as the leader's motives are pure and non-abusive. Thus, leadership power is value neutral and can either be positive for followers and society or negative, as abusive political leaders have demonstrated (i.e., Hitler, Lenin, Stalin, Saddam Hussein, etc.).

As a Christian psychologist in private practice and as a practical theologian, I am very passionate about this topic. In my work with personality disordered clients over the years, of whom several of them were Christian leaders, I have learned that personality disorders can reduce one's emotional awareness and often cause people to justify and rationalize sinful actions. I am passionate about interdisciplinary studies, in particular integrating my three academic backgrounds in this current study. I graduated with an MDiv degree in pastoral counseling and Christian formation from a Pentecostal seminary that has strong Wesleyan roots. My faith journey also includes practicing spiritual disciplines before and since that time. I had been raised Catholic and over the last six-plus years have revisited

---

1. Kessler, "Leadership and Power," 531.

these roots by attending silent retreats and by consulting a spiritual director now for five-plus years. I am a member of a Pentecostal church, but I have a deep appreciation for the contemplative Christian tradition. As an introvert by nature, I experience God the most in silence. I also studied clinical psychology (PsyD) and organizational leadership (Certificate of Advanced Graduate Studies) on a postgraduate level. This study is adapted from my thesis for a MTh degree in theological ethics with specialization in Christian leadership at the University of South Africa (UNISA). Thus, this study is the culmination of ten-plus years researching toxic leadership from a clinical/developmental psychology background and from a theological and organizational leadership perspective. In addition, this study includes what I have learned over the last twelve-plus years from working with personality-disordered clients in Christian and non-Christian contexts, of whom several were Christian leaders.

In this interdisciplinary study I address the problem of toxic leadership, especially in Christian contexts. Toxic leadership behaviors of narcissistic and obsessive-compulsive leaders will be emphasized. To counteract toxic Christian leadership, this study proposes a leadership development model, called formational leadership, which is based on Wesleyan spirituality. In particular, Wesleyan theology serves as a foundation for this study and Wesleyan spirituality, including Pentecostal and monastic spiritualities, provide the means for the formation process. Formational leadership emphasizes the spiritual, emotional, and ethical development processes in the leader and includes an analysis of *orthokardia*, *orthodynamis*, and *orthopraxis*. These components have a circular relationship with one another. *Orthokardia* ("right heart") includes the concepts of spiritual and emotional maturity, which a Christian leader needs to develop in order to become an ethical and effective leader. *Orthodynamis* ("right power") includes pure power and influence motives based on Christian affections, which should inform formational leadership. *Orthopraxis* ("right practices") refers to right and "just" leadership behaviors informed by Wesley's social holiness and justice values, which need to be adopted as organizational core values. The implications of these components for leadership development are outlined in chapters 4–6, which include practical steps for helping toxic leaders change their dysfunctional and sinful intentions and behaviors. In addition, after chapters 1–6 the reader will find reflection exercises and questions that could be utilized for one's personal formation process towards spiritual and emotional maturity and the development of Christian affections.

I wrote this book for pastors and other Christian leaders as well as for executive coaches and spiritual directors. It is also written for seminary students and for graduate students who study leadership at Christian universities. My hope is that this study will be both a manual for restoring toxic Christian leaders *and* a tool for preventing toxic Christian leadership. God loves his church and desires for all of his followers to be one (see John 17:21), which means to have unity in diversity and the absence of abusive behaviors.

Acknowledgements

First of all, I would like to express my appreciation and gratitude to Professor Kretzschmar at the University of South Africa (UNISA) for embodying the three Christian affections of humility, gratitude, and compassion. Her balanced approach of providing support and gentle challenge has made me a better researcher. In addition, I would like to thank Dr. Matt Thompson for inspiring me to explore Wesley's Eastern theological origins. I am also thankful to him for proofreading chapters 3 and 6 and for providing minor feedback comments on content, such as on Wesley's theology, American evangelicalism, and postmodernism. Furthermore, I would like to thank my wife, Dawn, for encouraging me to take time away from her and our children to work on this book. Above all, I am very grateful to our God, who inspired and guided me throughout this research and writing process. "For everything comes from him and exists by his power and is intended for his glory. All glory to him forever! Amen" (Romans 11:36, NLT).

Chapter 1

Introduction

IN THIS STUDY I propose a theoretical Christian leadership development model informed by Wesleyan spirituality. My purpose of writing this book was to provide a prophetic vision for ethical Christian leadership based on spiritual and emotional maturity in the leader. It is prophetic because Christian leaders are being used by God to affect their contexts.[1] Barna observed in the late 1990s that the church is "paralyzed by the absence of godly leadership."[2] The situation has not improved since then, but appears to have become worse due to the absence of moral absolutes prevalent in contemporary postmodern societies[3] and the narcissistic entitlement of the Millennial generation.[4] The Body of Christ is not immune to these post-Christian societal influences that often produce corrupt and abusive leadership practices. Because of these influences, Kretzschmar argues that spiritual formation is essential for Christian leadership development.[5] Therefore, this model will conceptualize the process of leadership formation based on the Wesleyan spiritual formation tradition. I will identify and define relevant Christian personality traits that need to be developed in Christian leaders to meet the challenges that the current postmodern society poses. There are various definitions of Christian leadership and leaders. Kretzschmar defines leaders as: ". . . people who have willing followers . . . have an impact on the lives and views of people, and on situations and structures . . . people who are able to inspire, encourage and guide others."[6] One emphasis within this defini-

1. Kretzschmar, "Indispensability," 351.
2. Barna, *Second Coming*, 101
3. Veith, *Postmodern Times*.
4. White, *Church in an Age*, 73; and Twenge and Campbell, *Narcissism Epidemic*, 123.
5. Kretzschmar, "Indispensability," 339.
6. Kretzschmar, "Authentic Christian Leadership," 46.

tion appears to be on inspiring and encouraging followers, which refers to visionary/charismatic leadership. Barna defines a Christian leader as ". . . someone who is called by God to lead and possess virtuous character and effectively motivates, mobilizes resources, and directs people toward the fulfillment of a jointly embraced vision from God."[7] This definition connotes the "being" and "doing" of effective Christian leadership and points to embodied virtue ethics. Thus, Christian leadership is inherently value-based and is informed by Christian traditions and perceptions of spirituality. For example, Christian leadership from a Catholic perspective may emphasize Thomas Aquinas's theology whereas a Lutheran perspective may emphasize Luther's theology that focuses on justifying grace. Christian spirituality (or in the Catholic tradition, spiritual theology) can be viewed as "first-order theology" and can be defined as "the act of reflecting on the mystery of God and his relationship with the created universe, especially the *human* experience of God" with the emphasis on the ordinary believer.[8]

Christian spirituality should include a strong communal orientation that also addresses social justice and ecological issues.[9] Wesleyan spirituality consists of both personal and social holiness. When it comes to personal holiness, Wesleyan spirituality emphasizes the process of sanctification, human freedom, and religious affections.[10] One of these three elements, sanctification, points to and implies the process of spiritual formation. Mulholland provides one of several definitions of spiritual formation from a Wesleyan perspective and views it as "a process of being conformed to the image of Christ for the sake of others."[11] This definition is particularly helpful for Christian leadership, since it includes how the effects of spiritual formation impact "others" and connotes the interdependent nature of the Body of Christ (cf. 1 Cor 12:12–31). This definition has powerful implications for Christian leadership development. Holt extends this definition by including love for God, self, others, and love for whole creation, which also addresses the leader's role of attending to the environment, social justice issues, etc.[12] In order to successfully participate in spiritual formation, the Christian leader needs self-awareness.[13] In the absence of self-awareness, the Christian leader needs to be humble enough to be open to feedback from others.

7. Barna, *Second Coming*, 107.
8. Maas and O'Donnell, "Introduction," 12.
9. Kretzschmar, "Indispensability," 343–44.
10. Kilian and Parker, *Spiritual Formation*, 201
11. Mulholland, *Invitation to a Journey*, 12.
12. Holt, *Thirsty for God*, 23–28.
13. Kretzschmar, "Indispensability," 345.

The Wesleyan tradition was influenced by the contemplative tradition as evidenced by Wesley's emphasis on spiritual disciplines, such as prayer and corporate confession (in his "societies") as well as the "disciplines of abstinence" (fasting from food, abstaining from sex for a short time, silence, simplicity, etc.).[14] It is well known that this movement heavily influenced Wesley. In turn, Wesleyan spirituality influenced the development of the Pentecostal movement and spirituality. Pentecostal believers, especially Wesleyan Pentecostals, belong to one of three groups that comprise evangelicalism in America.[15] More recently, evangelicalism also includes socially aware evangelicals or *left-wing* evangelicals.[16] The American neo-evangelical theologian, Carl Henry, included social ethics by emphasizing social transformation in addition to individual conversion, which provided an impetus for separating fundamentalism from evangelicalism.[17]

A contemporary example of socially aware evangelical theology is the American evangelical social activist, Jim Wallis, who established Sojourners in the early 1970.[18] Sojourners is a non-profit organization that focuses on bridging social justice with biblical spiritual renewal. Wallis writes about biblical politics (neither promoting left- nor right-wing party ideologies), anti-war, economic justice, and social issues (race, abortion, etc.). In one of his books he asserts,

> Sojourners has focused on the environment and the increasing Christian activism—much of it evangelical—that is rising up to offer new leadership. It may well be that only theology—good theology—can save the Earth now.[19]

Thus, socially aware evangelical theology integrates the evangelical emphasis on individual conversion and faith in Jesus Christ with social activism thereby following the biblical mandate in its entirety (pursuing individual and

---

14. Tracy, "Spiritual Direction," 127.

15. Oden states that there are "three houses" of evangelicalism: "Reformed, liturgical, and pietistic." The Reformed group includes classic Protestants (Lutheran, Reformed, Baptist); the liturgical group includes Anglican, Roman, and Eastern Orthodox evangelical believers; and the pietistic group is comprised of Wesleyan evangelicals, the "holiness traditions of evangelical revivalism," and Pentecostal (and charismatic) believers, which have come out of the holiness tradition. Noted in Oden, *John Wesley's*, 11. Among Pentecostals there are two types: the older Wesleyan/Methodistic type (Church of God in Christ, Church of God–Cleveland, TN, Pentecostal Holiness, etc.) and the newer baptistic type (Assemblies of God, etc.). Noted in Synan, *Holiness-Pentecostal*, 153.

16. Grenz, *Renewing the Center*.

17. Ibid., 95.

18. Wallis, *God's Politics*.

19. Ibid., 353.

corporate salvation and justice). Wesleyan spirituality has always emphasized the social activism that was inherent in Wesley's understanding of imparted righteousness as evidenced by Wesley's critiques of injustices in eighteenth-century England (slavery, inhumane prisons, etc.).[20] In chapter 6, I will also incorporate key insights from socially aware Wesleyan evangelicalism.

In this next section, I will define the concepts and terms that are utilized in this book:

Toxic leadership refers to the abuse of leadership power that *directly* results in interpersonal emotional, physical, and sexual harm in followers. Implied in this definition is the assumption that toxic leadership stems from personality disorder traits in leaders.

Wesleyan spirituality is defined as a form of Christian spirituality that focuses on personal and social holiness. In particular, it brings the believer:

> into the experience of sanctifying grace whereby inner sin is cleansed, the image of God restored, and the heart so filled with divine love that the believer can love God with all the heart, mind, soul and strength and the neighbor as one's self.[21]

Wesleyan spirituality includes experiencing the presence of God through the Holy Spirit.

While there are several definitions of *spiritual maturity*, I will define it according to Wesleyan spirituality. Spiritual maturity is Christian perfection that consists of the dynamic change process of the believer into God's image based on sanctifying grace and the believer's cooperation. Sanctification includes the cleansing of the heart from impurities to produce pure intentions within the heart to avoid voluntary or conscious sin.[22] Loving God, others, and self, are important indicators of spiritual maturity that reflect this change process.

Emotional maturity is defined as a psychological state that reflects a sufficiently developed *self*, characterized by the ability to "be an individual in a group" and by being "responsible for [oneself] and neither foster[ing] nor participat[ing] in the irresponsibility of others.[23]" Thus, emotional maturity equals interdependence that is achieved through the process of differentiation.[24] In addition, Godwin's "reasoning muscles" illustrate emotional maturity, which are awareness, humility, reliability, responsibility, and empathy.[25]

20. Thompson, "Social Involvement," 707–8.
21. Tracy, "Spiritual Direction," 116.
22. Oden, *John Wesley's*, 315; Lindström, *Wesley and Sanctification*, 129.
23. Kerr and Bowen, *Family Evaluation*, 97.
24. Cf. Fairbairn, *Object Relations Theory*.
25. Godwin, *How to Solve*, 65.

Formational leadership is the proposed dynamic leadership development model that consists of *orthokardia*, *orthodynamis*, and *orthopraxis*. Formational leadership is informed by Wesleyan spirituality and focuses on the development of spiritual and emotional maturity in the Christian leader, which includes the development of Christian virtues/affections. It is assumed that a Christian leader who cooperates with the Holy Spirit to become more like Christ (sanctification) produces right motives that result in right leadership behaviors.

Orthokardia is the first component in the proposed model and includes the concepts of spiritual maturity and emotional maturity. According to Scazzero,[26] we cannot separate spiritual maturity from emotional maturity. I have met many Christian clients and fellow church members over the years who claimed to be spiritually mature, but still displayed passive-aggressive behaviors, held grudges, or struggled with being assertive with others. For this reason, *orthokardia* includes both concepts.

Orthodynamis is the second component in the model and includes right power and influence motives that should inform formational leadership. These power motives are based on three key Christian affections (humility, gratitude, and compassion).

Orthopraxis is the third component in the model and refers to right and just leadership behaviors informed by Wesley's social holiness and justice values. In addition, the three key Christian affections (humility, gratitude, and compassion) are included in these values. These values need to be adopted as organizational core values that influence right leadership practices and behaviors.

Transformational leadership has been defined as an effective leadership style that emphasizes motivating, challenging, and empowering followers[27] and is concerned with "emotions, values, ethics, standards, and long-term goals."[28] I see transformational leadership as an aspect of formational leadership among other leadership styles and models (e.g., Primal Leadership).

Similar to transformational leadership and identified in transformational leadership research, *authentic leadership* generally refers to "*authenticity* of leaders and their leadership."[29] In particular, authentic leaders "are genuine people who are true to themselves and to what they believe," which refers to integrity and moral strength.[30] It relates to morality and virtuous character needed for Christian leadership.

26. Scazzero, *Emotionally Healthy Spirituality*.
27. Bass and Avolio, "Transformational Leadership."
28. Northouse, *Leadership*, 171.
29. Ibid., 205.
30. George and Sims, *True North*, 205.

Emotional intelligence is defined as a set of abilities that consist of "being able to motivate oneself and persist in the face of frustrations; to control impulses and delay gratification; to regulate one's moods [and]. . .to empathize."[31] "Emotional intelligence includes "self-awareness" and "self-management" skills.[32] It is related to emotional maturity regarding coping and relationship behaviors.

Very similar to emotional intelligence, *social intelligence* refers to skills that are informed by the "social brain," such as "interaction synchrony" (being able to read non-verbal cues, etc.), "empathy, social cognition, interaction skills, and concern for others" (compassion).[33] It includes skills that reflect "social awareness" and "social facility (or relationship management).[34]" Emotional intelligence can be viewed as the prerequisite for social intelligence. For example, we can empathize for others, but we may not have compassion or concern for others. Thus, social intelligence includes prosocial values and morality.

Primal leadership is a leadership model that focuses on leadership practices of emotionally intelligent leaders.[35] It consists of "self-awareness" and "self-management" that constitutes "personal competence" and "social awareness" and "relationship management," which refers to "social competence."[36] Personal competence refers to emotional intelligence and social competence resembles social intelligence, but it does not include "concern for others" or "compassion."

In this book I outline a relational leadership development model that incorporates various academic disciplines. It can thus be considered trans-disciplinary in character by integrating Wesleyan spirituality with two different sub-disciplines of behavioral sciences, namely leadership studies and developmental/clinical psychology. I would like to demonstrate that formational leadership informed by Wesleyan spirituality must begin with a "right" or pure heart resulting from sanctifying grace that includes loving God, others, and self. The second component of the model includes having pure motives, which refers to "right" power as opposed to abusive power motives. This part also includes Christian affections/virtues. Finally, the model includes "right" leadership practices and behaviors, which in turn affect the leader's heart and motives via feedback processes from others. Thus, formational leadership is a relational leadership development model that

---

31. Goleman, *Emotional Intelligence*, 34.
32. Goleman, *Social Intelligence*, 331.
33. Ibid., 329.
34. Ibid., 331.
35. Goleman et al., *Primal Leadership*, 38.
36. Ibid., 39.

emphasizes loving God first, loving others including creation,[37] and loving oneself. This model also emphasizes accountability relationships between the leader and God mediated through mature mentors and/or spiritual directors. It outlines practical steps to develop Christian virtues, prevent and remedy the abuse of power, and outlines a plan to develop effective leadership practices by emphasizing principles drawn from Wesleyan spirituality.

I hypothesize that the more the Christian leader has achieved spiritual and emotional maturity (*orthokardia*) and the presence of humility, gratitude, and compassion (*orthodynamis*) displayed by the Christian leader, the more effectively he or she practices godly leadership. Leadership effectiveness is defined here as being able to lead under stressful conditions by skillfully managing personal anxiety, by being able to engage in successful conflict resolution with followers and colleagues, and by promoting cooperation in groups and organizations, etc., which are similar to the self-management and relationship management leadership competencies in the *Primal Leadership model*.[38] The formational leadership development model assumes a circular causality, meaning a "right" or pure heart causes "right" power and influence processes in Christian leaders, which result in "right" and effective leadership practices. At the same time, "right" leadership practices affect the "heart" of the Christian leader including power and influence processes through feedback processes.

The main question that I wanted to answer in this book is, "how can Christian toxic leaders be developed through Wesleyan spirituality and insights from Bowen's Family Systems theory and Attachment theory to develop spiritual and emotional maturity that produce ethical behavior patterns?" The following questions illustrate this question more in detail:

1. What is toxic leadership and what are its psychological and spiritual causes?

2. What is Wesleyan spirituality and how do key theological concepts inform Wesleyan spirituality?

3. What is spiritual and emotional maturity and how can they be developed to counteract toxic leadership?

4. What are right power motives and which Christian affections and virtues are especially needed in Christian leaders to counteract toxic leadership?

---

37. The importance of attending to creation as part of the sanctification process will be addressed in chapter 6 of this book, where I discuss social holiness and justice.

38. Goleman et al., *Primal Leadership*, 39.

5. What are just leadership practices and how can Christian organizations be developed to reflect social holiness and justice?

In chapter 2 of this book I will answer question 1 by discussing toxic leadership in secular and Christian contexts and by outlining the development of personality disorders with the focus on narcissism and perfectionism. In chapter 3 I will answer question 2 by exploring Wesleyan spirituality. Chapter 4 of this book will answer question 3 by defining spiritual and emotional development (*orthokardia*[39]). The Wesleyan concept of entire perfection describes spiritual maturity, whereas emotional maturity is defined by drawing from two psychological theories, especially from family systems theory that emphasizes the concept of differentiation, which, along with spiritual maturity, will counteract toxic leadership. Question 4 will be answered by chapter 5 of this book in which three key Christian affections and virtues are proposed and right power motives are described (*orthodynamis*). Finally, chapter 6 answers question 5 by exploring just leadership practices that are needed to develop Christian organizations that reflect social holiness and justice (*orthopraxis*). The following figure illustrates the three components of the model:

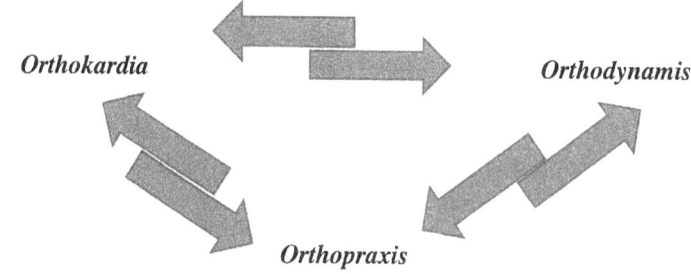

Figure 1: Relationships between Orthokardia, Orthodynamis, and Orthopraxis

Orthokardia is the starting point in the model based on God's prevenient, justifying, and above all, sanctifying grace, which requires the active cooperation of the believer.

---

39. *Orthokardia* is a neologism Clapper created (see Clapper, "Orthokardia"). *Orthokardia*, *orthopraxis*, and *orthodoxy* are components that were used in Clapper's dissertation as well as in Maddox's writings, as noted in Clapper, *Renewal*, 92. This study utilizes a similar threefold pattern, but adds *orthodynamis* due to its relevance to Christian leadership.

INTRODUCTION

Orthokardia refers to having pure motives as evidenced by loving God, others, and self ("'Love the Lord your God with all your heart and with all your soul and with all your mind.' ... 'Love your neighbor as yourself,'" Matt 22:37-39, NIV). *Orthodynamis* focuses on right power and influence which is associated with the Christian affections, in particular humility, gratitude, and compassion. *Orthopraxis* refers to right leadership practices. *Orthokardia* reflects an ontological change in the believer (the "pure heart") due to God's sanctifying grace and provides the spiritual and psychological foundation for the other two. Leffel, Fritz, and Stephens[40] proposed a model that describe "moral affective capacities" similar to the concept of Christian affections in this dissertation. The authors describe the following components:

> Specifically, our review suggests that the moral emotion-related capacities of *trust*, *love*, and *elevation* [or admiration] are associated (primarily) with the motive to bond (Attachment system); *empathy* and *compassion/sympathy* with the motive to help (Altruism); *gratitude* and *positive pride* with the motive to mutuality (Reciprocity); and *guilt*, *forgiveness*, and *humility* with the motive to "get it right"(Reparation).[41]

As I stated above, as the leader grows in sanctifying grace and increases his or her spiritual and emotional maturity, the leader increases his or her leadership effectiveness. Thus, this proposed leadership development model is dynamic and constitutes an expansion of current Christian leadership models that are mostly static in nature. It is dynamic due to its mutually informing constructs and its linear growth projections. The more the leader grows in sanctifying grace the more he or she improves his or her leadership effectiveness:

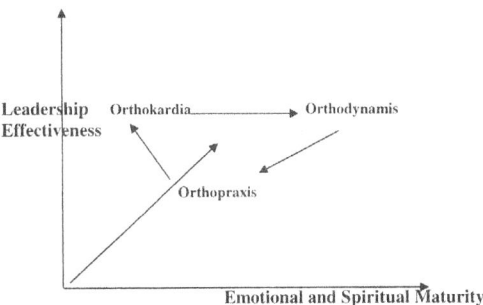

Figure 2: Relationship between Leadership Effectiveness and Emotional and Spiritual Maturity

40. Leffel et al., "Who Cares?," 202.
41. Ibid., 211.

This model is congruent with Wesleyan spirituality. Wesley's doctrine of entire sanctification and Christian perfection is one of the distinctions of Wesleyan spirituality, which is based on sanctifying grace.[42] Sanctification according to Wesley requires the circumcision and cleansing of the heart from impurities, which are sinful dispositions.[43] This process produces pure intentions within the heart to avoid voluntary or conscious sin.[44] This book includes Wesley's writing (primary sources) and Wesleyan theologians with the emphasis on spirituality. I used these findings to develop the theological basis of the model and integrated them with leadership studies and clinical/developmental psychology.

Now I will survey secular and Christian leadership theories as well as key sources on Wesleyan leadership. Secular leadership theories that are utilized for this study are transformational leadership, authentic leadership, and primal leadership. Since the 1980s, transformational leadership has gained wide acceptance in the field of leadership studies.[45] Transformational leadership is rooted in Burns's transforming leadership theory.[46] There are many models of transformational leadership.[47] All models share the focus on effective leadership behaviors, such as empowering and encouraging followers, vision casting, and considering the followers' needs.

A more recent leadership model, called authentic leadership, is also relevant for this study. There are also several authentic leadership approaches, but this book will only include George's practical authentic leadership approach that focuses on the characteristics of authentic leaders.[48] His approach includes five characteristic, such as having a purpose, possessing strong values, establishing trusting relationships, self-discipline, and be-

---

42. Kilian and Parker, "Wesleyan Spirituality," 205.

43. Oden, *John Wesley's*, 315.

44. Lindström, *Wesley and Sanctification*, 129.

45. Conger, "Charismatic."

46. Cf. Burns, *Leadership*. However, Meier ("Shedding Light," 139, 142) points out that Burns's transforming leadership is always concerned with the organizational goal (organizational success, etc.) as well as with the means to reach the goal by stressing the ethical motives and behaviors of the leader, whereas Bass's transformational leadership primarily focuses on the success of the organization while also emphasizing the moral character of the leader. Bass's transformational leadership reflects American economic pragmatism more than transforming leadership.

47. Bass, *Leadership*; Bass, *Transformational Leadership*; Bass and Avolio, *Improving Organizational*; Bennis and Nanus, *Leaders*; Conger and Kanungo, "Toward a Behavioral," 1987; Conger and Kanungo, *Charismatic Leadership*; Kouzes and Posner, *Leadership Challenge*; Sashkin, "Visionary Leader"; Sashkin and Sashkin, *Leadership That Matters*; Kotter and Heskett, *Corporate Culture*.

48. Northouse, *Leadership*, 211; George, *Authentic Leadership*.

ing passionate about one's mission (meaning to act from the heart, which includes compassion).⁴⁹

Primal leadership theory developed by Goleman, Boyatzis, and McKee⁵⁰ includes the concepts of emotional intelligence and social intelligence. It consists of two major competency domains: Personal and social competence. Personal competence consists of self-awareness (emotional self-awareness, accurate self-assessment, and self-confidence) and self-management (emotional self-control, transparency, adaptability, achievement, initiative, and optimism), whereas social competence includes social awareness (empathy, organizational awareness, and service) and relationship management (inspirational leadership, influence, developing others, change catalyst, conflict management, building bonds, and teamwork and collaboration)⁵¹ This model grew out of Goleman's emotional (and social) intelligence concept.⁵²

There are several Christian leadership models that emphasize and presuppose virtue ethics and Christian character development.⁵³ For example, Hayford mentions the "integrity of the heart" as the most important indicator of Christian leadership.⁵⁴ Ford's Character/Competency Model begins with Christian character development and includes four components: "spirituality-growing a leader's heart for God, leadership understanding and skills, evangelism understanding and skills, and kingdom seeking-commitment to the wider and global aspects of the Church."⁵⁵ The Life-Cycle Leadership model includes character development.⁵⁶ The first phase of this model is called Ministry Foundation, which includes character formation and values formation that continues in phase 2 (Early Ministry phase).⁵⁷ Blanchard's and Hodges's Servant Leadership Model starts with "the heart"

---

49. Northouse, *Leadership*, 212–12.

50. Goleman et al., *Primal Leadership*.

51. Ibid., 39.

52. More recently Goleman (*Social Intelligence*, 84) developed a similar construct, called social intelligence, which includes two main domains: social awareness (primal empathy, attunement, empathic accuracy, and social cognition) and social facility (synchrony, self-presentation, influence, and concern). Social intelligence is included in primal leadership (social competence and relationship management). However, compassion (concern for others) is missing in this leadership model.

53. Barna, "Nothing Is More"; Hayford, "Character."

54. Hayford, "Character," 68.

55. Ford, "Helping Leaders," 134–35.

56. Clinton and Clinton, "Life Cycle."

57. Ibid, 165–67.

of the leader and emphasizes the development of "leadership character."[58] Finally, Malphurs emphasizes the formation of godly character in Christian leadership (second section focuses on the "heart").[59] Thus, the proposed model is based on Wesleyan spirituality that shares with several Christian leadership approaches the emphasis on Christian personality development and Christian virtues.

In this introductory chapter I provided the background, purpose, and research questions for this book. I also provided a brief literature review of secular and Christian leadership approaches and theories. In the next chapter I will discuss toxic secular and Christian leadership and will outline the development of personality disorders that explain why toxic leadership occurs.

Reflection Questions and Exercises

(Please pray for the leading of the Holy Spirit before you answer the reflection questions and complete the exercises)

1. What are your thoughts and feelings about spiritual and emotional maturity? Reflect on your experiences with fellow church members.
2. The Bible includes both, personal piety and social justice. How can they be integrated?
3. Many evangelical Christians view "social justice" as liberal and irrelevant. Do you agree or disagree?
4. In your opinion, what is the difference between leadership in secular and Christian contexts?
5. Journal about your formational experiences as a Christian leader (defining moments, calling, crises, successes, etc.).

---

58. Blanchard and Hodges, *Servant Leader*, 17.
59. Malphurs, *Being Leaders*.

Chapter 2

Toxic Secular and Christian Leadership

FORMER VIRGINIA GOVERNOR BOB McDonnell was found guilty of public corruption charges in September 2014 according to the *Wall Street Journal*.[1] McDonnell is a Christian leader who committed a moral failure that has become public. He uttered the following statement as he left the courthouse: "All I can say is my trust remains in the Lord."[2] Christian leaders are not perfect and society should not judge Christian leaders more harshly than secular leaders. However, the question can be posed as to why Christian leaders make moral mistakes, abuse their power, or harm their subordinates. Why do some Christian leaders do not follow the Bible and why do they fail to internalize Christian morality and ethics? In this chapter I will answer these questions by discussing the concept of personality disorders, especially narcissistic and obsessive-compulsive personality disorder traits. Narcissistic personality disorder traits explain why even Christian leaders may be oblivious to what motivates them to pursue leadership and why they tend to compartmentalize, rationalize, and justify their unethical behaviors. Obsessive-compulsive leaders often focus on rules and regulations, and other control mechanisms that followers often experience as micromanagement and emotional abuse.

What is toxic leadership? Lubit lists five types of toxic managers: Narcissistic, unethical (antisocial), aggressive (bullying, sexual harassment, etc.), rigid (compulsive), and impaired (alcohol abuse, depressed, etc.).[3] Two of these, narcissistic and compulsive leaders, are the focus of

---

1. Bauerlein and Chase, "Jury Finds," A4.
2. Ibid.
3. Lubit, *Coping with Toxic*.

this book.[4] Furnham asserts that the basic idea underlying Lubit's model is based on the premise that "toxic personality traits make one vulnerable to toxic behaviour under stress."[5] For the purpose of this book, I will define toxic leadership as the abuse of leadership power that *directly* results in interpersonal emotional, physical, and sexual harm in followers. Implied in this definition is the assumption that toxic leadership stems from personality disorder traits in leaders. This means leadership behaviors that are more passive-aggressive can be harmful as well, but their effects are not as damaging as overt aggressive behaviors (bullying, verbal shaming, verbal or physical threats, sexual perpetration, etc.). In the first part of this chapter I will discuss the effects of toxic leadership, often perpetrated by narcissistic, (and briefly) psychopathic, and obsessive-compulsive leaders which will introduce the problem this book attempts to solve.

Abuse of Power in Secular and Christian Leadership

Secular Contexts

The twentieth century has witnessed several destructive political leaders. Maladaptive narcissistic/psychopathic leaders, such as Hitler, Stalin, and Saddam Hussein can be counted among them and are well known for their cruelty and grandiosity.[6] Whether one reflects on the Holocaust, Stalin's mass executions, or Saddam Hussein's abuse and oppression of the Kurds, many people are disgusted by their actions. However, narcissistic and psychopathic leaders can also be found in corporate settings, where their effects on the organization are just as destructive as the legacy of the political tyrants.[7]

Toxic leadership is abusive leadership that harms followers and reduces leadership effectiveness. It has been recently associated with the Dark Triad, which refers to narcissism, Machiavellianism, and psychopathy.[8] Narcissism and psychopathy are personality traits or disorders, whereas Machiavellianism is not technically a personality trait but "is considered an

---

4. There appears to be some overlap in Lubit's model. Narcissistic leaders can also be aggressive and unethical, especially those narcissistic leaders with narcissistic and antisocial personality traits. Compulsive leaders also tend to be aggressive when they fear loss of control, change in routine, etc.

5. Furnham, *Elephant in the Boardroom*, 45.

6. Post, "Current Concepts"; Glad, "Why Tyrants Go."

7. Kernberg, "Regression in Organizational"; Kets de Vries and Miller, "Narcissism and Leadership"; Lubit, "Long-Term."

8. Paulhus and Williams, "Dark Triad," 557.

attitudinal, belief or stylistic variable." [9] All three share a lack of empathy for others (Goleman 2006). According to Furnham, the Dark Triad includes three interrelated personality features:

1. Arrogance, self-centeredness, self-enhancement
2. Duplicitousness, cynicism, manipulativeness
3. Emotionally cold, impulsive thrill-seeking and frequently engaged in illegal, dangerous, anti-social behavior.[10]

Leaders who possess Dark Triad personality traits have high self-interest, are low in empathy, and are not interested in longer term relationships.[11] These traits render leadership less effective or even ineffective. O'Boyle, Forsyth, Banks, and McDaniel performed a meta-analysis of the Dark Triad regarding its relationship to work performance and counterproductive work behavior (CWB), which refers to abusive leadership practices.[12] The authors incorporated original papers about Dark Triad traits and behaviors that were published between 1951 and 2011 of 245 independent samples ($N=43,907$). The results indicated that, as predicted, Machiavellianism was negatively associated with the leader's work performance and positively related to CWB. Narcissism was unrelated to job performance (opposite was hypothesized), but it was associated with CWB. Finally, as predicted, psychopathy was negatively related to job performance and positively associated with CWB. The authors commented on the insignificant relationship between narcissism and job performance:

> The negative relation between narcissism and performance was stronger for individuals in positions of authority. The adage "Power corrupts; absolute power corrupts absolutely" seems apt when discussing the handing of authority over to a narcissist.[13]

This means that narcissistic leaders who have less authority in organizations tend to display a better work performance than narcissistic leaders who have more organizational power. The following is a brief description of Machiavellianism and psychopathy.

Machiavellianism is rooted in the sixteenth-century book *The Prince*, written by Machiavelli. Machiavelli's leadership style has been associated

---

9. Furnham, *Elephant in the Boardroom*, 90.
10. Ibid., 17–18.
11. Ibid., 90.
12. O'Boyle et al., "Meta-Analysis."
13. Ibid., 571.

with "cynicism, deceit, and guile."[14] Machiavellian leaders make promises, alliances, and promises and often break them. Furnham likens the Machiavellian leadership style with Theory X of McGregor Theory, since these leaders are "cynical about workers" and therefore perceive a need to force subordinates to work.[15] Furnham concludes his section on Machiavellianism by discussing its relation to ethics and virtues, which is relevant for Christian and moral leadership:

> Machiavellianism is a philosophy. It is a value or belief system that has a Hobbesian rather than Rousseauian view of Human Nature. To some it seems like a form of naïve Darwinianism which has no place for altruism, selflessness, and virtue.[16]

Psychopathic leaders are drawn to leadership positions that include risk-taking and frequent change based on psychopaths being thrill-seeking and prone to boredom. Furnham lists some of the job situations that psychopathic leaders pursue: "when an organization is changing rapidly, in decline, or under investigation" psychopathic leaders "like outwitting the system—opportunistically exploiting who and what they can."[17] Due to the low prevalence of psychopathy in the general population (1 percent) and its limited relevance for Christian leadership, I will focus on narcissistic and obsessive-compulsive leaders, which I will discuss next.

People "whose personalities are organized around maintaining their self-esteem by getting affirmation from outside themselves" are considered narcissistic in psychoanalytic theory.[18] Narcissism can be mild and subtle as in some very successful people, as well as more severe (and maladaptive) as in the case of toxic political leaders, such as Hitler and Saddam Hussein. Various researchers have explicitly noted the presence of narcissists in organizational and political leadership[19] and Kets de Vries asserts that "narcissism and leadership are intricately connected."[20] Narcissistic leaders pose a paradox since narcissism, like any other personality trait, occurs on

---

14. Furnham, *Elephant in the Boardroom*, 140.
15. Ibid., 149.
16. Ibid., 151.
17. Ibid., 106.
18. McWilliams, *Psychoanalytic Diagnosis*, 176.
19. Kets de Vries and Miller, "Narcissism and Leadership"; Kets de Vries, *Leadership Mystique*; Kernberg, *Ideology, Conflict*; Sankowsky, "Charismatic Leader"; Downs, *Beyond the Looking*; Schell, *Management*; McFarlin and Sweeney, *House of Mirrors*; Lubit, "Long-Term Organizational"; Maccoby, "Narcissistic Leaders"; Maccoby, *Productive Narcissist*; Post, "Current Concepts."
20. Kets de Vries, *Leadership Mystique*, 83.

a continuum ranging from adaptive to maladaptive and abusive narcissism. On the one hand, maladaptive narcissism leads to lowered productivity, increased staff dissatisfaction, and has been linked to executive derailment. On the other hand, adaptive narcissism has been found to produce positive outcomes such as self-confidence, persuasiveness, assertiveness and charisma, which are important in effective leadership.[21] Kets de Vries notes that "a considerable percentage of [leaders] are driven by reactive [maladaptive] narcissism."[22] Reactive narcissism, unlike constructive (adaptive) narcissism, develops in individuals who have been wounded in the past and are "reparation seekers" by over compensating their perceived sense of inferiority.[23] Thus, for secular and Christian leadership development, organizational leaders should be able to recognize when narcissism becomes maladaptive. In particular, it is beneficial to know how the behaviors of leaders or leadership styles (e.g., transformational and transactional leadership) are affected by adaptive and maladaptive narcissism in organizational leaders.

Sashkin and Sashkin and Maccoby provide a strong argument for the link between transformational leadership and narcissism.[24] Sashkin and Sashkin argue that transformational leaders "have a strong sense of self-confidence" as well as a high need for power, which are components of narcissism.[25] Maccoby associates productive (adaptive) narcissism with visionary leadership, which can be considered as synonymous with transformational leadership. The author asserts that adaptive narcissistic leaders have two strengths, among others, that characterize transformational leadership: the ability for visioning and charisma.[26] He views the ability to develop a vision as the key aspect in adaptive narcissism.[27] Thus, there is a strong link between effective leadership and narcissistic traits.

Stone, in describing the "zone just beyond normal narcissism," lists some traits of the "supernormal" narcissist, which are charisma, assertiveness and competitiveness.[28] Charisma is related to leadership and refers to the ability of individuals to make people feel loved and appreciated. Charisma as well as power are value neutral and can be negative (e.g., Hitler,

---

21. Kets de Vries and Miller, "Narcissism and Leadership"; Millon, "DSM Narcissistic Personality"; Stone, "Normal Narcissism."

22. Kets de Vries, *Leadership Mystique*, 86.

23. Ibid., 88.

24. Sashkin and Sashkin, *Leadership That Matters*; Maccoby, *Productive Narcissist*.

25. Sashkin and Sashkin, *Leadership That Matters*, 86.

26. Maccoby, *Productive Narcissist*.

27. Ibid., 96.

28. Stone, "Normal Narcissism," 14–15.

etc.) or positive (e.g., Martin Luther King Jr.). Charismatic leaders share the attributes of having a "tremendous self-confidence" and the "unshakable conviction of being right."[29] The various definitions of charismatic leadership have resulted in a "muddled field."[30] However, one definition of charismatic leadership is provided by House and Howell:

> [Charismatic leadership] emphasizes symbolic leader behavior, visionary and inspirational ability, nonverbal communication, appeal to ideological values, intellectual stimulation of followers by the leader, and leader expectations for follower self-sacrifice and for performance beyond expectations.[31]

These behaviors are adaptive, positive, and very similar to transformational leadership. However, Burns views "pure" charismatic leadership as "distort[ing] constructive and mutually empowering leader-follower relationships."[32] Furthermore, Sashkin and Sashkin argue that the difference between the charismatic and the transformational leader concerns the personality of the leader.[33] Both charismatic and transformational leaders display the same leader behaviors, such as effective communication, consistency in their actions, and showing respect, etc., but charismatic leaders "do these things only as a matter of appearance." Thus, according to Sashkin and his associates, effective leadership behaviors flow from the personality and authentic character of a truly transformational leader. However, Meier cautions us not to jump to premature conclusions regarding the *intention* of a charismatic leader, as it is elusive and difficult to assess.[34]

When it comes to the intention of charismatic leaders, we need to examine the leadership power motive.[35] McClelland found that men with a personalized power orientation tended to "collect more 'prestige supplies' (like convertibles or Playboy Club keys), prefer man-to-man competitive sports, and display more impulsive aggressive actions."[36] On the other hand, men with a socialized power orientation tended to "have more hesitation about expressing power in a direct interpersonal way . . . [and] exercise

---

29. Ibid., 15.
30. Meier, "Shedding Light," 118.
31. House and Howell, "Personality and Charismatic," 82.
32. Burns, *Transforming Leadership*, 27.
33. Sashkin and Sashkin, *Leadership That Matters*, 9.
34. Meier, "Shedding Light," 130.
35. More detail about power motives and power sources will be addressed in chapter 5 of this book.
36. McClelland, *Power*, 258.

power for the benefit of others (altruistic power)."[37] Thus, leaders with a personalized power orientation tend to be egotistical, whereas leaders with a socialized power orientation tend to be altruistic. Sashkin and Sashkin link charismatic leadership to personalized power and transformational leadership to socialized power.[38]

According to Stone, self-regard and self-confidence are important ingredients of effective leadership.[39] In addition to self-confidence, he comments on the obvious relationship between assertiveness and leadership (to take charge, speak his or her mind, etc.):

> the "narcissism" (here in quotation marks, because it is not maladaptive) of the ideal leader may extend to the outer edge of what we can still consider normal—in contrast to the clearly maladaptive narcissism of the arrogant, grandiose, or bullying leader.[40]

Thus, we can say that many leaders display adaptive narcissistic traits, which make people more effective as leaders. Maccoby argues that a large number of adaptive narcissists function as corporate leaders.[41] The author further claims that adaptive narcissistic traits make leaders effective, but refers to secular not Christian organizations. I argue that adaptive narcissistic leaders can be effective in Christian organizations as long as they remain humble and teachable. Adaptive narcissists can become "unproductive" or maladaptive when they succumb to "stress and inner conflict."[42] Thus, self-care and burnout prevention are crucial to prevent ineffective leadership and moral failures, which is often absent in Christian contexts according to what I have observed and heard from Christian leaders over the years and is one of five areas to foster in pastors according to Burns, Chapman, and Guthrie who researched pastoral ministry.[43]

Competitiveness is another trait that is shared with adaptive narcissism. Taking credit for something one has invented, written, etc. is still within the limits of adaptive narcissism.[44] However, when individuals fail "to give others credit for their contributions" by plagiarizing or stealing the

---

37. Ibid., 258.
38. Sashkin and Sashkin, *Leadership That Matters*, 64.
39. Stone, "Normal Narcissism," 15.
40. Ibid., 16.
41. Maccoby, "Narcissistic Leaders."
42. Maccoby, *Productive Narcissist*, 88.
43. Burns et al., *Resilient Ministry*.
44. Stone, "Normal Narcissism," 17.

ideas of others, they go beyond the bounds of adaptive narcissism.[45] In these cases, competitiveness is a manifestation of maladaptive narcissism. Thus, charisma, assertiveness, and competitiveness can be adaptive aspects of narcissism.

Conger, in describing the *dark side of leadership*, refers to maladaptive narcissistic leadership when he comments on flawed visioning, communication, and general management practices.[46] The vision of a narcissistic leader, which is often compelling and inspiring, reflects the leader's selfish needs and seldom the needs of the organization. In addition, maladaptive narcissistic leaders manipulate their followers by exaggerated impression management and by "gaining [followers'] commitment by restricting negative information and maximizing positive information."[47] Finally, maladaptive narcissistic leaders display flawed management practices by "poor management of people and networks" and by displaying "an informal/impulsive style that is disruptive and dysfunctional."[48] Moreover, these leaders tend to "alternat[e] between idealizing and devaluing others," which, according to Kernberg, refers to the defense mechanism of splitting, and seem to fail "to manage details and effectively act as an administrator," etc.[49] Overall, maladaptive narcissistic leaders perform poorly as leaders and managers. In particular, two aspects of organizational leadership are the focus of the next few paragraphs: decision-making and corporate culture. Toxic or maladaptive narcissistic leadership negatively impacts these two areas.

Kets de Vries and Miller describe decision-making by maladaptive narcissistic leader as "risk-laden" and impulsive, meaning that the leader consults no one and he or she "tends to do very little scanning and analysis."[50] Consequently, the decisions are often wrong, for which the leader tends to blame his or her subordinates. Kernberg illustrates the circular process of the deteriorating performance of narcissistic leaders in terms of critical thinking and decision-making:

> The danger is that the leader's narcissistic tendency might be reinforced by adulation. Such adulation may bring about a circular process wherein artificially inflated self-esteem derived from idealization and admiration gradually diminishes the leader's

---

45. Ibid., 17.
46. Conger, "Dark Side."
47. Ibid., 256.
48. Ibid., 258.
49. Kernberg, *Ideology, Conflict*, 298.
50. Kets de Vries and Miller, "Narcissism and Leadership," 201, 208.

capacity for self-criticism and leads to a chronic narcissistic regression that may become unfitted to leadership.[51]

Thus, followers reinforce the faulty decision-making, and other leadership responsibilities in general, which eventually renders the leader incompetent for the leadership task. A similar phenomenon can be seen in group dynamics. Brown compares denial, which is a defense mechanism of narcissistic individuals, at the group level with Janis's groupthink.[52] Groupthink refers to the symptom of uncritically accepting what the group has decided as a result of self-deceptions. The (maladaptive) narcissistic leader, based on his or her denial, is impaired in his or her critical thinking ability, and the group members who admire the leader, either uncritically conform or share the leader's denial. The flawed decision-making is exacerbated by the fact that narcissistic leaders prefer to be totally in charge of the organization, which leads to over-centralization.[53] Thus, a narcissistic leader does not tolerate participative decision-making and delegation of power. This means that the organization is doomed to eventually become a closed system.

Regarding organizational culture, Kets de Vries and Miller hypothesized that the more maladaptive the personality traits of the leader are, the more the culture is shaped by dysfunction. In a narcissistic/dramatic corporate culture, "everything seems to revolve around the leader" and leaders are "seen as infallible," which abbreviates the tenure of "independent-minded managers."[54] In addition, "an effective information system" is absent: downward communication seldom occurs.[55] Employees receive key information from media and/or grapevine. Finally, "narcissistic" companies are known for "audacity, risk taking, and diversification," which represents their impulsive nature.[56] In short, the narcissistic corporate culture reflects the maladaptive traits of its narcissistic leader. But how do obsessive-compulsive leaders relate to followers and how do they affect organizational cultures?

Hogan and Fernandez describe the "perfectionist manager" as one of "six dominant syndromes of mismanagement," along with mistrustful, fearful, aloof, stubborn, and arrogant managers.[57] Obsessive-compulsive and perfectionistic will be used interchangeably for the purpose of this book. Perfectionistic leaders are "industrious, careful, dutiful about planning,

---

51. Kernberg, *Ideology, Conflict*, 112.
52. Brown, "Narcissism, Identity"; Janis, *Victims of Groupthink*.
53. Downs, *Beyond the Looking*.
54. Kets de Vries and Miller, "Narcissism and Leadership," 254.
55. Ibid., 255.
56. Ibid., 254.
57. Hogan and Fernandez, "Syndromes," 29–30.

meticulous, and have high standards of performance."[58] They are often well esteemed by their superiors due to their high work performance and perfectionism is "admired and rewarded" in some organizations.[59] However, under pressure, they feel compelled to work on their own and refuse to delegate to subordinates.[60] They also alienate subordinates by nitpicking and micromanagement. This may often develop into verbal abuse, which inflicts emotional harm in followers. Since leaders need to be hard working and competent, we can say that this personality trait requires more balance. Thus, similar to the model in this study below, Kaplan and Kaiser propose an approach to diagnose "lopsided leadership" and "lack of balance:"

> What is needed, then, is a way of measuring leadership that allows for the possibility, in fact the reality, that sub-par managerial performance can result not only from a deficiency of certain skills and behaviors, but also from an excess of them as well. Aristotle made this deceptively simple truth central to his "Ethics." He thought of virtue, or efficacy, as the midpoint between excess and deficiency.[61]

The authors describe a continuum from "forceful leadership" to "enabling leadership" with "virtues" and "vices" for each.[62] The "vice" of the "forceful leader" resembles the obsessive-compulsive leader and is described in the following way: "dominant to the point of eclipsing subordinates," "doesn't hear and value others' opinions," is "insensitive and callous," and "rigid."[63]

A similar approach to measuring traits for leaders is using the Big Five personality model, which includes five domains: Openness to experience, conscientiousness, extroversion, agreeableness, and neuroticism.[64] Obsessive-compulsive personality traits equal high conscientiousness among others. Toegel and Barsaux describe high conscientiousness and state that the leader with this profile micromanages and thereby "inhibits subordinates and delays problem recognition" and the leader "lose[s] sight of the big picture."[65] In addition, these leaders tend to burn out faster and have work-life balance issues.[66] A moderate level of conscientiousness is most

---

58. Ibid., 31.
59. Furnham, *Elephant in the Boardroom*, 172.
60. Hogan and Fernandez, "Syndromes," 31.
61. Kaplan and Kaiser, "Developing Versatile Leadership," 21.
62. Ibid., 22.
63. Ibid.
64. Costa and McCrae, *Revised NEO Personality*.
65. Toegel and Barsaux, "How to Become," 55.
66. Ibid.

effective, which means a leader is responsible and demonstrates excellence regarding work ethics and attention to detail, but he or she is able to delegate authority and task to followers and he or she does not lose sight of the big picture. The Big Five model is helpful here, since it suggests optimal levels of health when people endorse a moderate elevation on all five personality domains.

Obsessive-compulsive leaders often experience a deep sense of shame and try to unconsciously cover it up by striving for perfection. Therefore, these leaders tend to be "indecisive, cautious, and fearful about making mistakes."[67] In addition, these leaders are preoccupied "with orderliness, perfectionism, and mental and interpersonal control, at the expense of flexibility, openness, and efficiency."[68] Emotional abuse can occur because these leaders can be "tyrannical bosses," "mean," and are driven by "oughts and shoulds," which they expect from followers.[69] Due to their reduced emotional literacy, they often struggle with interpersonal relationships and are often insensitive as stated above.[70]

What does an obsessive-compulsive organizational culture look like? The assumption is that an obsessive-compulsive top management that usually includes more than one leader creates an organizational culture that resembles his or her personality through the process of reinforcement and reward processes. This reinforcement process ensures that only executives who "love to follow rules" and are bureaucrats themselves stay at the company.[71] The obsessive-compulsive organizational culture is defined as a:

> bureaucratic group culture [that] is depersonalized and rigid, permeated by top management's preoccupation with control over people, operations, and the external environment. Leaders manage by rules rather than through personal guidance or directives.[72]

The obsessive-compulsive organizational culture often monitors internal operations, dictates dress codes, demands frequent staff meetings, etc. Its strategy is inwardly focused and emphasizes on "stale product lines" versus "incremental innovation."[73] An example of an obsessive-compulsive

---

67. Furnham, *Elephant in the Boardroom*, 171.
68. Ibid., 172.
69. Ibid., 173.
70. Ibid.
71. Kets de Vries, *Leadership Mystique*, 124.
72. Ibid.
73. Ibid., 125.

organization is the early Ford company that conveyed Henry Ford's slogan: "Any color as long as it's black." [74] Therefore, bureaucratic organizational cultures only do well when external environments are relatively stable and innovation is obsolete. The obsessive-compulsive leaders needs to manage his or her shame more effectively and needs to learn to reduce his or her unrealistic expectations of perfection for him- or herself and others. This is not easy and it may take some time to change these toxic patterns. In the next section I will outline how toxic narcissistic and obsessive-compulsive leadership is carried out Christian contexts.

Christian Contexts

"I wrote to the church about this, but Diotrephes, who *loves to be the leader*, refuses to have anything to do with us" (3 John 9, NLT, my emphasis).

Diotrephes appears to have been a narcissistic leader in the early church. He does not submit to spiritual authority and displays passive-aggressive and aggressive behaviors:

> When I come, I will report some of the things he is doing and *the evil accusations he is making against us*. Not only does he *refuse to welcome* the traveling teachers, he also *tells others not to help them*. And when they do help, *he puts them out of the church*. (3 John 10, NLT, my emphasis)

Another good example for narcissistic leaders in the Bible, according to McIntosh and Rima, is King Solomon, who was "obsessed with his image."[75] The authors hypothesize that Solomon was a narcissistic leader based on:

> Solomon's contrived route to the throne, his youthfulness and inexperience, the legendary success of his father, as well as his probable awareness of the circumstances of his own birth that followed the death of David and Bathsheba's child born of adultery all combined to provide a sense of inferiority and a powerful drive within the young king to make a name for himself.[76]

In addition, Solomon's focus on prestige, accomplishments, accumulation of wealth and status, as well as his excessive number of wives and concubines further point to his narcissistic personality. There are probably more biblical characters with narcissistic traits. It is encouraging for us that the

---

74. Ibid.
75. McIntosh and Rima, *Overcoming the Dark*, 112.
76. Ibid., 63.

Bible does not portray perfect individuals and the Bible is very honest about sinful behavior patterns and how they impact the narcissistic individual and people close to them. King Solomon was said to have left his faith in God at the end of his life as a result of his choices, which affected Israel and resulted in a divided kingdom. How can contemporary toxic leadership in Christian contexts be described?

Wikipedia lists twenty religious leaders who committed violent crimes, which includes several Christian leaders who committed murder, rape, and molestation, and nine religious leaders who committed non-violent crimes. Among them are Christian leaders, such as Jim Bakker who was convicted of fraud, Henry Lyons, former president of the National Baptist Convention, who was convicted of grand theft, Barry Minkow, former head pastor of a large church, who was convicted of fraud, and Kent Hovind ("Dr. Dino"), founder of the Creation Science Evangelism ministry, who was convicted of tax evasion. The former governor of Virginia could be included on that list, but his leadership was confined to a secular context.

How has toxic and narcissistic leadership been exemplified in current Christian contexts? McIntosh and Rima discuss some indicators or signs of (maladaptive) narcissistic church leaders, which are being obsessed with whether a sermon was good, destroyed churches due to energetic and costly projects, the pastor's comments that the church would be negatively impacted if he left, and the constant launching of new ministries in the absence of sufficient resources to staff them.[77] Unfortunately, Christian churches "provide a fertile soil for budding" narcissistic leaders because kingdom work is often used to justify "grandiose visions and risky ventures."[78] Too often followers do not feel comfortable with challenging these leaders because the work is done for God. The authors view Jim Bakker as having narcissistic personality disorder because of his grandiose visions, his drive to achieve greatness for approval, and his resolve to do anything to obtain the "approval and recognition he craved."[79] In addition, some Christian leaders have abused their authority and power to commit sexual sins. For example, Jim Bakker and Jimmy Swaggart engaged in illicit sexual conduct, which became public.[80] Sheafer describes narcissistic ministers as:

> . . . having superficial charm ("seems to understand others . . . confidence and answers to big problems"), grandiose ("God talking or working directly through him"), attention and

---

77. Ibid., 117.
78. Ibid.
79. Ibid., 116.
80. Heggen, *Sexual Abuse*, 100.

admiration seeking ("enjoys theatrics during church, and using over-dramatic speech"), power seeking (pressure "to commit to serve in several ministries, attend several services each week and put the desires of the pastor to grow the church above the needs of their families"), and exploitativeness (large range from minor to major abuse, but insensitivity to financial needs of church members: "will ask for money, even when it puts members at financial risk").[81]

The author further notes that narcissistic pastors tend to use the Bible to manipulate and control their followers. These control tactics can range from being aggressive (demanding obedience by making threats) to passive-aggressive (ignoring church members who do not comply, telling members that they may experience spiritual consequences if they do not comply, etc.). Similar to McIntosh and Rima's observations above, Sheafer explains why church members fail to question the authority of the Christian leader: "Unfortunately, narcissists in a religious setting tend to "get away with it" for longer than in other settings because the religious community wants to give people the benefit of the doubt."[82] It is important to differentiate between the biblical mandate to submit to authority and the warning to critically discern the motives of fellow Christians, which includes pastors and ministers. Church members may often feel uncomfortable about the leader's actions, but may suppress their suspicions because they do not want to be perceived as rebellious or oppositional. As an American who grew up in Germany I find resistance to Hitler's evil regime biblically sound (Bonhoeffer, etc.) We need to discern the motives of Christian leaders and speak up assertively if they abuse their power and authority.

What about Christian obsessive-compulsive leadership? Furnham states that perfectionistic leaders tend to be "fanatical and fundamentalist about moral, political, and religious issues."[83] This does not mean we cannot hold conservative Christian values, but it does mean we should avoid being rigid and legalistic like the Pharisees Jesus condemned.

It is not surprising that legalistic churches attract these leaders through the reinforcement process described above. The perfectionistic church leader may perpetuate a toxic faith system that deemphasizes grace over works and may put too much pressure on followers to serve in the church at the expense of the follower's family relationships, etc. According to Berry "faith becomes toxic when individuals use God or religion for personal gain in

---

81. Sheafer, *Narcissist Next Door*, 162–63.

82. Ibid., 173.

83. Furnham, *Elephant in the Boardroom*, 173.

profit, power, pleasure, or prestige."[84] In this case, since the author includes other dysfunctional leader types, the perfectionist church leader may use his or her power to impose personal unrealistically high pious standards on his or her congregants and only affirm and recruit followers who have similar personality traits. This can constitute spiritual abuse, which is often part of a toxic faith system. However, these leaders can also be emotionally abusive to others. McIntosh and Rima state that perfectionist Christian leaders can be "overly moralistic . . . and judgmental both of themselves and others."[85] They can be angry at times and express it in "violent outbursts" followed by immediate apologies.[86] As mentioned above, perfectionism is a cover up for excessive shame and individuals with this personality are often unaware of it, since they tend to de-emphasize emotions and repress negative emotions. The obsessive-compulsive church culture includes striving for perfection, which is usually an "extension and reflection" of the perfectionist pastor.[87]

A biblical example is Moses who was a "man in control."[88] One can see obsessive-compulsive personality traits in Moses due to his struggles with delegating authority. His father-in-law, Jethro, suggested delegating authority, which resulted in a more effective leadership and in a more efficient organization (Exod 18:17–18).[89] However, Moses also had an anger issue:

> Moses was subject to occasional public eruptions of anger. In fact one of his public outbursts resulted in his being forbidden to enter the Promised Land, the ultimate purpose of his leading the people out of Egypt (Num. 20:1–13).[90]

Both narcissistic and obsessive-compulsive leaders can be toxic. However, it appears that narcissistic leaders tend to be identified more often based on the church's disdain for pride. Obsessive-compulsive Christian leaders may often be celebrated as "faithful Christian servants" regardless of the fact that these Christian leaders often neglect their family relationships and tend to micromanage their followers. The lack of self-care and inevitable propensity to burn out is also often falsely viewed as a virtue in our Christian churches. The Christian leadership model discussed below will provide Christian leaders with insights to discern their general motives ("heart"), their specific

---

84. Berry, *Spiritual Abuse*, 96.
85. McIntosh and Rima, *Overcoming the Dark*, 106.
86. Ibid., 107.
87. Ibid.
88. Ibid., 104.
89. Ibid., 105.
90. Ibid., 105.

power motives, and will suggest leadership practices that glorify God. Below the concept of personality disorders with the focus on narcissistic and obsessive-compulsive personality disorders is explored.

How do sin and vice relate to narcissism and obsessive-compulsive personality traits? Regarding sin and narcissism, the Lutheran theologian Ted Peters discusses the progression of the sin of pride, which stems from idolatry, which in this sense refers to trust in oneself as opposed to trust in God.[91] The "illusion of independence" is the foundation of pride and results in narcissism.[92] Pride manifests in narcissism, in the desire to have "power over" people, in "tribalism and group evil," and in "patriarchy."[93] In short, narcissistic behaviors stem from the sin of pride and can have destructive consequences for all parties involved. The sin of pride is included in the list of the seven deadly sins. The Egyptian ascetic and theologian Evagrius in the late 4th century identified eight deadly sins as opposed to seven, and he originally referred to them as "disruptive thoughts or obsessive feelings."[94] One can say that these obsessive thoughts lead to sinful behavior if they are put to practice. The goal of Evagrius's teaching was *apatheia*, which was freedom from these sinful thoughts.[95] The eight sinful and obsessive thoughts were the following:

> gluttony, lust, avarice (greed), anger, sadness (depression or dejection), *acedia* (sometimes called sloth, but better as restless despairing), vainglory, and pride. In general, the sequence moves from thoughts presenting lesser dangers to the soul toward the more dangerous.[96]

These eight sinful thought patterns can be correlated with narcissistic and obsessive-compulsive personality disorder traits. The sin of pride according to Evagrius, Cassian, and Gregory is the "queen of sins" and the root cause

91. Peters, *Sin*, 94.
92. Ibid., 94.
93. Ibid., 95, 98, 101, and 105.
94. Vest, *Desiring Life*, 68.
95. Ibid. *Apatheia* refers to an "abiding sense of peace and joy that comes from the full harmony of the passions, a habitual state developed through discipline (*ascesis*), which is why we call it a virtue," and includes the ability "to remain calm and peaceful even while remembering situations or events" that are negative (Okholm, "To Vent," 173). This state of harmony then "enables one fully to love others and God." *Apatheia* resembles the psychological characteristics of differentiation, which I will discuss in chapter 4.
96. Ibid., 70. The Benedictine monk Gregory, who later became a pope (Gregory the Great), modified the list by removing *vainglory* and by viewing *pride* as the "root of all sins" (Okholm, "To Vent," 166). He also merged *acedia* with *sadness* into *sloth*, and added *envy*. This final list became the *seven deadly sins* in the Christian tradition.

of all other sins, which we can correlate with narcissism above.[97] However, pride (and vainglory) according to Vest are also distorted ways of knowing the truth and refers to "perverted love."[98] This describes the narcissist well, since he or she is overly self-focused and neglects to focus on God. Vest views pride as "the complete perversion of reason, for it takes our capacity for union with God and turns it inward on ourselves, centered in our enclosed little world," whereas she defines vainglory as "taking credit for everything good that happens as if we alone had caused it."[99] Vainglory thus applies to both narcissistic and perfectionistic leaders. The plagiarism of intellectual property is another example of vainglory, which some politicians and celebrities have committed. Pride refers to ignoring God when it comes to our being and existence in the universe, but vainglory ignores God's actions as if we have done everything ourselves. Both distort the truth about God's presence and actions, and/or the contribution of others. Thus, narcissistic pride and vainglory is being inauthentic and living a lie. The virtue of humility is a correction of both distorted perceptions, namely by "*recognizing* the truth" regarding the nature of God and his involvement in the world in one's personal life[100] and our interdependence.

The obsessive thought of anger[101] according to Evagrius's system is relevant for both narcissistic and obsessive-compulsive personalities and refers, along with sadness and despair, to "our human power of refusing or rejecting," which constitutes a "distortion" of "our "rejecting powers *against other people* rather than against our own inner willfulness."[102] Both personalities are prone to anger outbursts, but for different reasons. The narcissistic person often gets angry when he or she perceives being humiliated (narcissistic injury), whereas the obsessive-compulsive person may feel enraged when he or she loses control or needs to change a routine.

Lust and greed are also relevant for narcissists and obsessive-compulsive personalities. Lust, greed, and gluttony are an "expression of excessive love" and are "distortions of our power to desire."[103] Narcissistic leaders may give in

97. Okholm, *Dangerous Passions*, 161.

98. Vest, *Desiring Life*, 78. Okholm (*Dangerous Passions*, 158) views pride and vainglory as essentially interchangeable, but defines pride as referring more to our relationship with God whereas vainglory concerns our relationship with others.

99. Vest, *Desiring Life*, 81, 80.

100. Ibid., 89.

101. Anger here refers to the definition provided above as an obsessive thought or excessive feeling that is frequent and disruptive. Anger as a feeling is not sinful, but the sinful expression of anger is. Ephesians 4:26 reminds us that we should not sin when we are angry, which normalizes the experience of anger.

102. Vest, *Desiring Life*, 74--75.

103. Ibid., 72--73.

to lust, whereas both personality styles and leader types may feel tempted to be greedy in accumulating material goods and wealth. Acquiring leadership status, even in the church, can also be added to the vice of greed, which refers to a distortion of a desire to have power and influence. Finally, Gregory's addition of envy is very relevant for narcissistic leaders, since narcissistic individuals often experience envy (see below). Christian narcissistic leaders are prone to envying others' abilities, power and influence, status, etc. The corresponding virtue of gratitude can reduce envy in Christian leaders.

The pursuit of humility is the primary way to acquire virtue according to the Benedictine spirituality.[104] Humility is knowing the truth about ourselves, which means being aware of our strengths and weaknesses.[105] Humility requires emotional stability "for withstanding the storms of life . . . to control ourselves when there is nothing else in life that we can control."[106] Humility is a Christian affection and virtue that I will explore in chapter 5. The question can now be posed as to how personality disorders develop.

Development of Personality Disorders

Personality is often defined as: "A complex pattern of deeply embedded psychological characteristics that are expressed automatically in almost every area of psychological functioning."[107] This is contrasted with the concept of character, which the authors define as: "Characteristics acquired during our upbringing and connot[ing] a degree of conformity to virtuous social standards."[108] While both constructs overlap somewhat, this in this book I will focus on the personality construct when it comes to leader types, but its relationship to ethical behavior patterns is addressed as well.

Personality disorders originate from biological and genetic factors (nature) and from external factors (nurture), which refers to the diathesis stress model.[109] According to Millon and his associates, personality and per-

---

104. Ibid., 88.

105. Ibid., 89.

106. Chittister, *Rule of Benedict*, 87. Stability is one of the three Benedictine vows. The other two are obedience to the voice of God and openness to change by "saying yes to following Christ's call to discipleship" (De Waal, *Seeking God*, 13). The vow of stability is "achieved through perseverance, through holding on even under great strain, without weakening or trying to escape" (ibid., 58). The vows of stability along with openness to change resemble the psychological characteristics of differentiation in chapter 4.

107 Millon et al., *Personality Disorders*, 2.

108. Ibid.

109. Kring et al., *Abnormal Psychology*, 58.

sonality disorders develop as result of a "complex interplay" of internal and external factors, especially the interactional patterns between a person and his or her environment.[110] In addition, a leading geneticist and DNA scientist asserts that heredity is only one of three predictive factors when it comes to personality traits with childhood experiences and human free will being the two remaining factors.[111] Thus, the person's temperamental dispositions (inborn characteristics), genetic predispositions, and his or her attachment experiences (see chapter 4 for details) are etiological factors. Specific etiological factors will be explored below. Millon et al. view personality disorders on a continuum from adaptive personality style to personality disorder. This continuum includes traits that can range from being "adaptive" to "severely disordered" (with "subclinical" and "disordered" in between).[112] They also equate personality disorders with the body's immune system:

> Robust immune activity easily counteracts most infectious organisms, whereas weakened immune activity leads to illness. Psychopathology should be conceived as reflecting the same interactive pattern. Here, however, it is not our immunological defenses, but our overall personality pattern—that is, coping skills and adaptive flexibilities—that determine whether we respond constructively or succumb to the psychosocial environment.[113]

People with personality disorders usually have poor coping skills, are inflexible, and often develop depressive and anxiety disorders among others. The *Diagnostic and Statistical Manual of Mental Disorders* (5th edition) (*DSM-5*) defines a personality disorder as "enduring pattern of inner experience and behavior that deviates markedly from the expectations of the individual's culture" with the enduring pattern being "inflexible and pervasive across a broad range of personal and social situations."[114] It lists ten personality disorders organized in three clusters: Cluster A (paranoid, schizoid, and schizotypal), Cluster B (antisocial, borderline, histrionic, and narcissistic), and Cluster C (avoidant, dependent, and obsessive-compulsive). Antisocial (similar to psychopathic above), narcissistic, and obsessive-compulsive personality disorders are especially relevant for the topic of toxic leadership as defined above, since people with these three personality disorders have a wish to control others, which may often motivate them to pursue leadership positions.[115]

110. Millon et al., *Personality Disorders*, 78.
111. Collins, *Language*, 263.
112. Millon et al., *Personality Disorders*, 12.
113. Ibid., 9.
114. APA, *Diagnostic and Statistical Manual* (5th ed.), 646.
115. Benjamin, *Interpersonal Diagnosis*, 387. Benjamin also includes paranoid

Model of Four Personality Styles and Leader Types

A dimensional conceptualization of personality disorders resembles psychodynamic models that focus on personality styles. The German psychologist and psychoanalyst, Fritz Riemann uses a dimensional model when he discusses four personality styles.[116] The author outlines four basic anxieties or fears that point to four underlying personalities. He differentiates between the schizoid personality whose fear is not to lose one's self and its opposite personality: the depressive personality whose fear is to become or assume a separate self. The two other personalities he discusses are the compulsive personality whose fear is transience or change and its opposite personality, the hysterical personality whose fear is limitedness. While this model is interesting and relevant for the concept of leadership, it is limited due to its outdated personality labels. Depressive personality was removed in the *DSM-III* and subsumed under mood disorders and is therefore no longer included in the current *DSM-5*.[117] In addition, schizoid personality is less relevant for leadership, since people with this personality style usually do not seek Christian leadership positions or may not be encouraged to pursue leadership positions in Christian contexts, which is due to their cold and detached interpersonal style. A leader with schizoid personality traits is more common in hospital administrative contexts.[118]

An adaptation to Riemann's model is to include the following four personality styles that serve as four different leader types[119]: narcissistic,

---

personality disorder on this list, but I did not discuss it here, since it can be assumed that Christians with paranoid traits are often not considered for leadership positions. One example of a paranoid religious leader is the Rev. Jim Jones, who initiated the 1978 mass suicide in Jonestown, Guyana (Millon et al., *Personality Disorders*, 447). In addition, individuals with antisocial personality disorder are less relevant for Christian leadership due to a history of criminal behavior that often disqualifies them from entering Christian leadership positions. Furthermore, Goldman ("High Toxicity Leadership," 733) refers to leaders with borderline personality disorder and labels their leadership "high toxicity leadership" or "extreme levels of dysfunctional leadership." The author suggests that leaders with borderline personality disorder traits require interventions by psychologists or psychiatrists, not merely by executive coaches or HR professionals (744). Thus, individuals with borderline personality disorder traits tend to be too unstable for leadership positions in general and are even less likely to be selected for Christian leadership positions. Borderline personality disorder is defined as "a pervasive pattern of instability of interpersonal relationships, self-image, and affects [intense episodes of rage, anxiety and/or depression, etc.], and marked impulsivity [substance abuse, promiscuous sexual behaviors, etc.]" (APA, *Diagnostic and Statistical* [5th ed.], 653). Therefore, in this book I focus on narcissistic and obsessive-compulsive leaders.

116 Riemann, *Grundformen der Angst*.

117. McWilliams, *Psychoanalytic Diagnosis*, 236.

118 Kernberg, "Regression in Organizational," 49.

119. As stated above, Lubit's (*Coping with Toxic*) model consists of five types of

obsessive-compulsive (formerly compulsive), histrionic (formerly hysterical), and dependent personality. The fear of a person with narcissistic personality is being dependent (or the loss of power) whereas the fear of its opposite personality style, the dependent personality, is the fear of independence (or assuming power). The fear of a person with an obsessive-compulsive personality style is change, whereas the fear of its opposite personality, histrionic, is routine or limitedness:

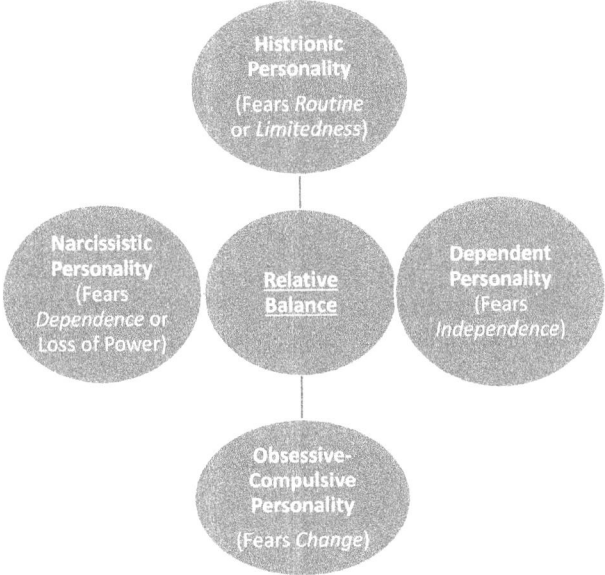

Figure 3: Four Personality Styles/ Leader Types

---

toxic managers: narcissistic, unethical, aggressive, rigid, and impaired. McIntosh and Rima's (*Overcoming the Dark*) model also includes five leader types: compulsive leaders, narcissistic leaders, paranoid leaders, codependent leaders, and passive-aggressive leaders. Dependent and histrionic leaders often display passive-aggressive behaviors because they usually lack assertiveness and tend to avoid conflict, fearing a direct expression of anger. However, similar to passive-aggressive leaders in McIntosh and Rima, they occasionally tend to express short anger outbursts. Passive-aggressive personality disorder last appeared in the *DSM-IIIR*, 356. The current *DSM* does not contain passive-aggressive personality disorder. As previously mentioned, Christian leaders with paranoid personality traits tend to be scarce. Narcissistic and obsessive-compulsive leaders are often verbally aggressive, which followers experience as harmful according to the definition of toxic leadership noted above. This current model depicts four leader types with extreme personality disorder traits that appear on two continua, with the middle point depicting the most balanced and effective personality in leaders. However, in this book I focus on two leader types that personify toxic leadership, namely narcissistic and obsessive-compulsive leaders.

This model provides a general map for leadership development. The narcissistic leader needs to become less independent so that he or she is able to accept more influence from others, whereas the dependent leader needs to decrease dependence and develop more independence. Thus, both leader types should move toward relative balance and interdependence (see chapter 4). The obsessive-compulsive leader will benefit from being more flexible so that he or she is able to embrace change, whereas the histrionic leader needs more stability and consistency.

In addition, this model explains why dependent personalities rarely seek leadership position and if they do, often display incompetent leadership. These individuals are often incompetent leaders because of their pervasive "submissive and clinging behavior."[120]

McIntosh and Rima assert that these leaders lack assertiveness, have an excessive need to please others, and often produce "burnout and other debilitating maladies."[121] The histrionic leader is also less competent as a leader because he or she fears routine and may overwhelm his or her subordinates by imposing frequent organizational changes and growth campaigns. This is due to their tendency to be highly suggestible, meaning their "opinions and feelings are easily influenced by others and current fads" and they tend to "adopt convictions quickly."[122] This can impair the stability and structure of an organization. Their tendency to change organizational core values, mission and vision statements frequently may frustrate many followers.

This model points to potential leadership pitfalls in narcissistic leaders, namely the potential abuse of power, which was described above. The obsessive-compulsive leader fears change, which prevents organizational learning and flexibility, and he or she struggles with delegating authority. In addition, obsessive-compulsive leaders based on their excessive needs for control and orderliness, create or reinforce bureaucratic organizational structures.[123] While these leaders quite frequently assume leadership positions, organizations can only tolerate mild to moderate obsessive-compulsive personality traits.[124] Leaders with severe obsessive-compulsive personality traits usually do not reach upper management positions. However, this may not apply to pastoral leadership, since these leaders tend to be attracted to churches that hold legalistic theologies and these churches often view these leaders as a good fit. An emotionally mature leader draws from all four personality

---

120. APA, *Diagnostic and Statistical* (5th ed.), 675.
121. McIntosh and Rima, *Overcoming the Dark*, 136.
122. APA, *Diagnostic and Statistical* (5th ed.), 668.
123. Kernberg, "Regression in Organizational," 51.
124. Ibid., 50.

styles in a balanced way in order to develop effective leadership practices. As noted earlier, the focus of this book is on narcissistic and obsessive-compulsive leaders.

Narcissism and Perfectionism

The term narcissism can be traced to Greek mythology. Narcissus adored his beauty so much that, while looking at his reflection in the waters of a spring, he fell into the water and drowned. As mentioned above, people who rely on deriving constant affirmation from others are considered narcissistic.[125] The *DSM-5* describes narcissistic personality disorder, which is the most maladaptive form of narcissism. It refers to a "pervasive pattern of grandiosity (in fantasy or behavior), need for admiration, and lack of empathy" and five or more of the following:

1. Has a grandiose sense of self-importance . . .
2. Is preoccupied with fantasies of unlimited success, power, brilliance, beauty, or ideal love.
3. Believes that he or she is "special" and unique and can only be understood by, or should associate with, other special or high-status people (or institutions).
4. Requires excessive admiration.
5. Has a sense of entitlement, i.e., unreasonable expectations of especially favorable treatment or automatic compliance with his or her expectations.
6. Is interpersonally exploitative, i.e., takes advantage of others to achieve his or her own ends.
7. Lacks empathy . . .
8. Is often envious of others or believes that others are envious of him or her.
9. Shows arrogant, haughty behaviors or attitudes.[126]

The prevalence estimates of narcissistic personality disorder range from 0 percent to 6.2 percent in community samples according to the APA. This means that the prevalence of people with a narcissistic personality style (having traits and personality features) can be assumed to be much higher.

125. McWilliams, *Psychoanalytic Diagnosis*, 176.
126. APA, *Diagnostic and Statistical* (5th ed.), 669--70.

Individuals with this personality disorder are usually reluctant to seek treatment unless their romantic partners require that they (mostly males) accompany them to marital or couple therapy. Thus, it can be hypothesized that the actual prevalence rate of narcissistic personality disorder may be higher, especially among influential and famous people (Benjamin, 1996a).

The following further describes the nature of narcissism. Narcissistic individuals experience two main emotions, shame and envy.[127] Ronningstam adds anger to this list, which is generally considered as a secondary emotion following the perception of threat towards one's self-esteem.[128] For example, the narcissist feels ashamed and reacts with anger after being criticized, which increases feelings of shame. Shame is "the sense of being *seen* as bad or wrong" based on perceived inadequacies.[129] Feelings of envy are based on "an internal conviction that [one] is lacking in some way and that [one's] inadequacies are at constant risk of exposure."[130] This internal self-doubt makes one vulnerable to envy those who seem to have the qualities one lacks. In addition, envy may be the basis for critically judging oneself and others. Due to their perceived inferiority, narcissists develop certain defenses, which serve to protect their fragile egos. Narcissists utilize the following defenses: Idealization and devaluation (seeing the world as either all good or all bad), perfectionism ("holding [oneself] up to unrealistic ideals"), denial, and rationalization.[131] Narcissists also tend to use the following behavioral and cognitive strategies: ego aggrandizement (overestimating one's abilities), attributional egotism (attributing favorable results to oneself), and possessing a sense of entitlement (believing to have the right to exploit others).[132] Ronningstam discusses two types of narcissists: the arrogant and the shy type.[133] The arrogant type displays "strong reactions to criticism, defeats, or other threats to the self-esteem" and anger reactions can range from "silent contempt to overt hostility and explosive rage outbursts."[134] The interpersonal pattern of the arrogant type is characterized by an "overtly arrogant and haughty attitude."[135] Both overt aggressive and passive-aggressive behavior pat-

---

127. McWilliams, *Psychoanalytic Diagnosis*, 180.

128. Ronningstam, "Narcissistic Personality," 753.

129. McWilliams, *Psychoanalytic Diagnosis*, 180.

130. Ibid., 180.

131. Kets de Vries and Miller, "Narcissism and Leadership," 206; McWilliams, *Psychoanalytic Diagnosis*, 181; Brown," Narcissism, Identity," 643.

132. Brown, "Narcissism, Identity," 643--47.

133. Ronningstam, "Narcissistic Personality," 753--54.

134. Ibid.

135. Ibid., 754.

terns can be observed. I remember when I was a teenager in Germany, before my Christian conversion, I told friends that I majored in business administration so that I could become very rich by pursuing a career as a CPA. I was aware of my arrogance and felt guilty afterwards.

The shy type is "constricted interpersonally and vocationally" and he or she is "sensitive, inhibited, vulnerable, shame ridden, and socially withdrawn."[136] Unlike the arrogant type, the shy narcissistic type regulates his or her self-esteem by shaming. The shy narcissistic type is not easily recognizable due to the absence of arrogance and haughtiness. Especially in Christian contexts, he or she may be perceived as displaying Christian "humility" due to his or her frequent statements that reflect self-criticism and devaluation. Interestingly, Furnham correctly conceptualizes narcissism as a "*disorder* of self-esteem."[137]

When it comes to the subtypes and the etiology of narcissism, there are various hypotheses derived from personality and clinical theories, which I will discuss next. Theories of narcissism are mainly derived from psychoanalytic theories, such as Kernberg's object relations, and Benjamin's interpersonal theory, which can be considered as a combination of psychodynamic theory and social learning theory. These theories are the most popular in the field of personality and clinical theory and will be briefly reviewed.

Kernberg views narcissism as being on a continuum ranging from normal (adaptive) narcissism to maladaptive narcissism.[138] The etiology of maladaptive narcissism, according to Kernberg, can be traced to "parents who are cold and rejecting but admiring." In turn, based on specific types of childhood experiences, narcissistic individuals internalize the good attributes of significant others but devalue real objects by "project[ing] onto others all the negative aspects of themselves and others."[139]

Benjamin's Interpersonal theory views maladaptive narcissism as "internalization of unrealistic adoration."[140] Interpersonal theory posits that one's personality is shaped by interpersonal experiences with significant others which, in turn, are internalized, which either results in imitating behaviors and/or seeking relationships with people that resemble their caregivers. Thus, unlike Kernberg's conceptualizations, Benjamin's theory views the etiology of narcissism as a consequence of parental adoration, which

---

136. Ibid.
137. Furnham, *Elephant in the Boardroom*, 128.
138. Kernberg, *Severe Personality*; Kernberg, "Pathological Narcissism."
139. Kernberg, "Pathological Narcissism," 41.
140. Benjamin, *Interpersonal Diagnosis*, 147.

results in "the child becom[ing] 'hooked' on false glory."[141] "False glory" refers to a distortion of truth, which the narcissistic individual internalizes. Later in life, the narcissistic individual expects others to adore him or her. In addition, Benjamin argues that narcissism can be learned through interpersonal situations that foster narcissistic tendencies later in life. Famous and influential people are especially susceptible to developing narcissism:

> . . . single episodes do not create the disorder, but many repetitions of such episodes can. The public can and will deliver noncontingent adoration as well as deferential nurturance to the rich and famous. Given the right conditions, it is never too late to develop NPD [narcissistic personality disorder].[142]

Twenge and Campbell (2009) similarly observe that narcissism results from "overpraising" children, by being obsessed with and wanting to be like celebrities, and by being influenced by social networking (e.g., MySpace, Facebook, Twitter, etc.).[143] The preoccupation with receiving affirmations from Facebook friends via "likes" can be said to foster narcissism as well. Thus, personality is dynamic and changing depending on interpersonal feedback and regular exposure to stimuli that can reinforce negative personality traits, such as narcissism. Furthermore, implied in Benjamin's theory is a dimensional view of personality disorders, meaning that the degree of severity of narcissism is on a continuum. Lubit, a psychiatrist and executive coach, combines psychoanalytic and social learning theories by concluding that influences from one's early childhood along with reinforcement of behavior patterns throughout one's life can result in destructive narcissism.[144] Obsessive-compulsive personality traits or perfectionism is the second foci of this book, which I will be explore next.

People who idealize reason and whose personalities are "organized around thinking and doing abound in Western societies."[145] However, people who overemphasize thinking and doing can be described as having obsessive-compulsive personality disorder.[146] Obsessive-compulsive personality disorder is defined in the *DSM-5* as:

1. A pervasive pattern of preoccupation with orderliness, perfectionism, and mental and interpersonal control, at the expense of flexibility,

---

141. Ibid., 145.
142. Ibid., 147.
143. Twenge and Campbell, *Narcissism Epidemic*, 83, 91, 108.
144. Lubit, "Long-Term Organizational," 133.
145. McWilliams, *Psychoanalytic Diagnosis*, 289.
146. Ibid.

openness, and efficiency, beginning by early adulthood and present in a variety of contexts, as indicated by four (or more) of the following:

2. Is preoccupied with details, rules, lists, order, organization, or schedules to the extent that the major point of the activity is lost.
3. Shows perfectionism that interferes with task completion (e.g., is unable to complete a project because his or hers own overly strict standards are not met).
4. Is excessively devoted to work and productivity to the exclusion of leisure activities and friendships (not accounted for by obvious economic necessity).
5. Is over-conscientious, scrupulous, and inflexible about matters of morality, ethics, or values (not accounted for by cultural or religious identification).
6. Is unable to discard worn-out or worthless objects even when they have no sentimental value.
7. Is reluctant to delegate tasks or to work with others unless they submit to exactly his or her way of doing things.
8. Adopts a miserly spending style toward both self and others; money is viewed as something to be hoarded for future catastrophes.
9. Shows rigidity and stubbornness.[147]

The overemphasis on thinking and doing means that these personalities use isolation of affect as a primary defense.[148] Isolation of affect refers to "isolating feeling from knowing," which has great value when people need to work as medical doctors with patients who require severe surgical interventions, etc.[149] The chronic isolation of feelings from one's thinking and doing describes the obsessive-compulsive personality. However, anger and shame are two feelings obsessive-compulsive personalities often experience.[150] Perfectionists tend to be conscious of shame and they view anger as an acceptable emotion. I can identify with the perfectionistic personality the most and used to be more devoid of feelings, which was apparent during my CPE (clinical pastoral education) internship at a hospital in Atlanta for my MDiv degree. My CPE peers were shocked when I remained stoic after watching a movie that portrayed a genocide of a people group. Over the years during

---

147. APA, *Diagnostic and Statistical* (5th ed.), 678--79.
148. McWilliams, *Psychoanalytic Diagnosis*, 132.
149. Ibid., 131.
150. Ibid., 293.

my clinical psychology training by learning from mentors, and later from my spiritual director, my wife, and the Holy Spirit, I am now aware of my feelings and can express them more easily.

Another common defense in these personalities is reaction formation, which refers to saying or doing something that is the opposite of what the person desires. The obsessive-compulsive person uses reaction formation "against tolerating ambivalence" which can include "cooperation and rebellion, initiative and sloth, . . . order and disorder," and the following statement nicely illustrates this process: "Paragons of virtue may have a paradoxical island of corruption."[151] McIntosh and Rima observe that the compulsive leader "can be angry, rebellious individuals who believe it is wrong to express their true feelings."[152]

Regarding the origin of obsessive-compulsive personality from an Object Relations perspective, obsessive-compulsive personality is copied from controlling parents unlike Freud who "depicted the anal phase as engendering a prototypical battle of the wills."[153] Similarly, contemporary Interpersonal theory views the "[i]dentification with the behaviors and ideals of a cold and controlling parent" as the primary etiological factor for obsessive-compulsive personality disorder in addition to parental neglect.[154] As a result, the developing child fears "making a mistake or being accused of being imperfect" and has internalized "harsh self-criticism" and "neglect of the self."[155] Consequently, he or she treats others critically and harshly as well. As mentioned above, the excessive shame these personalities experience is covered up by the wish to be perfect. However, contemporary scholarship acknowledges genetic predispositions to this personality type as well.[156]

This personality is one of the most prevalent personality disorder with prevalence rates "ranging from 2.1% to 7.9%" in the general population.[157] It must be kept in mind that this book views personality on a continuum, which means that the prevalence may be even higher when we include people with obsessive-compulsive personality traits or features. People who choose professions that require much attention to detail and excellence, such as accountants, surgeons, even corporate managers, tend to select these professions because their obsessive-compulsive personality traits appear to be a natural fit for practicing these professions.

151. Ibid., 296.
152. McIntosh and Rima, *Overcoming the Dark*, 106.
153. McWilliams, *Psychoanalytic Diagnosis*, 297.
154. Benjamin, *Interpersonal Diagnosis*, 245.
155. Ibid., 244.
156. McWilliams, *Psychoanalytic Diagnosis*, 291.
157. APA, *Diagnostic and Statistical* (5th ed.), 681.

Conclusion

I this chapter I discussed the effects of toxic leadership in secular and Christian contexts and answered the question as to why even Christian leaders are able to commit moral failures and harm their followers. I correlated the two toxic personalities with the eight sinful thought patterns. The narcissist tends to struggle with pride, vainglory, anger, lust, and gluttony, whereas the obsessive-compulsive person has a propensity to struggle with anger, lust, and gluttony. The truth that we are dependent on God and others means developing the virtue of humility, which can produce emotional stability. The discussion on personality disorders provided information on emotions, defenses, behavior patterns, and on the etiology of personality disorders with the focus on narcissistic and obsessive-compulsive personalities. The narcissistic individual relies too much on receiving affirmations from others. Narcissists tend to be grandiose regarding their fantasies or behavior, have an exaggerated need for admiration, often experience envy, and above all, lack empathy, which often results in abusive behaviors towards others. Leaders with narcissistic personality traits display toxic leadership behaviors. Individuals with obsessive-compulsive personality traits tend to idealize reason. People with more severe perfectionistic traits overemphasize thinking and doing. They are often perceived as cold, unemotional, and lack emotional awareness. Both, the narcissistic and the perfectionistic leader can become verbally aggressive. The narcissistic leader often experiences narcissistic rage when he or she is being ignored, not promoted or praised, rejected, etc., whereas the perfectionistic leader expresses anger inappropriately when he or she perceives that organizational rules have not been followed or when he or she is encouraged to change a routine behavior. The four-leader type model suggests that these two leaders need to move toward the middle point toward relative balance. The narcissistic leader needs to become less independent so that he or she is able to accept more influence from others, whereas the obsessive-compulsive leader needs to become more flexible so that he or she is able to embrace change. In the next chapter I will discuss Wesleyan spirituality that will provide a theological foundation for this book. I argue that a Wesleyan spirituality with its focus on personal and social holiness provides a remedy for the problems posed in this chapter.

Reflection Questions and Exercises

(Please pray for the leading of the Holy Spirit before you answer the reflection questions and complete the exercises)

1. Take the Leader Personality Style Questionnaire in the appendix and explore, if you do not know already, what leader type matches yours. Also take the following online personality screens: http://drjeffszymanski.com/are-you-a-perfectionist and https://psychcentral.com/quizzes/narcissistic.htm.

2. We tend to struggle with the same sin(s) on a daily basis, which are often called "signature sins." Which of the seven deadly sins do you struggle the most with: gluttony, lust, greed, impatience or aggression (anger), sloth, pride, or envy?

3. Whom were you closest to in your family of origin? Which parent do you imitate the most or the least?

4. Make a list of events that have caused you to experience shame, depression, anxiety, etc. Discuss these with a trusted friend, professional coach, therapist, or spiritual director.

5. List positive traits of people you strongly dislike and make a list of negative traits of people you idealize and/or are envy of.

6. List incidents during which you tended to deny, minimize, or rationalize your contributions to interpersonal conflicts.

7. Journal your feelings on a daily basis and include them in your prayer life.

Chapter 3

Wesleyan Spirituality

IN THIS CHAPTER I will provide a discussion Wesleyan spirituality that will provide the theological framework of this book. It is important to first discuss Wesley's historical and social context, what influenced him and his formation. This chapter will then briefly summarize Wesley's key theological positions, which include his theological insights regarding anthropology, hamartiology, and soteriology. These theological concepts are especially relevant for my formational leadership model because of their correspondence to psychology. Anthropology is congruent with personality psychology (see chapter 4), hamartiology corresponds to psychopathology (see chapter 2), and soteriology is compatible with developmental psychology and psychotherapeutic interventions (see chapter 4 as well as implications sections in chapters 4–6).[1]

The Historical and Social Context

Wesley's historical context was eighteenth-century Great Britain, which was under the influence of the Enlightenment. The Enlightenment stressed liberty and autonomy and renounced oppressive forces in religion, politics, and morality.[2] The Enlightenment also emphasized reason and science. However, traditional forces, such as the Reformation, among other historical movements, equally influenced Wesley.[3] As a result, Wesley combined piety with reason. The Church of England had adopted Arminian theology including universal redemption, which was consistent with the Enlighten-

---

1. Carter and Narramore, *Integration*, 50; Ridgway, "Psychology," 888.
2. Outler, "Pietism," 249.
3. Gregory, "Long Eighteenth Century," 23.

ment thought through its emphasis on optimism, perfectability, etc.[4] Wesley followed Arminianism to some extent, but also drew from other theological sources, which I will discuss below.

The British Enlightenment also emphasized empiricism and sensation, which Wesley adopted in his theology. Wesley appreciated the role of emotion and experience in his theology informed by his own spiritual experience. Wesley's quadrilateral (scripture, reason, tradition and experience) also integrates reason with tradition. This means reason, experience, and church tradition all need to be considered for the interpretation of Scripture.[5] Thus, Wesley's theology can therefore be considered a balanced approach regarding the roles of reason and experience.

While Wesley was influenced by Lockean empiricism, he was equally influenced by traditional forces. The Wesleyan movement can even be viewed as a counter-enlightenment movement in some respects, especially when one considers Wesley's reaffirmation of "old wives' medical remedies, the casting of lots, the belief in diabolic possession and in exorcism by prayer, etc."[6] These supernatural practices enabled Wesley to reach the English lower class and were partly responsible for the growth of Methodism in eighteenth-century England. Most important among these various contextual forces was the state of the Church of England in the eighteenth century, which had lost much of its spirituality:

> [T]he eighteenth-century Church of England has frequently been a byword for lax standards and pastoral negligence, indicating an institution that had fallen far short of the ideals of the Church of the sixteenth and seventeenth centuries . . .[7]

Thus, Wesley sought to reform the Church of England by restoring higher moral standards and pastoral responsiveness to the needs of parishioners. There is a striking resemblance to Martin Luther's context—the sixteenth-century Catholic Church.

In addition, the "Toleration Act" of 1689 contributed to the growth of Methodism within the Anglican Church. [8] This was accomplished by

---

4. Ibid., 38.
5. Oden, *John Wesley's*, 55.
6. Hempton, "Wesley in Context," 66.
7. Gregory, "Long Eighteenth Century," 26.
8. The *Toleration Act* ensured that ministers of dissenting groups (Baptists, Presbyterians, Quakers, etc.) in seventeenth-century England followed the Thirty-Nine Articles of the Church of England (except regarding baptism and church government), which resulted in tolerance of dissenting church groups (Gregory, "Long Eighteenth Century," 36).

tolerating the Methodist movement and by encouraging dissenters to join the Anglican Church.[9]

Another factor was Wesley's social context. Wesley sought to reform the immoral culture in eighteenth-century England.[10] It included unjust societal practices, such as slavery, inhumane work conditions, immoral sexual behaviors, etc. Thus, Wesley provided an impetus for reforming English morals as well as for restoring scriptural holiness in Anglican churches.[11] In essence, by the 1770s, Wesley had influenced his social context by opposing radicalism, materialism, slavery, Catholicism, corruption and theological heterodoxy.[12] In addition, Wesley and his early Methodist leaders protested against luxury and rampant alcoholism.[13] Wesley's remedy and starting point consisted of "the individual's moral transformation."[14] The next section will discuss Wesley's influences and formation.

Wesley's Influences and Formation

Wesley was born on June 17, 1703 and died in 1791 having lived for eighty-eight years, which was more than twice the average life expectancy in the eighteenth century. The influences that had an impact on Wesley can be categorized as informal, formal and non-formal. Wesley's *informal* educational experiences were provided by his family, especially by his mother's (Susanna) teaching during the first 10 years.[15] Susanna Wesley appeared to have provided a delicate balance of nurture as well as of discipline. Thus, she was a strong disciplinarian, but also devoted at least one hour per week with each of her children.[16] Susanna Wesley had a profound influence on John Wesley's theology with "John Wesley [having been] the founder of Methodism [while] Susanna Wesley [having given] Methodism its methodical nature."[17] Thus, John Wesley learned discipline and self-control in his home. He also developed an appreciation for a systematic way of living out his faith. Wesley's father influenced him as well. As an Anglican pastor, his

9. Ibid., 37.
10. Hempton, "Wesley in Context," 66.
11. Ibid., 66.
12. Ibid., 71.
13. Marquardt, *John Wesley's Social*, 131.
14. Ibid., 131.
15. Maddix, "John Wesley's Formational," 1.
16. Ibid., 2.
17. Ibid., 3–4.

father inspired John to pursue his academic training, and he modeled an appreciation for the sacraments.

Wesley's *formal* education began at age ten when he entered Charterhouse Boarding School.[18] Attending a private boarding school was a common practice in eighteenth-century England. Wesley's experiences were not always positive while he was at his boarding school and these experiences shaped his view of childhood education. After graduating from boarding school, John entered Christ Church at Oxford University to obtain his bachelor's degree. There he became proficient in classical studies.[19] His educational experiences at Oxford fostered his academic preparation and provided exposure to "practical divinity" by reading devotional literature.[20] In particular, John Wesley read Thomas à Kempis's *Imitation of Christ*, which exposed him to the "nature and extent of inward religion."[21] While at Oxford he also read Jeremy Taylor's *The Rule of Exercise of Holy Living* and *The Rule of Exercise of Holy Dying* that emphasized holy love as the goal of religion. As stated below, love toward God and others was evidence for sanctification in a believer's life. His mother, due to her Puritan heritage, influenced John to focus on "experiential divinity," whereas his father urged him to become proficient in technical aspects of theology, such as biblical languages and other academic subjects.[22] Wesley followed British empiricism and Aristotle in that he viewed knowledge as being derived from the senses.[23] This led to Wesley's claim that God creates in believers "spiritual senses" in addition to physical senses that can be directly affected by "spiritual realities."[24]

John Wesley became an ordained deacon in the Church of England in 1725 and graduated from Oxford in 1729.[25] That same year Wesley read William Law's *Christian Perfection* and *A Serious Call to a Devout and Holy Life*, two works that profoundly influenced his theology.[26] Also in 1729, after his graduation from Oxford, John Wesley became a fellow at Lincoln College where he tutored undergraduate students in both academic and spiritual disciplines.[27] Wesley met with his students four nights a week to study

18. Ibid., 4.
19. Collins, "Wesley's Life," 43.
20. Maddix, "John Wesley's Formational," 4.
21. Collins, "Wesley's Life," 44.
22. Maddix, "John Wesley's Formational," 4.
23. Miles, "Instrumental Role," 86.
24. Maddox, "Enriching Role," 118.
25. Maddix, "John Wesley's Formational," 5.
26. Collins, "Wesley's Life," 44.
27. Maddix, "John Wesley's Formational," 5.

the classics, to read the Greek New Testament, and to practice spiritual disciplines (such as prayer, fasting, confession). He and his group also frequently partook of the sacraments. In addition, "the students served others by visiting the sick, elderly, and imprisoned, and provided clothing and financial aid where they could."[28] The group became known as "the Holy Club, Bible Moths, Sacramentarians" and, by 1732, "Methodists."[29]

Wesley's *non-formal* education, as far as significant influences on his theology are concerned, consisted of his missionary journey to Georgia, his Aldersgate experience, and the influence of Moravianism.[30] In 1735, John and his brother Charles and two others sailed for Georgia to preach to the Native Americans and to come to terms with his own salvation.[31] While on the ship, Wesley became very afraid during a severe Atlantic storm. He was impressed by "the serenity of the Moravian community on board who calmly sang" during the storm.[32] He concluded that the Moravians "were delivered from pride, anger, and revenge" while other passengers feared for their lives during the storm.[33] Wesley realized that something was missing when it came to his Christian faith. Shortly after arriving in Georgia, Wesley sought advice from a Moravian leader, August Spangenberg, who asked him direct probing questions about his personal salvation: "Does the Spirit of God bear witness with your spirit that you are a child of God?" Wesley was perplexed and did not know how to answer this question. When asked, "do you know Jesus Christ?" Wesley responded that he had had a global belief that Jesus is the Savior of the world to which Spangenberg further probed, "but do you know he has saved *you*?" Wesley responded that he hoped that Christ died for him and continued with similar vague answers. This interview experience was Wesley's second significant influential factor and showed Wesley that he lacked the witness of the Holy Spirit.[34] He was also made aware of the importance of instantaneous justification when a person is born-again, which is accompanied by the assurance of faith and that he is a child of God.[35] The Moravians, especially Peter Böhler, taught that justification and the new birth experience eliminates the power of sin,

---

28. Ibid., 5.
29. Collins, "Wesley's Life," 45.
30. Maddix, "John Wesley's Formational," 5.
31. Ibid., 5; Collins, "Wesley's Life," 46.
32. Collins, "Wesley's Life," 46.
33. Maddix, "John Wesley's Formational," 6.
34. Collins, "Wesley's Life," 46.
35. Maddix, "John Wesley's Formational," 6.

which Wesley adopted in his theology.[36] However, Moravian theology also included the elimination of "the being of sin," which Wesley did not adopt.[37]

In addition, the Moravians along with Isaac Watts, a Congregationalist, influenced the Wesley brothers to begin the practice of singing hymns during worship services, which had been forbidden in the Church of England.[38] Charles Wesley's hymns contributed greatly to Wesleyan spirituality. For example, Hymn 129 on the "doctrine of deification" illustrates the awareness of the indwelling Trinity in the believer:

> THE Father, Son, and Spirit dwell
> By faith in till his saints below.
> And then in love unspeakable
> The glorious Trinity we know
> Created after God to shine.
> Filled with the Plentitude Divine.[39]

Wesley's Aldersgate experience, shortly after his return from Georgia, was the third significant influential factor on his theology. On May 24, 1738, while under Böhler's spiritual direction, John listened to the reading of Martin Luther's "Preface to the Epistle to the Romans" at a religious society meeting on Aldersgate Street.[40] He recorded his spiritual experience in his journal:

> . . . I felt my heart strangely warmed. I felt I did trust in Christ, Christ alone, for salvation, and an assurance was given me, that He had taken away my sins, even mine, and saved me from the law of sin and death.[41]

Thus, Wesley experienced justification and forgiveness of his past sins, and his Aldersgate experience "represented an important actualization of saving grace."[42]

In 1738, after his Aldersgate experience, Wesley went to Herrnhut, which was a Moravian settlement, where he met with Count Zinzendorf, a Moravian leader, and became further aware of the theological differences between Moravian theology and his own theological reflections. Moravian

36. Collins, "Wesley's Life," 48.
37. Ibid., 46.
38. Westerfield Tucker, "Wesley's Emphases," 231.
39. Vickers, "And We," 342.
40. Collins, "Wesley's Life," 47.
41. Wesley, *Works*, 1:14.
42. Collins, "Wesley's Life," 47.

theology was based on Lutheran theology. Luther viewed justification and sanctification "as interrelated and interlocked," since "[p]eople always require justification because they are sinners: And people always require the sanctification of the justified life."[43] This theological difference between Luther and Wesley was apparent during the conversation with Count Zinzendorf:

> Count Zinzendorf (Z): "I acknowledge no inherent perfection in this life. This is an error of errors. . . . Whoever follows inherent perfection, denies Christ."
>
> John Wesley (W): "But I believe, that the spirit of Christ works this perfection in true Christians."
>
> Z: "By no means. All our perfection is in Christ. All Christian Perfection is, Faith in the blood of Christ. Our whole Christian Perfection is imputed, not inherent. We are perfect in Christ: In ourselves we are never perfect."
>
> and later . . .
>
> Z: "Our whole justification, and sanctification, are in the same instant, and he receives neither more nor less."
>
> W: "Does not a true believer increase in love to God daily? Is he *perfected* in love when he is justified?"[44]

This interview excerpt nicely illustrates the difference between Moravian theology and Wesleyan theology when it comes to sanctification and constituted the starting point of a gradual departure from Moravian theology. In addition to the theological differences between Wesley and the Moravians, Wesley noticed "their levity in behavior" and that Moravians do not fast.[45] His theological difference from Moravian and Lutheran theology regarding sanctification, in particular, was due to Wesley's preference for Greek theologians over Latin theologians.[46] Wesley drew from Eastern theology the emphasis of (therapeutic) gradual salvation, meaning believers becoming more like Christ during sanctification.[47] However, "Wesley's Aldersgate experience resulted in

---

43. Moltmann, *Spirit of Life*, 163.
44. Ibid., 169–70.
45. Collins, "Wesley's Life," 49.
46. Maddox, "John Wesley," 30.
47. Maddox, *Responsible Grace*, 152.

a 'heart-felt' religion that became the central thrust and aim of Methodism."⁴⁸ What were Wesley's views on anthropology, hamartiology, and soteriology?

Theological Foundations: Anthropology, Hamartiology, and Soteriology

Wesley's theological framework included creation, fall, and redemption.⁴⁹ Wesley taught universal atonement, which was aligned with Arminianism. For him, creation was tied to the covenant of works, in particular Adam before the Fall rather than the Mosaic covenant.⁵⁰ As stated above, Wesley drew from Eastern theology and integrated it with Western theology, especially Anglican Arminian theology. Thompson's comment is particularly helpful here:

> Wesley is, in my opinion, the integrative theologian *par excellence* in synthesizing the best of Eastern and Western theology into a coherent whole. This preference for both/and thinking rather than the dominant either/or thinking characteristic of the post-Enlightenment West is most likely the chief reason Wesley is so often misunderstood in the West.⁵¹

Thus, Wesley developed a theology that integrated Eastern and Western theological insights, thereby restoring the early church's emphasis on sanctification as understood as real (inherent) changes in the believer post-conversion. He drew more heavily from Eastern theologians, such as "Basil, Chrysostom, Clement of Alexandria, Clement of Rome, Ephraem Syrus, Ignatius, Irenaeus, Justin Martyr, Origen, Polycarp and (Pseudo-) Macarius."⁵² He especially integrated John Chrysostom's writings into his theology, which included the centrality of love and the balanced perspective of "*grace* and *demand*." ⁵³ The following is a brief summary of Wesley's anthropology, hamartiology, and soteriology.

Wesley's view of humanity was inherently relational and he viewed proper relationships as essential to human existence.⁵⁴ Wesley recognized four basic relationships, which were with God, with other humans, with

---

48. Maddix, "John Wesley's Formational," 7.
49. Vickers, "Wesley's Theological," 193.
50. Ibid., 193.
51 Thompson, "Kingdom Come," 108.
52. Maddox, "John Wesley," 30.
53. Ibid., 30.
54. Maddox, *Responsible Grace*, 68.

animals, and with oneself. Four moral human actions correspond to each of the four relationships; the relationship with God consists of "knowing, loving, obeying, and enjoying God eternally"; proper relationships with others includes "loving service"; with animals, "loving protection"; and with oneself, "self-acceptance."[55] Important is his inclusion of the love for oneself, which includes treating oneself compassionately. It is also worth noting that Wesley included love towards animals, which has often been neglected by other theologians. This resembles Holt's definition of Christian spirituality by including love for the whole creation in addition to having love for God, self, and others.[56]

Wesley's anthropology can also be considered dichotomist, since he believed that humans live as "embodied souls/spirits."[57] Note that this view does not differentiate between "soul" and "(human) spirit." Dichotomism is still the most common view in theology and became the universal belief of the church after the Council of Constantinople in 381.[58]

In addition, Wesley's anthropology included various other aspects, such as the understanding, will, liberty, and conscience:

> Wesley's writings after the transitions of Aldersgate reflect a self-conscious adoption of [an] empiricist-inspired *affectional* moral psychology. This adoption takes formal expression in his list of the faculties that constitute the Image of God in humanity: understanding, will, liberty, and conscience. "Will" is used in this list as an inclusive term for the various affections.[59]

Thus, Wesley saw humans as created in God's Image. The image of God, according to Wesley, consists of three aspects: The natural image, the political image, and the moral image.[60] The natural image, as quoted above, includes "[human] understanding, freedom of the will, and various affections."[61] The political image refers to human's duty to lead the animal kingdom and the moral image refers to righteousness and holiness. Though exegetically weak, Wesley followed Irenaeus's dual distinction between the image of God, which corresponds to Wesley's natural image, and the likeness of God, which refers to Wesley's moral image.[62]

55. Ibid., 68.
56. Holt, *Thirsty for God*, 23–28.
57. Maddox, *Responsible Grace*, 71.
58. Erickson, *Christian Theology*, 522.
59. Maddox, "Psychology," 103.
60. Lodahl, "Wesley and Nature," 23.
61. Ibid., 23.
62. Most biblical scholars today view the usage of "image of God" and "likeness of

It is worth noting the major differences between Western and Eastern theology when it comes to human nature:

> Western Christians have generally assumed that humans were created in a complete and perfect state—the epitome of all that God wanted them to be. God's original will was simply that they retain this perfection. However, humans were created in the Image of God, which included—in particular—an ability for self-determination.... Eastern anthropology differs from the West on nearly every point. First, Eastern theologians have generally assumed that humanity was originally innocent, but not complete. We were created with a dynamic nature destined to progress in communion with God. This conviction lies behind their typical distinction between the "Image of God" and the "Likeness of God." The "Image of God" denoted the universal human potentiality for life in God. The "Likeness of God" was the *realization* of that potentiality. Such realization (often called *deification*) is only possible by *participation* in divine life and grace. Moreover, it is neither inevitable nor automatic. Thus, the Image of God necessarily includes the aspect of human freedom, though it centers in the larger category of capacity for communion with God.[63]

These differences are reflected in Wesley's coherent theological system in which he integrated both views. In particular, Wesley believed that humans were created in a perfect state (Western), but he also differentiated between the image of God (natural image) and likeness of God (moral image), thereby following the Eastern view. The consequences of the Fall in Western theology included:

> 1) the loss of self-determination (we are free now only to sin), and 2) the inheritance of the *guilt* of this original sin by all human posterity. Since this fallen condition is universal, the West has a tendency to talk of it as the "natural" state of human existence; i.e., they base their anthropology primarily on the Fall, emphasizing the guilt and powerlessness of humans apart from God's grace.[64]

And in Eastern theology:

> First, they [Eastern theologians] reject the idea of human posterity inheriting the guilt of the Fall, we become guilty only when we imitate Adam's sin. Second, they argue that the primary

---

God" in Genesis 1:26 as an expression of parallelism (ibid., 24, 25).

63 Maddox, "John Wesley," 34.

64. Ibid., 34.

result of the Fall was the introduction of death and corruption into human life and its subsequent dominion over humanity. Finally, while Orthodoxy clearly believes that the death and disease thus introduced have so weakened the human intellect and will that we can no longer hope to attain the Likeness of God, they do not hold that the Fall deprived us of all grace, or of the responsibility for responding to God's offer of restored communion in Christ.[65]

Again, Wesley's theology integrated both views by affirming humanity's inherited guilt, but his theology emphasized "how the Fall introduced spiritual corruption into human life."[66] Prevenient grace universally cancels this inherited guilt based on Christ's redemption.[67] However, the restoration of the moral image in humans is gradual and achieved through sanctifying grace (see below). Original sin is thus better described as *inbeing sin* in Wesley's theology because of the Eastern understanding of "sin's present infection of our nature" as opposed to the focus in the West on the origin of sin.[68] The later Wesley believed in a biological transmission of Adam's corrupted nature (infected).[69]

Wesley emphasized original or inbeing sin based on adopting the concept of deification during the process of sanctification.[70] Wesley differentiated between inbeing (original) sin and specific or personal sins. Inbeing sin is an "innate corruption of the innermost nature of man [and] is compared to an evil root bearing like branches and like fruits" whereas specific sins "which proceed from original sin are compared to evil sprouts proceeding from the same evil root."[71] Personal sins are "actual transgressions" and consist of inward, outward, and "sins of omission (the failure to do good)," which are "negative inward sins."[72] Inward sins refer to "pride, wrath, and foolish desires," whereas outward sins include actual sinful behaviors, which develop from inward sins.[73] It is important to note that Wesley saw personal sins as *intentional* and *voluntary* transgressions as opposed to *unintentional*

65. Ibid., 34.
66. Ibid., 35.
67. Maddox, *Responsible Grace*, 75.
68. Ibid., 75.
69. Maddox asserts that the late Wesley followed Tertullian's traducianism—meaning the "entire nature (body and soul) of human persons are transmitted (traduced) from their parents" (ibid, 76, 80).
70. Lindström, *Wesley and Sanctification*, 31.
71. Ibid., 38.
72. Ibid.
73. Ibid., 39.

transgressions of God's law.[74] Thus "human imperfections and unintentional offenses . . . do not fall into the category of sin," which means for Wesley personal sin is based on evil motives and intentions.[75] We can conclude that pure and sanctified motives and intentions reduce and potentially eliminate *intentional* personal sins in believers.

The focus in Wesley's theology is on sanctification, which entails real character changes in believers based on God's sanctifying grace and human cooperation. What, then, was Wesley's view of the way of salvation? According to Maddox, Wesley's view of salvation has three dimensions that consist of deliverance: "(1) immediately from the *penalty* of sin, (2) progressively from the *plague* of sin, and (3) eschatologically from the very *presence* of sin and its effects."[76] As mentioned above, Wesley integrated the Western judicial soteriology with the Eastern therapeutic emphasis on deification (*theosis*), especially the late Wesley.[77] The Eastern theology's emphasis on the concept of *theosis* can be traced back to Irenaeus and especially Athanasius's well-known statement: "God became human in order that human beings might become God."[78] Wesley's soteriology views God's grace as operative in several ways toward several ends.[79] According to Wesley, humans do not initiate salvation; they are given *prevenient grace*, which paves the way for *convicting grace*. This also means that humans are able to resist this grace. If convicting grace is accepted, it leads to *justifying grace*. Justifying grace provides the restoration to the favor of God including the elimination of guilt, which refers to the Western judicial emphasis. The Eastern therapeutic emphasis can be seen in Wesley's view of *sanctifying grace*, which saves the believer "from the power and root of sin, and restore[s] the believer to the image of God."[80] Thus, *sanctifying grace* fosters actual change of the believer through a transformation into God's image. The focus of Wesley's soteriology is on sanctifying grace, meaning the Eastern therapeutic emphasis. In chapter 4 of this book I will further discuss and develop Wesley's concept of sanctification/perfection.

It is important in this section to further discuss prevenient grace. Prevenient grace is universally given to all humans based on Christ's

---

74. Carter, "Hamartiology," 271.
75. Ibid., 271.
76. Maddox, *Responsible Grace*, 143.
77. Ibid, 142.
78. Thunberg, "Eastern Christianity," 308.
79. Kilian and Parker, "Wesleyan Spirituality," 205.
80. Oden, *John Wesley's*, 247.

atonement.[81] Wesley followed Augustine's conception of grace, but modified it. According to Augustine, prevenient grace "goes ahead" and prepares "the human will for conversion," which is then followed by "operative grace" that "effects the conversion of sinners without any assistance on their part."[82] Unlike Augustine, Wesley perceived human cooperation in each phase of grace not merely in Augustine's "cooperative grace" phase that occurs after conversion.[83] Prevenient grace resembles the Eastern Orthodox view that some measure of human freedom remained after the Fall for humans to turn to God.[84] In this view, similar to Eastern theology, Wesley believed that grace was given to all enabling human freedom, which contradicted Augustine's view. It is a free gift and not a reward for humanity.[85] For this reason, Wesley is said to have adopted a Semi-Augustinian theological position.[86] However, there are other benefits of prevenient grace, such as a basic knowledge of the attributes of God, reinscription of the moral law, conscience, and the restraint of wickedness.[87]

Regarding a basic knowledge of the attributes of God, Wesley refers to general revelation derived from Romans 1:19, which "forms the basis for a natural theology" according to some theologians.[88] The second benefit (moral law being reinscribed) is based on Wesley's assertion that God would not leave humans in an utterly depraved state without giving them a glimpse of God's moral law written upon their hearts. This aspect of prevenient grace also explains moral behavior in non-Christians, such as humanists, philanthropists, atheists, etc. Thus, moral behavior, regardless of who performs it, ultimately originates in God's prevenient grace. This aspect is based on Wesley's view that every person has a desire to please God, even the unbeliever.[89] The third benefit, conscience, is a supernatural gift based on God's grace. It is important to note that, according to Wesley, the human conscience is

81. Collins, *Theology of Wesley*, 74.
82. McGrath, *Christian Theology*, 450.
83. Ibid., 451.
84. Maddox, "John Wesley," 34.
85. Runyon, *New Creation*, 37.
86. Walton, *Chronological and Background*, 47. Semi-Augustinianism can be considered a "diluted form of Augustinianism" that was adopted at the Council of Orange (AD 529) after Semi-Pelagianism was condemned. Semi-Augustinianism means that the "the first step of faith—*initium fidei*—is not in human nature, but in divine grace" (Gonzalez, *History of Christianity*, 61–62). It also rejected Augustine's more extreme views, such as predestination and irresistible grace.
87. Collins, *Theology of Wesley*, 78.
88. Ibid., 77.
89. Marquardt, *John Wesley's Social*, 93.

not derived from nature (parents, biology, etc.), but from God. However, Wesley also acknowledged that the conscience can be "scrupulous" and evil, which necessitates a correction through Scripture.[90] The conscience has a key function during the salvation process because the Holy Spirit uses one's conscience to motivate the sinner to repent.[91] The fourth benefit, restraint of wickedness, is similar "to Luther's orders of creation and preservation" and refers to God's "restraining grace" to limit wickedness in society.[92]

Conclusion

This chapter explored Wesley's historical and social context, influences and formation. Wesley addressed the social ills of eighteenth-century Great Britain. He equally stressed personal moral transformation and social transformation, but insisted that the transformation begins in the individual. In this chapter I also provided an outline of his theological views regarding anthropology, hamartiology and soteriology. These foci are relevant for this book due to their correspondence to personality, developmental, and psychotherapeutic psychology, which can add important insights for Christian leadership development. Wesley provided an excellent synthesis of both Western and Eastern theology. His emphasis was on the therapeutic nature of salvation that produces real character changes in believers. This resembles the Eastern theological concept of *theosis*, which is another important insight for later sections and for leadership development in general. In the next chapter I will outline *orthokardia* and will focus on Wesley's view of sanctification and perfection, which consists of loving God with all one's mind, soul, etc., and loving others as one loves him- or herself. I will also discuss healthy human development that will provide important insights for the concept of emotional maturity.

Reflection Questions and Exercises

(Please pray for the leading of the Holy Spirit before you answer the reflection questions and complete the exercises)

1. Make a time line of your salvation (dates of your spiritual experiences, etc.).

---

90. Runyon, *New Creation*, 32.
91. Ibid., 33.
92. Collins, *Theology of Wesley*, 80.

2. Prior to your conversion, did you ever experience a time when you wanted to please God (cf. prevenient grace)?
3. When did you experience the desire to be more like Christ (cf. sanctifying grace)? If you have not experienced it, pray for the Holy Spirit to give you this desire for Christ-likeness.
4. How can you cooperate with God on a daily, weekly, monthly, etc. basis?
5. How can you relate to Wesley's Aldersgate experience?
6. Reflect on Wesley's differentiation between sins and transgressions, with sins being *intentional* and *voluntary* as opposed to *unintentional* rule-breaking behaviors. How can this help you with self-compassion?

Chapter 4

Orthokardia

Spiritual and Emotional Maturity

ORTHOKARDIA INCLUDES THE CONCEPTS of spiritual maturity and emotional maturity. According to Scazzero we cannot separate spiritual maturity from emotional maturity.[1] In this chapter I will explore Wesley's understanding of entire sanctification/Christian perfection with the focus on loving God, others, and self. Perfect love as a result of God's sanctifying grace constitutes spiritual maturity. I will also outline healthy emotional development drawing from two psychological theories, Bowlby's Attachment theory and Bowen's Family Systems Theory. These theories contribute to a foundational understanding of emotional maturity that will be correlated with spiritual maturity. It is important to re-emphasize that *orthokardia* presupposes *orthodoxy* as mentioned in chapter 1. Kretzschmar points out that the conversion of the leader's "head" (one's intellect) involves the development of prudence:

> Prudence goes beyond information and knowledge: it is practical wisdom which is attuned to things as they really are, and it pursues goodness. It is both a knowledge of reality and the realisation of the good: it is related to both the good life and good persons.[2]

In addition, *orthodoxy* refers to "knowing what is right" which includes knowing God and being known by him.[3] Knowing God "is linked to goodness, self-control and the ongoing experience of God's grace" and not only

1. Scazzero, *Emotionally Healthy Spirituality*.
2. Kretzschmar, "Formation," 30.
3. Kretzschmar, "Education," 5.

includes the acquisition of information, but also includes understanding others and relating to them.[4] It is important to note that the mind is the starting point for moral transformation and the development of virtue. Wright's statement is helpful here:

> The key to virtue lies precisely, as we have seen, in the transformation of the mind. The point is not that the practices are wrong, or inadequate, *but that our conscious mind and heart need to understand, ponder, and consciously choose* the patterns of life which these practices are supposed to produce in us and through us.[5]

This means that knowing God and choosing the good is an essential prerequisite for moral transformation of the heart. Obstacles or hindrances to knowing prevent the successful development of the moral life. Kretzschmar lists some obstacles to knowing, which are pride, "ignorance of self, the scriptures, others and life in general," a distorted image of God, and separation of faith and reason.[6] *Orthokardia* presupposes that Christian leaders have removed these obstacles, turned towards God in worship, internalized orthodox doctrine, are in the process of renewing their minds, integrate faith and reason according to Wesleyan theology, and are in the process of developing practical wisdom. Next I will discuss *orthokardia*, which includes Wesley's understanding of sanctification resulting in a pure heart.

Christian Perfection: Love for God, Others, and Self

Orthokardia ("right heart") includes and presupposes Wesley's concept of entire sanctification or Christian perfection. The heart is the "center of moral agency" according to Clapper.[7] It is also the "seat of values, the home of the deep and abiding emotions" and it is:[8]

---

4. Ibid., 5.
5. Wright, *After You Believe*, 259 (my emphasis).
6. Kretzschmar, "Education," 5.
7. Clapper, "John Wesley," 49. According to Ogletree ("Agents and Moral," 36), moral agency includes the following three components: "(1) a primal *disposition* to live a moral life; (2) the *capacity* to act morally; and (3) a sound *moral judgment*." According to Wesleyan theology, all three components are provided by God's prevenient grace (regarding moral disposition) and sanctifying grace in cooperation with the believer's volition to act morally. The third component refers to our rational faculties and the renewing of one's mind (cf. Romans 12).
8. Clapper, "John Wesley," 51.

the source of our strongest desires and the guide for our deepest choices, the home of our most intense yearnings and of our greatest hopes, fears, loves, and dreams. The heart carries our identity, that sense of who we are that is composed of both our history (how we have been formed in the furnace of life up to this point) and our vision of what we want to become (how we hope to be formed in the future). *The heart is a metaphor for who we really are, that vision of self we see when, in our frankest moments of honesty and insight*, we name what we are really after in life, what brings our greatest fulfillment.[9]

Thus, the heart is a vision of our true self informed by truth and honesty. Clapper links the heart with one's self-understanding.[10] We can say that the heart is part of our personality. Our personality provides a sense of identity and is shaped by our past and present and will inform our future. The heart has been affected by the Fall and is thus deceitful (Jer 17:9), which requires correction from the outside. The Holy Spirit is an external Being that is able to correct and change one's heart, which is initiated by salvation that includes the process of sanctification. As mentioned above, Wesley's view of salvation has three dimensions that include deliverance: "(1) immediately from the *penalty* of sin, (2) progressively from the *plague* of sin, and (3) eschatologically from the very *presence* of sin and its effects."[11] Justifying grace provides the restoration to the favor of God including the elimination of guilt, which refers to the Western judicial emphasis. The Eastern therapeutic emphasis can be seen in Wesley's view of *sanctifying grace*, which saves the believer "from the power and root of sin, and restore[s] to the image of God."[12] Thus, *sanctifying grace* fosters actual change of the believer through a dynamic process of transformation into God's image towards Christian perfection, which constitutes spiritual maturity.

Christian perfection does not include absolute perfection, but it rather refers to purity of intention not to sin anymore. This purity of intention is a work of sanctifying grace and is imparted by the Holy Spirit. The term "perfection" in the Bible has also been translated as "maturation" or "completeness" (cf. Matt 5:48). The static notion of "perfection" stems from a Western interpretation of the text (cf. the Latin Vulgate, *perfectus*) rather than an Eastern understanding of the Greek original (*teleiotes*), which implies a

---

9. Ibid., 17 (my emphasis).
10. Ibid., 70.
11. Maddox, *Responsible Grace*, 143.
12. Oden, *John Wesley's*, 247.

dynamic process towards holiness.[13] Similarly, according to Wesley, "but neither in this sense is there any *absolute perfection* on earth. There is no perfection of degrees; none which does not admit of a *continual increase.*"[14] Loving God is the primary benefit of sanctification according to Wesley:

> "Whatsoever things are just, whatsoever things are pure, whatsoever things are amiable, or honorable; if there be any virtue, if there be any praise," they are all comprised in this one word,— *love. In this is perfection, and glory, and happiness.* The royal law of heaven and earth is this, "Thou shalt love the Lord thy God with all thy heart, and with all thy soul, and with all thy mind, and with all thy strength." (Sermon 17)[15]

It is worth noting that perfect love does not imply "some constancy of inner feeling," but love for God and one's neighbor is more an enduring affective state.[16] Clapper distinguishes between feelings that are transitory and emotions that are longer lasting.[17] Christians should not be controlled by feelings and Wesley warns against "reducing religion into feeling states" but rather Christians should develop "affective capacities," which refers to Christian affections that will be revisited and further developed in chapter 5.[18]

Perfect love during the process of sanctification can purify one's heart according to Wesley:

> Love has purified his heart from envy, malice, wrath, and unkind temper. It has cleansed him from pride, whereof only "cometh contention:" and he hath now "put on bowels of mercy, kindness, humbleness of mind, meekness, long-suffering." And, indeed all possible ground for contention on his part is cut off.[19]

A pure heart, based on the process of sanctification, produces pure love, pure motives and intentions that reduce and potentially eliminate intentional personal sins in believers. Pure motives and intentions will be emphasized in chapter 5. Wesley's own definition of Christian perfection is helpful here:

---

13. Ibid., 320.
14. Wesley, *Plain Account*, 16 (my emphasis).
15. Wesley, *Works*, 5:I/11 (my emphasis).
16. Clapper, "Orthokardia," 61.
17. Clapper, *Renewal*, 66.
18. Ibid., 66, 65.
19. Wesley, *Plain Account*, 12–13.

> The loving God with all your heart, mind, soul, and strength. This implies that no wrong temper, none contrary to love, remains in the soul; and that all the thoughts, words, and actions are *governed by pure love*.[20]

In the remaining sections I will discuss Wesley's foci of love (love for God, others, and self)[21] and the quality and nature of love. It is important to emphasize that according to Wesley, one's ability to love God is based on God's grace and love towards the sinner, meaning God's love is the source of human love.[22] Wesley continues to emphasize the centrality of love here, which is the result of sanctifying grace:

> Let your soul be filled with so entire a love of him, that you may love nothing but for his sake. "Have a pure intention of heart, a steadfast regard to his glory in all your actions." "Fix your eye upon the blessed hope of your calling, and make all the things of the world minister unto it." For then, and not till then, is that "mind in us which was also in Christ Jesus . . ." (Sermon 17).[23]

The second commandment of Jesus is equally important for Wesley, which refers to love for others:

> "Thou shalt love thy neighbor as thyself." *Thou shalt love,*—Thou shalt embrace with the most tender goodwill, the most earnest and cordial affection, the most inflamed desires of preventing or removing all evil, and of procuring for him every possible good,—*Thy neighbor;*—that is, not only thy friend, thy kinsman, or thy acquaintance; not only the virtuous, the friendly, him that loves thee, that prevents or returns thy kindness; but every child of man, every human creature, every soul which God hath made; . . . (Sermon 7).[24]

It is important to note that Wesley emphasizes the passionate desire to do anything in one's power to provide goodness to others and to remove evil regardless of status, ethnicity, gender, etc., which refers to the human tendency

---

20. Ibid., 42 (my emphasis).

21. This is contrasted with Augustine's alternate conception of love. He viewed love as desire, "as morally neutral," and as "not essentially connected to helping, benevolence, giving, *shalom*, or increasing genuine blessedness" (Oord, *Nature of Love*, 60). Augustine also rejected loving others for "their own sakes" as well as self-love (ibid., 64).

22. Lindström, *Wesley and Sanctification*, 177.

23. Wesley, *Works*, 5:II/10.

24. Ibid., 5:I/140–41.

of *prejudging* others or prejudice. The human tendency to be prejudiced will be addressed in chapter 6.

Finally, loving oneself is the prerequisite of loving others. While Wesley did not emphasize the love one should have for oneself he implied that sanctified Christians should be kind to others as they are kind to themselves:

> Him thou shalt love *as thyself*; with the same invariable thirst after his happiness in every kind; the same unwearied care to screen him from whatever might grieve or hurt either his soul or body. (Sermon 7)[25]

Proper self-love is not sinful, but unregulated self-love is.[26] By emphasizing love for oneself we go beyond Wesley's eigtheenth-century worldview and context to a twenty-first-century *self-help* and therapeutic worldview. The Christian psychologist Beck depicts the triangle of love and describes love for God as "cultic," love for others as "humanistic," and love for self as "therapeutic."[27] Beck provides a regulation of self-love based on humility. He associates the concept of *kenosis* (cf. Phil 2:7) with proper self-love and argues that loving others needs to be coupled with humility:

> This "welcoming others" requires that the ego be strong enough to set aside self-interest, resilient enough to suffer relational damage when others take advantage (one thinks of the relationship between Jesus and Judas), and assertive enough to not allow this process to spiral into victimhood in the face of chronic relational abuse and neglect. All these traits can be described as a form of "self-love."[28]

Thus, a sanctified Christian will keep the three foci of love in balance by loving God and others based on proper self-love. These foci constitute the essence of entire sanctification/Christian perfection and again constitute spiritual maturity. This requires self-awareness of deficiencies in one's love for oneself that pose potential barriers to loving others resulting from one's derailed psychological development, which I will discuss below.

The quality and nature of love will be outlined next. Wesley's emphasis on love as a mark of sanctification was heavily influenced by his reading of

---

25. Ibid., I/140.

26. Lindström, *Wesley and Sanctification*, 196.

27. Beck, "Love in the Laboratory," 168. Beck's choice of the word "cultic" is a not a good one and can be easily misunderstood. He appears to mean that love for God has a "spiritual" or "transcendent" nature as opposed to one's love toward others or self.

28. Ibid., 171.

Jeremy Taylor, Thomas a Kempis, and William Law.[29] He was especially influenced by William Law's ideas on love.[30] Wesley adopted from William Law the emphasis on human transformation based on sanctification and cooperation with God's grace.[31] Law, as a "practical mystic," saw salvation primarily as an imitation of Christ (similar to Thomas a Kempis) with love toward God and one's neighbor being essential for Christianity.[32] Law even perceived proper self-love as a standard for brotherly love.[33] However, unlike Wesley, Law put heavier emphasis on the love for others yet still asserted that "all love comes from God."[34] However, there are key differences between Law's conception of Christian love and Wesley's.[35] One difference is that Wesley emphasized God's love toward humans as a starting point based on the Atonement. Wesley put more emphasis on the causes of love (Atonement), whereas Law emphasized the ends (human love as a result of sanctification). As I discussed in chapter 2, the Fall rendered human beings incapable of approaching and loving God, which necessitated prevenient grace and subsequent graces. Therefore, Wesley argued, love must come from God.

The idea of love is also closely tied to the notions of law and reason. Wesley saw love and moral law as compatible, since love fulfills God's moral law.[36] Reason implies that love needs to be ordered and regulated.[37] Lindström views this connection as a result of the prevailing rationalism in Wesley's time. Thus, love is not merely an emotion, but a Christian affection or virtue to honor and worship God and to do what is good for others as a duty and requirement of the moral law. Love toward God is gradual and progressive with its end of attaining a perfect unity with God, a notion that Wesley most likely adopted from William Law and Christian mysticism.[38]

29. Collins, *Theology of Wesley*, 125.
30. Lindström, *Wesley and Sanctification*, 162.
31. Ibid., 162–63.
32. Ibid., 164.
33. Ibid., 167.
34. Ibid., 170.
35. Ibid., 174.
36. Ibid., 180.
37. Ibid., 182.

38. Ibid., 186. The Christian mystical tradition adopted three steps toward divine union: purgation, illumination, and perfect union (Reininger, "Christian Contemplative," 41). The last stage is closely related to divine love: "The Christian experience of unity with God is not a state of consciousness or awareness but a *state of love* where the soul participates in the true nature of the Trinity and *infinite love*" (ibid., 45; my emphasis).

Loving others includes "tender good-will" toward others.[39] Self-love adds to brotherly love and serves as a prerequisite and is associated with the Golden Rule.[40]

The Wesleyan theologian Thomas Oord defines love as acting "intentionally, in sympathetic/empathetic response to God and others, to promote overall well-being."[41] He means by well-being "health, healing, happiness, wholeness, medicine, and flourishing" and by "overall" he refers to "promoting the common good" and well-being of enemies, strangers, and the poor.[42] His definition combines love with justice. By sympathy and empathy, Oord denotes the emotional or feeling aspect of love, which marks a slight departure from Wesley's conception of love that tends to de-emphasize emotion, which again was most likely informed by rationalism.[43] He asserts that "any act of love involves intention and feeling."[44] Similarly, the New Testament theologian, Matthew Elliott, argues that the notion of Christian love being a human emotion is biblical.[45] He further notes that love without emotion is not genuine love. He views the emotion of love as "vital for authentic Christian spirituality."[46] The author equates the human emotions of love, joy, and hope (fruits of the Spirit) as evidence for one's transformation in Christ, which resembles Wesleyan theology.[47] Elliott further argues that when Jesus commanded his disciples to love God and others he intended for his disciples to experience an emotional transformation: "[Jesus] used feelings as a measure *because feelings get at the truth of what is actually inside us*. Duty-driven love is counterfeit."[48] This resembles a Wesleyan Pentecostal view of love and sanctification:

> The *measure of love* given in new birth, along with the graces therein implanted come to full fruitfulness in sanctification. This entire sanctification is a *"burning passion for souls"* that enables one to forgive one's persecutors.[49]

---

39. Lindström, *Wesley and Sanctification*, 191.
40. Ibid., 195.
41. Oord, *Nature of Love*, 17.
42. Ibid., 19–20.
43. Ibid., 22.
44. Ibid., 30.
45. Elliott, "Emotional Core," 108.
46. Ibid.
47. Ibid., 110.
48. Ibid., 114.
49. Land, *Pentecostal Spirituality*, 128 (my emphasis).

This passion goes beyond a duty-driven love and includes an experiential aspect caused by the Holy Spirit that enables us to forgive enemies. Thus, in this book I view love and other Christian affections as ethical virtues *and* as emotions. Emotions, however, should not be overemphasized as we should not base our Christian spirituality solely on how we feel. Neither should we neglect emotions altogether to become "Christian stoics." A balanced view of emotions is needed, which we will explore below.

When it comes to prioritizing love, Oord, based on Wesley's sermon 92, "On Zeal," uses a series of concentric circles to depict Wesley's order of love: Love for God, self, and others is in the center, then are holy tempers (virtues or attitudes), works of mercy (e.g., helping the needy), works of piety (e.g., prayer and Eucharist), and love for fellow Christians is last.[50] He points out that one's "love for those in need often lay closer to the center of Christian commitment than either love expressions of piety or love for fellow believers in the Church." This reminds us of Oord's definition of love that includes the promotion of well-being and social justice.[51] This aspect will be the focus of chapter 6. We explored the nature of spiritual maturity and defined it as having a pure heart to love God, others, and self. What, then, is emotional maturity from a psychological perspective?

Healthy Emotional Development

Healthy emotional development is essential for becoming an empowering leader. Hence, an examination of human development provides important insights as to the emotional maturity of adult leaders. A healthy attachment to caregivers and the incorporation of the caregivers' positive traits constitute an important foundation for adaptive personality development. In this section I will discuss two essential theories that are relevant for the conceptualization of healthy emotional development. These theories are relevant for this study because of their emphasis on interpersonal relationships that have important implications for the communal character of spiritual formation and for emotional maturity.

Attachment Theory

Attachment theory is credited to John Bowlby who developed his theory based on the research trend during 1950s and 60s that focused on the

---

50. Oord, "Love, Wesleyan Theology," 152.
51. Oord, *Nature of Love*.

effects of maternal deprivation among other influences.⁵² He defines attachment as:

> [A]ny form of behavior that results in a person attaining or maintaining proximity to some other clearly identified individual who is conceived as better able to cope with the world.⁵³

This means the infant "perceives" the caregiver as being more able to cope with and manage negative mood states. Coping also refers to the infant and alludes to managing the underlying mood state of anxiety and/or sadness resulting from separation from and/or loss of significant others. In other words, the infant clings to his or her caregivers to modulate his or her negative mood states. If caregivers provide a sense of safety to their children the "children's anxiety will be relieved," which is "the safe haven function of attachment" or "secure base."⁵⁴ By providing warmth and structure to their children, parents ensure a secure attachment relationship.⁵⁵

There are three attachment patterns: secure, ambivalent, and avoidant.⁵⁶ Securely attached infants and children "confidently explore their environments . . . and when distressed, they seek contact with their caregivers."⁵⁷ Children (or infants) who fall into the avoidant attachment pattern avoid their caregivers when distressed, whereas children with the ambivalent (anxious) attachment pattern display "a mix of contact seeking and angry resistance."⁵⁸ Main and Solomon added a fourth attachment pattern called a disorganized pattern, which is often the result of extreme abuse of neglect.⁵⁹ Children with this pattern are the most disturbed and display an inconsistent "strategy for handling stress."⁶⁰

In 2001, Daniel Siegel, a child psychiatrist, introduced an interdisciplinary field of study called interpersonal neurobiology (IPNB). IPNB includes various disciplines, such as psychiatry, neurobiology, psychology including attachment theory, etc.⁶¹ He defines attachment as:

---

52. Bowlby, *Attachment and Loss*; Bowlby, "Attachment and Loss," 666.
53. Ibid., 668.
54. Batholomew et al., "Attachment," 197.
55. Benjamin, "Interpersonal Theory," 187.
56. Ainsworth et al., *Patterns of Attachment*.
57. Ibid., 197.
58. Ibid., 197.
59. Main and Solomon, "Procedures for Identifying."
60. Ainsworth et al., *Patterns of Attachment*, 197.
61. Siegel, *Developing Mind*.

an inborn system in the brain that evolves in ways that influence and organize motivational, emotional, and memory processes with respect to significant caregiving figures.[62]

He eloquently integrates neuroscience with attachment theory when he notes:

Repeated [attachment] experiences become encoded in implicit memory [unconscious memory that stores mental models, experiences, etc.] as expectations and then as mental models or schemata of attachment, which serve to help the child feel an internal sense of what John Bowlby called a "secure base" in the world.[63]

These early patterns of relating correlate with how we as adults interact with others in the future, especially romantic partners. Siegel calls them "adult states of mind" and summarizes them accordingly.[64] The secure attachment style, or later in life called the autonomous adult state of mind, refers to individuals having been securely attached to caregivers and their ability to securely attach to people later in life. People with a dismissing (avoidant in childhood) adult state of mind, dismiss attachment-related experiences and struggle with recalling personal events in their lives.[65] They often minimize negative experiences in childhood and tend to emphasize rationality. These people tend to avoid emotional closeness and are extremely independent. In addition, individuals with a dismissing adult state of mind can be described as having a "false self" and believe the "illusion of self-sufficiency."[66] Individuals with an ambivalent /preoccupied adult state of mind are "preoccupied with or by past attachment relationships [and] experiences" and appear "angry, passive, or fearful."[67] They are obsessively preoccupied with their relationships, tend to cling to people, and "seek attachment at the expense of autonomy."[68] These individuals can be described as "submissive, acquiescent, [and] suggestible" needing "excessive reassurance."[69] We can say that these individuals prefer to depend on others and do not value autonomy. Finally, people with an unresolved/disorganized adult state of mind tend to dissociate during discussions of past traumatic events and have difficulties

62. Ibid., 91.
63. Ibid.
64. Ibid., 99.
65. Ibid., 126.
66. Brown and Elliott, *Attachment Disturbances*, 108.
67. Siegel, *Developing Mind*, 99.
68. Brown and Elliott, *Attachment Disturbances*, 109.
69. Ibid.

with affect regulation especially if past trauma has not been resolved.[70] This tendency to dissociate points to a poorly developed and often fragmented self.[71] In additions, these adults tend to be passive and unassertive, but can often vacillate between dependency and controlling behaviors.[72]

Thus, they can alternate between dismissing and preoccupied adult states of mind.

How do people with various attachment patterns cope with stressful events? This question refers to one's emotional self-regulation abilities. Generally speaking, people with a secure attachment have an adaptive emotional regulation, which means they deal with stress successfully most of the time. Similarly, Schore views attachment as "the right-brain regulation of biological synchronicity between organisms."[73] In particular, he refers to the right orbitofrontal cortex (OFC) that provides emotional regulation including emotional self-control, which is not present at birth:

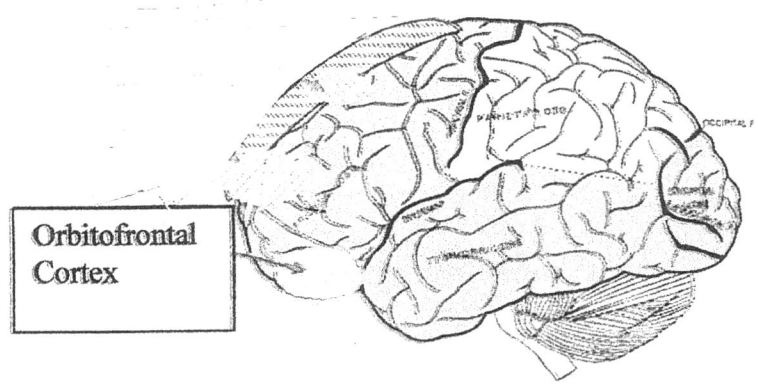

Figure 4: Orbitofrontal Cortex (OFC)

The OFC connects "three major regions of the brain: the cortex (or 'thinking brain'), the amygdala (the trigger point for many emotional reactions), and the brain stem (the 'reptilian' zones for automatic responses)."[74] The OFC is also the key region for social emotions, such as empathy and compassion, and it provides the experience of "love and warmth" when two people are securely attached.[75] Insecure attachment results in "inefficient patterns of

70. Siegel, *Developing Mind*, 137.
71. Brown and Elliott, *Attachment Disturbances*, 119.
72. Ibid., 118.
73. Schore, *Affect Regulation*, 41.
74. Goleman, *Social Intelligence*, 64.
75. Ibid., 64.

organization of the right brain, especially the right orbitofrontal areas."[76] This causes problems with empathy as well as causes difficulties with modulating emotions, such as "shame, rage, excitement, elation, disgust, panic-terror, and hopelessness-despair."[77] This explains why people with insecure attachment styles often struggle with shame, anger, depression, anxiety, etc. Regarding specific insecure states of mind, individuals with a dismissing state of mind tend to deny or block emotion-related thoughts or (negative) memories in order to avoid the perception of vulnerability, which they view as threatening.[78] Whereas people with a preoccupied state of mind tend to exaggerate these negative emotions in order to communicate to others that they need support and protection.[79] Individuals with a disorganized state of mind tend to be most impaired and ill equipped when it comes to coping. They tend to struggle the most with emotional self-regulation and social competence.[80]

In general, insecurely attached individuals tend to struggle with interpersonal forgiveness, which is mediated by a "lack of empathy."[81] Since there is ample research support for the fact that narcissists (often have a dismissing state of mind) struggle with forgiving others, narcissistic Christians also struggle with forgiving God for their problems and suffering in their lives.[82] While "forgiving God" may be theologically problematic, we can conclude that people who do not struggle with narcissistic traits tend to accept suffering and submission to God's will more easily. Forgiveness is a common Christian concept and the following will outline how attachment relates to Christian spirituality. The Christian psychiatrist Thompson explains how attachment informs our emotional experience of God:

> Our brains through the forces of various emotional states and implicit as well as explicit memory, *construct our experiences* of God—sometimes in ways that contradict what we assent to theologically. In this way, paying attention to our attachment means we are invariably paying attention to our connection with God.[83]

---

76. Schore, *Affect Regulation*, 47.
77. Ibid.
78. Shaver and Mikulincer, "Adult Attachment," 240.
79. Ibid., 241.
80. Brown and Elliott, *Attachment Disturbances*, 118.
81. Shaver and Mikulincer, "Adult Attachment," 243.
82. Twenge and Campbell, *Narcissism Epidemic*, 245.
83. Thompson, *Anatomy of the Soul*, 118.

Thus, our attachment to caregivers predicts our attachment to God, which has been empirically validated.[84] In particular, Hall and his colleagues found that securely attached individuals feel more connected to a spiritual community and experience less anxiety in their relationship with God than insecurely attached individuals. I was securely attached to my father, but not to my mother who died from cancer when I was eleven years old. My God image has been mostly positive, but at times negative in the past when I felt that God would be mad at me for having sinned and made me feel ashamed.

This has important implications for spiritual formation and Christian leadership development in particular. The good news is that insecurely attached leaders can "learn" secure attachment patterns to relate better to others as well as to God.[85]

How do adult states of mind relate to leadership behavior? Wallin integrated attachment theory with an interpersonal therapy approach, which was written for therapists to become aware of their attachment style as it influences the therapeutic relationship.[86] His insights can also be applied to leaders. For example, leaders should operate from an autonomous/secure state of mind when they interact with their followers/subordinates or with colleagues. In a secure state of mind, leaders are able to set boundaries with their subordinates, can provide constructive feedback and say "no," and are able to be empathic and compassionate. In a dismissing state of mind, leaders tend to focus on themselves and struggle with empathy and compassion. They also tend to focus on task, power, and may be too directive or even verbally aggressive at times. Leaders in a preoccupied state of mind tend to over-identify with others, often work too hard to be liked at all costs, and tend to struggle with setting boundaries. These leaders often get burned out very fast. How can leaders become emotionally mature, which means becoming interdependent?

Bowen's Family Systems Theory

Bowen's Family Systems theory in particular and other family therapy models in general emerged from Interpersonal and Object Relations theories.[87]

84. Coe and Hall, *Psychology in the Spirit*, 247.
85. Thompson, *Anatomy of the Soul*.
86. Wallin, *Attachment in Psychotherapy*.

87. Interpersonal theory was developed by Harry Stack Sullivan (*Interpersonal Theory*) and belongs to relational models or theories that emphasize internalized and interpersonal relationships as opposed to aggressive and sexual (biological) drives, which were the focus in Freudian theory. Relational models include object relations theories, such as by Ronald Fairbairn, Melanie Klein, D. W. Winnicott, Margaret Mahler, Otto Kernberg, Edith Jacobsen, and the American interpersonal school, among

In particular, Bowen was influenced by his clinical work at the Menninger Clinic where he focused on studying "mother-child symbiosis,"[88] which "led to his concept of *differentiation of self*."[89] Bowen's Family Systems Theory emphasizes the differentiation of self.[90] His theory is therefore another helpful theory to further illustrate healthy development toward emotional maturity throughout life. Differentiation of the self is a concept some theologians, such as Moltmann, Pannenberg, and Grenz, have used to describe the relationships within the Trinity.[91] For example, Grenz describes the Trinity as "a community and fellowship among three equal persons, rather than a monarchy of one person over the others."[92] Wesley viewed the relationships

---

others (Greenberg and Mitchell, *Object Relations*). However, Fairbairn's theory, along with Sullivan's, is the most original and purest relational model (ibid., 151). For Fairbairn, "libido is primarily object-seeking (rather than pleasure seeking, as in the classic [Freudian] theory)" meaning, "the real libidinal aim is the establishment of satisfactory relationships" (Fairbairn, *Object Relations*, 82, 138). Regarding developmental stages, Fairbairn's object relations theory includes three stages of human development from dependence, to independence, to interdependence. During the final stage in Fairbairn's theory, the *mature* stage, the individual must "renounce dependent relations with" one's parents and must "renounce . . . intense attachments to his [or her] compensatory internal objects," which is a lifelong process (Greenberg and Mitchell, *Object Relations*, 161). This means the individual needs to fully differentiate from his family of origin in order to become emotionally mature. Mature dependence is characterized by "a capacity on the part of a differentiated individual for co-operative relationships" with others (Fairbairn, *Object Relations*, 145). Thus, mature dependence involves interdependence, which includes the recognition that one is separate from another person (Greenberg and Mitchell, *Object Relations*, 161; Fairbairn, *Object Relations*, 145). Therefore, mature dependence involves mutuality, giving and taking, but primarily giving (Greenberg and Mitchell, *Object Relations*, 161). Fairbairn's emphasis on differentiation from one's parents and attachment to significant others resembles Bowen's theory. Interpersonal theory explains how children copy their parents' behaviors, which Bowen implicitly adopted as well. For example, children who experience compassion from their parents or caregivers will expect compassion from their parents (principle of complementarity) and are more likely to be more compassionate towards themselves (principle of introjection). In addition, they are more likely to be empathic and compassionate towards others (principle of similarity) (Benjamin, *Interpersonal Diagnosis*, 47; Benjamin, "Interpersonal Theory," 144).

88. The term "symbiotic relationship" between mother and child is borrowed from object relations and was coined by Margaret Mahler. It refers to the first three to four months of life (Greenberg and Mitchell, *Object Relations*, 274). Differentiation of self means autonomy of the self along with one's ability to distinguish thoughts from feelings (Nichols, *Family Therapy*, 32).

89. Nichols, *Family Therapy*, 32.
90. Kerr and Bowen, *Family Evaluation*.
91. Holeman and Martyn, *Inside the Leader's*, 61.
92. Grenz, *Social God*, 45.

within the Trinity very similar as "being-in-another" and as an "interpenetration of roles" without confusing them within the Trinity.[93]

Differentiation includes the concept of interdependence. We can say that differentiation is the process, whereas interdependence is one of the outcomes among others (emotional self-regulation, etc.). "Complete differentiation" is defined as existing "in a person who has fully resolved the emotional attachment to his [or her] family."[94] Further characteristics of a differentiated person are the following:

> He [or she] has attained *complete emotional maturity* in the sense that his [or her] self is developed sufficiently that, whenever it is important to do so, he [she] can be an individual in a group. He [she] is responsible for himself [herself] and neither fosters nor participates in the irresponsibility of others.[95]

This means he or she is a separate self and interdependent from others, which resembles Fairbairn's mature stage of development. He or she can take responsibility for self and is capable of remaining neutral when others act irresponsibly. Taking responsibility requires that one has the ability, power and opportunity to act.[96] In addition, Christian leaders need "to act freely in the service of what is right and good, that is to say, not to act because of fear or intimidation."[97] Similarly, regarding togetherness and individuality, Steinke summarizes differentiation as:

- Defining yourself and staying in touch with others
- Being responsible for yourself and responsive to others
- Maintaining your integrity and well-being without intruding on that of others
- Allowing the enhancement of the other's integrity and well-being without feeling abandoned, inferior, or less of a self
- Having an "I" and entering a relationship with another "I" without losing [one's] self or diminishing the self of the other.[98]

Thus, individuals can truly be separate from others when it comes to identity, values, hobbies, convictions, etc. without being disconnected from

---

93. Collins, *Theology of Wesley*, 92. According to Collins, Wesley used the early Greek concept of *perichoresis* (circumincession or interpenetration) in his formulation of the Trinity.

94. Kerr and Bowen, *Family Evaluation*, 97.

95. Ibid., 97 (my emphasis).

96. Kessler, "Leadership and Power," 527–50.

97. Kretzschmar, "Entering through," 8.

98. Steinke, *How Your Church*, 11.

them. They can agree to disagree and feel content about it. People who have differentiated can truly be happy for others and at the same time do not feel devastated when they are exposed to the suffering of others, but can remain emotionally supportive to people in need. Romans 12:15 illustrates this concept: "Rejoice with those who rejoice; mourn with those who mourn" (NIV), which means believers can truly connect with others in happiness and grief.

Further, differentiated people do not feel inferior to others nor do they feel superior. Their self-esteem is balanced similar to what Paul says in Romans 12:3: "Do not think of yourself more highly than you ought, but rather think of yourself with *sober judgment, in accordance with the faith God has distributed to each of you*" (NIV, my emphasis). Our self-evaluation should be sober and realistic based on the gifts God has provided to us believers. Being interdependent also means remaining a self in close relationships with others, such as in marriage, even in one's relationship with God.[99] Differentiation further includes the ability to "make meaningful sacrifices in relationships" without losing oneself.[100]

Regarding a numerical representation of differentiation, Bowen arbitrarily assigned a scale value of 100 to denote complete differentiation. The scale of differentiation traces complete differentiation (100) and complete "undifferentiation" (0) and degrees of differentiation in between.[101] Complete "undifferentiation" consists of the absence of emotional separation from one's family of origin, having "no-self," and being "incapable of being an individual in the group."[102]

Differentiation also includes the ability to distinguish thoughts from feelings, which is helpful for coping with negative emotions. This means, the level of differentiation is positively related to the level of stress and anxiety tolerance. In other words, individuals with lower levels of differentiation do not cope as well and struggle with emotional self-regulation.[103] Friedman's definition of differentiation illustrates this capacity and refers to the concept as:

> Defin[ing] [one's] own life's goals and values apart from surrounding pressures, to say "I" when others are demanding "you" and "we." It includes the capacity to maintain a (relatively) non-anxious presence in the midst of anxious systems, to take maximum responsibility for one's own destiny and emotional being.

99. Kilian and Parker, "Wesleyan Spirituality," 207.
100. Yarhouse and Sells, *Family Therapies*, 86.
101. Kerr and Bowen, *Family Evaluation*, 97.
102. Ibid.
103. Ibid., 99.

It can measured somewhat by the breadth of one's repertoire of responses when confronted with crisis . . . Differentiation means the capacity to be "I" while remaining connected.[104]

In addition, differentiation is a "lifelong process" of becoming "oneself out of one's self, with minimum reactivity to the positions or reactivity of others." [105] It also entails "being clear about one's own personal values and goals," which is extremely important for leading others.[106]

Thus, the differentiation of the self and its role in reducing anxiety are very helpful concepts for leadership development and can be well integrated with spiritual maturity according to Wesleyan spirituality.

A related concept is chronic anxiety, which is another major contribution of Bowen's theory.[107] Chronic anxiety is defined as an emotional response to "imagined threats and it is not experienced as time-limited" versus acute anxiety, which is a time-limited response to a real threat.[108] Reduced levels of differentiation, meaning emotional dependence on one's family of origin, increases chronic anxiety.[109] People cope with chronic anxiety in different ways, which Kerr and Bowen refer to as the "binding of anxiety."[110] Relationships serve to alleviate chronic anxiety, which can be adaptive and healthy if it does not lead to dependency. True interdependence includes healthy relationships between people in a balanced way. Balance includes, as Steinke's descriptions above indicate, the absence of extreme dependence and independence. Other ways to manage or bind chronic anxiety include drug and alcohol abuse, overeating, over-and underachievement, and other unhealthy behaviors (promiscuity, etc.).[111] Even personality traits constitute a mechanism for binding anxiety, such as obsessiveness, perfectionism, aggressiveness, hysteria, grandiosity, etc., which is an important insight and link to the four leader types in the previously described model.[112]

How does systems theory relate to leadership? Friedman describes differentiated leaders with the following characteristics:

---

104. Friedman, *Generation to Generation*, 27.
105. Friedman, *Failure of Nerve*, 194.
106. Ibid., 195.
107. Kerr and Bowen, *Family Evaluation*, 112.
108. Ibid., 113.
109. Ibid., 115.
110. Ibid., 119.
111. Kerr and Bowen, *Family Evaluation*, 119.
112. Ibid., 120.

- the capacity to separate oneself from surrounding emotional processes;
- the capacity to obtain clarity about one's own principles and vision;
- the willingness to be exposed and to be vulnerable;
- persistence in the face of inertial resistance; and
- self-regulation in the face of reactive sabotage.[113]

This illustrates the ability of differentiated leaders of maintaining a non-anxious presence among organizational systems comprised of colleagues, followers, superiors, etc. Holeman and Martyn developed a leadership model that incorporates both the concept of differentiation and Wesleyan theology.[114] The authors call this model relational holiness and include three components: spiritual maturity, emotional maturity, and relational maturity.[115] Spiritual maturity refers to Wesley's theological emphasis on entire sanctification, which includes one's relationship to God and others. Emotional maturity includes Bowen's concept of differentiation. Holeman notes how emotional maturity is fostered through human and divine relationships (also through earned secure attachment as described below):

> . . . healthy, caring relationships (human and Divine) are incredibly helpful for undoing some of the emotional and relational damage that was caused by a dysfunctional family of origin. Therefore we cannot underestimate the degree of transformation, spiritually, relationally, and neurologically, that one may experience through salvation and sanctification.[116]

Thus, relational holiness results from experiencing healthy interpersonal relationships with others and with God and can be said to be therapeutic. Holeman and Martyn illustrate "relational holiness" in Christian leaders:

> [C]hurch leaders with deepening levels of relational holiness are those whose identities are rooted and grounded in a vibrant and growing relationship with Christ. While such leaders also have vibrant and growing relationships with others, they are comfortable working closely with others in the church and they are capable of acting independently [or better interdependently]. These leaders

---

113. Friedman, *Failure of Nerve*, 96–97. Friedman defines sabotage as a "systemic phenomenon connected to the shifting balances in the emotional processes of a relationship system [organization, etc.]" (ibid., 12).

114. Holeman and Martyn, *Inside the Leader's*, 8.

115. Ibid., 8.

116. Holeman, "Wesleyan Holiness," 86.

> model personal and social holiness in their everyday living as well as in the midst of difficult interpersonal relationships[117]

When it comes to stressful and anxiety-producing interpersonal relationships, leaders with increased levels of differentiation including emotional and spiritual maturity, have more resources to cope with anxiety and potentially grow spiritually throughout the process. Therefore, Holeman and Martyn equate leadership with a crucible that serves as a container for the spiritual, emotional, and interpersonal transformation of the Christian leader:

> Leadership is a crucible into which leaders and their followers are thrust. When things heat up, as they inevitably will, leaders and those they lead experience anxiety. But notice that this anxiety contains within it the *potential for spiritual, emotional, and interpersonal transformation*, for going on to maturity in Christ.[118]

Thus, higher levels of differentiation not only help a Christian leader to manage anxiety more effectively, but also potentially enhance spiritual maturity in the leader. The leadership crucible also refers to various biblical examples of sacrifice for the cause of Christ, such as the example of Paul and Silas who sacrificed greatly for the sake of Christ when they were imprisoned (Acts 16:22–30). They were severely beaten before they were put in in prison (Acts 16: 23), but were "praying and singing hymns to God" (verse 25).

In our culture, individualism encourages independence in adolescence and adults. Many adults stay stuck in this second stage of development and have not established satisfying emotional relationships with others, not even in marital relationships, which is especially true for narcissistic and obsessive-compulsive leaders. For this reason, many toxic leaders only care for themselves, which can result in abuse toward followers and colleagues. Christian leaders need to acknowledge that nobody is good at everything and that they need help from others. The body of Christ is supposed to be interdependent as Paul talks about members of the body needing one another (1 Cor 12:12–31) and the following passage:

> But God has put the body together, giving greater honor to the parts that lacked it, so that there should be no division in the body, but that its parts should have equal concern for each other. If one part suffers, every part suffers with it; if one part is honored, every part rejoices with it. (1 Cor 12:24–26, NIV)

---

117. Holeman and Martyn, *Inside the Leader's*, 7.
118 Ibid., 34.

Thus, Christian leaders who are emotionally mature have developed interdependence, which includes receiving and asking for help if needed, helping others, and being connected to others by having deep relationships with their spouses, friends, and ministry partners. In the next few paragraphs I will provide suggestions for Christian leadership development based on psychotherapeutic approaches that inform the strategic application of the methods of spiritual formation.

Implications for Leadership Development

The Christian tradition has excellent resources for matters of the "heart." Approaches from the spiritual formation tradition can be very helpful for correcting flawed personality traits in toxic Christian leaders. In the Wesleyan tradition:

> The goal of [Wesleyan] spirituality . . . is to bring the converted believer into the experience of sanctifying grace whereby inner sin is cleansed, the image of God restored, and the heart so filled with divine love that the believer can love God with all the heart, mind, soul and strength and the neighbor as one's self.[119]

This requires that toxic Christian leaders open themselves to the discipline of guidance, which often includes spiritual direction, coaching, Christian counseling, among other modalities.[120] Formal spiritual direction can be very helpful for Christian leaders, but trained spiritual directors in Protestant circles are more difficult to find.[121] Spiritual direction can occur in individual and group formats, such as in the Wesleyan tradition which has included class meetings and bands The role of the spiritual director, whether direction takes place in groups or in individual sessions, is "simply and clearly to lead us to the real Director" and the director is the "means of God to open the path to the inward teaching of the Holy Spirit."[122] Since toxic narcissistic and obsessive-compulsive Christian leaders tend to be very individualistic, they often resist guidance and mentoring. Dietrich Bonhoeffer addresses individualistic German evangelical Christians when he writes:

> The Christian needs another Christian who speaks God's Word to him [and] he needs him again and again when he becomes

---

119. Tracy, "Spiritual Direction," 116.
120. Foster, *Celebration of Discipline*.
121. Kretzschmar, "Indispensability," 357.
122. Foster, *Celebration of Discipline*, 185.

uncertain and discouraged for by himself he cannot help himself without belying the truth.[123]

This means toxic Christian leaders need to become interdependent. They further benefit from mutual accountability to avoid being self-deceived. Toxic leaders with a narcissistic personality are especially defensive and often rationalize and justify their actions. Emotional maturity equals interdependence, which is included in the process of differentiation. A secure attachment is the foundation for differentiation and emotional maturity. Toxic leaders often experience insecure attachment and tend to have a dismissing state, which often manifests in narcissistic or obsessive-compulsive personalities (see figure below).[124] Dismissing leaders tend to be very individualistic and tend to struggle with receiving interpersonal support, warmth, and accountability whereas preoccupied leaders struggle with independence and interpersonal boundaries. Differentiated leaders are securely attached to others while at the same time have the ability to function autonomously from others. They either have experienced a secure attachment in their childhood or have obtained "earned" secure attachment later in life through satisfying and rewarding relationships with others and/or with Jesus Christ. Secure attachment is characterized by a relatively high level of differentiation. The figure below places secure attachment and relatively high levels of differentiation in the center. Leaders with a dismissing attachment style with either narcissistic or obsessive-compulsive personalities are on two extreme poles, whereas leaders with a preoccupied attachment style with either histrionic or dependent personalities are on the opposite extreme pole:

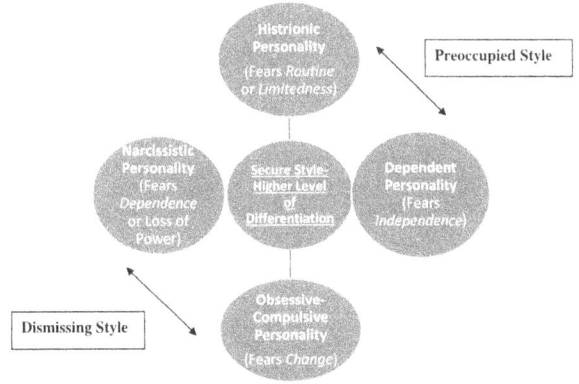

Figure 5: Personality Styles and Attachment Styles

123. Bonhoeffer, *Life Together*, 23.

124. Wallin, *Attachment in Psychotherapy*, 211. Leaders with a preoccupied state of mind often have dependent and histrionic personalities (224).

A pragmatic and useful approach to working with toxic leaders who are very defensive is conceptualizing personality as consisting of different sub-personality parts or selves. By conveying to toxic leaders that there are "bad" parts and "good" parts within him or herself may make him or her more open to change. The Christian tradition has a rich tradition of conceptualizing original or inbeing sin (see Wesley's concept above). Our sinful nature is pervasive and will never be fully eliminated in this life. This sinful nature "part" is a direct effect from the Fall and includes one's propensity to harm others, not caring about consequences, justifying or minimizing them, as well as using aggressive or passive-aggressive behaviors. Our sinful nature often produces the following defensive processes: Denial, rationalization, suppression, acting out, etc. These occur more frequently in personality disorder, such as narcissistic and obsessive-compulsive personality disorder among others. However, one can conceptualize a more positive personality part that is present in both, Christians and non-Christians, which can be named the "God image part." It is the result of God's prevenient grace and includes the following: Practicing goodness, being more emotionally mature, being compassionate, and being assertive as opposed to being aggressive or passive-aggressive. Adaptive coping skills motivated by this personality part include altruism, anticipation, humor, and sublimation (redirecting aggressive and inappropriate sexual impulses to engage in alternative behaviors, i.e., artistic and prosocial behaviors). Note that non-Christian leaders can practice goodness and sometimes do more philanthropic works than Christian leaders, which again can be attributed to Wesley's understanding of prevenient grace. After Christian conversion and the ongoing process of sanctification toward entire sanctification/Christian perfection, this personality part most resembles the moral image of God. While not a Wesleyan theologian, Johnson articulates well how human defenses can be eliminated through sanctification:

> The cross is God's redemptive, therapeutic intervention for undoing false defenses. On the cross, all sins, including all our desires to hide from reality were overcome. Now, through the gospel of the cross, the grace of God works to melt away our defenses. Grace is God's indirect means for purifying our hearts. We cannot purify ourselves; we are purified only through Christ. *By grace we are freed from our need for defenses because we are eternally protected by God's forgiving love and power.*[125]

---

125. Johnson, "Protecting One's Soul," 187 (my emphasis).

In addition, the Princeton theologian, James Loder argues that our ego defenses need to be transformed by the Holy Spirit.[126] He references Calvin when he talks about the transformed conscience ('inner integrity of the heart'), which entails "knowing within oneself by and with the spiritual presence of Christ that . . . one may act freely and with integrity."[127] Christian coaches, therapists, or even spiritual directors who assist Christian leaders would benefit from having indicators that serve as intervention targets. Emotionally mature and differentiated leaders possess "reason muscles" or better described as interpersonal muscles that help us resolve conflict, which are:

1. Awareness (the "ability to [notice] actual personal [shortcomings]")
2. Empathy ("the ability to be bothered if your personal [shortcomings] hurt others")
3. Humility (the "ability to acknowledge potential personal [shortcomings]")
4. Responsibility (the ability to admit personal shortcomings)
5. Reliability (the "ability to correct personal [shortcomings]")[128]

These indicators serve as indicators of emotional maturity. Godwin's interpersonal "muscles" are also good indicators for *orthokardia* and some are shared with *orthodynamis*, such as humility and empathy. These indicators can be developed in non-Christian toxic leaders based on the Wesleyan concept of prevenient grace. However, in toxic Christian leaders due to conversion and the process of sanctification these can be further strengthened by cooperating with the Holy Spirit.

Awareness can be fostered by asking toxic leaders to journal about their emotions, especially vulnerable feelings, such as anxiety, sadness, depression, and envy and shame, which are very common in toxic leaders. This awareness and a willingness to own these feelings render these leaders less defensive and helps them develop emotional maturity. Self-awareness and acceptance is also needed to develop authenticity.[129] By accepting oneself the leader is less vulnerable to getting hurt and is able to operate more from his or her authentic self.[130] It includes seeing "yourself clearly and accurately,

---

126. Loder, *Logic of the Spirit*, 197.
127. Ibid.
128. Godwin, *How to Solve*, 83.
129. George and Sims, *True North*, 82.
130. Ibid., 83.

and [to] know what you truly believe."[131] This requires loving oneself and being compassionate with one's self.[132] Once toxic Christian leaders are taught, in the context of a supportive relationship, how to become aware of their feelings and how to truly accept themselves they can learn to manage them and become more emotionally mature. This would ensure adequate coping and thereby avoiding sinful behavior patterns.

Responsibility (along with humility) are other indicators that could be developed in cooperation with the Holy Spirit. They involve being willing to admit that one is wrong, which paves the way for apologies. Toxic leaders are very "protective" and often use the following defenses: rationalization (including justification and minimization), devaluation/idealization, and perfectionism, reaction formation, and isolation from affect. Therefore, the parts language is particularly promising for toxic leaders to reduce defensiveness, since it is easier to acknowledge that he or she has a sinful part that is responsible for abusive behavior, impulse control problems, and moral failures.

The final indicator is reliability, which is defined as the "ability to correct personal wrongness" based on the interpersonal muscles concept.[133] Toxic leaders could be encouraged to makes small steps to change their destructive behaviors patterns. It is important that these steps are realistic and achievable for these leaders to implement.

To sum up, the Christian leader needs to develop awareness, humility, responsibility, and reliability, which would ensure that the leader takes active steps to correct shortcomings. Correcting mistakes, shortcomings, etc. can be accomplished by allowing the Holy Spirit to transform the Christian leader, which often includes the practice of spiritual disciplines. Spiritual disciplines are a "means of receiving [God's] grace."[134] Disciplines, such as prayer, fasting, and service, etc. develop a spiritual habit that enables the Holy Spirit to transform the heart of the Christian leader. Humility, and empathy, along with compassion, are included in the concept of *orthodynamis* and will be thoroughly developed in the next chapter.

How can narcissistic and obsessive-compulsive Christian leaders be motivated to change? In general, toxic narcissistic leaders need to become more interdependent by being open to influence from others, meaning becoming more "dependent." The toxic leader with a perfectionistic personality style needs to develop more flexibility. Narcissistic leaders tend to be very "protective" and often resist correction and/or constructive feedback. A

---

131. Ibid., 82.
132. Ibid.
133. Ibid., 83.
134. Foster, *Celebration of Discipline*, 7.

narcissistic leader needs to learn empathy through being in a therapeutic or coaching relationship where he or she can put himself or herself in someone's else's situation.[135] The therapist or coach needs to balance affirmation with a gentle confrontation so that the narcissistic leader can see and accept his or her faults, which can also be modeled by the therapist or coach.[136] By using the therapeutic or coaching relationship, the therapist or coach can let the leader with a dismissing attachment style know how he or she is being experienced.[137] However, these confrontations should be minor and gentle "embedded in strong support" when it comes to narcissistic leaders.[138] However, it is important not to reinforce the leader's grandiose self-perceptions.[139] The "sandwich technique" (support-confrontation-support) works well with narcissistic leaders due to their fragile egos and protectiveness. If support and gentle confrontations are balanced, narcissistic leaders can learn empathy slowly, become more grounded in reality, and gradually become more attuned to the core values of his or her company.[140] Another approach of motivating Christian narcissistic leaders to change is to ask them to draft their personal core values (e.g., integrity, respect, etc.) and then to explore discrepancies between their drafted core values and their leadership and interpersonal behaviors. This will raise awareness and may help the Christian leader align his or her behaviors with the core values the leader aspires to live out.

Regarding Christian obsessive-compulsive leaders, it is important for a therapist or coach not to engage in a power struggle with the leader.[141] Since the obsessive-compulsive leader values rationality and reason, he or she is tends to be more open to exploring "antecedents and consequences" of his or her interpersonal behavior patterns (coldness, reduced emotionality, etc.).[142] Once the leader gains some insight about the origins of his or her interpersonal patterns, the leader will be more motivated to work with the therapist or coach. However, this insight is confined to the intellectual level and he or she needs to learn emotional awareness, which includes "work[ing] on experiencing feelings."[143] Journaling feelings can be assigned as homework to help the leader raise his or her emotional awareness. The goal for the

135. Benjamin, *Interpersonal Diagnosis*, 157.
136. Ibid., 157.
137. Wallin, *Attachment in Psychotherapy*, 213.
138. Benjamin, *Interpersonal Diagnosis*, 157.
139. Kets de Vries, "Coaching the Toxic," 104.
140. Ibid., 104.
141. Benjamin, *Interpersonal Diagnosis*, 257.
142. Ibid.
143. Ibid.

obsessive-compulsive leader is to develop compassion for him- or herself.[144] Christian leaders can be reminded that God loves them unconditionally and that sanctification also includes loving oneself. Another intervention for perfectionistic leaders is helping them overcome their dichotomistic thinking style ("black-and-white thinking"), which causes them to perceive themselves and others as all good or all bad. Conceptualizing their or others' performance on a continuum from perfection to below average or poor[145] helps them to slowly develop a more flexible thinking style. This also helps them develop more compassion for themselves and others.

Conclusion

This chapter introduced the reader to *Orthokardia*, meaning Wesley's concept of sanctification with the focus on loving God and others based on loving one's self. God's love toward humans enables one to love others as one loves oneself, which is defined as spiritual maturity. In addition, in this chapter I discussed two relevant theories of human development with the focus on emotionally maturity. A secure attachment between the infant and the caregiver results in independence and ultimately in interdependence. Secure attachment also ensures adaptive coping and emotional self-regulation. Many individuals differentiate and achieve interdependence, which equals emotional maturity and constitutes a robust predictor for emotional health. Thus, healthy development requires secure attachment and differentiation from caregivers. However, insecurely attached individuals often display either a preoccupied style or a dismissing style of relating. Christian leaders with a dismissing style often have narcissistic or obsessive-compulsive personality traits. By working with a coach, therapist, or spiritual director, he or she can gradually change if the leader is open to God's grace and the Holy Spirit thereby achieving earned secure attachment. Christian leaders who have not securely attached to caregivers or others later in life, have not achieved interdependence, and tend to display interpersonal behavior problems. In particular, these leaders may struggle with developing empathy and compassion and may have difficulties with establishing healthy relationships with their followers, which is required for effective leadership.

Peter Scazzero argues successfully that one cannot separate spiritual maturity from emotional maturity.[146] His main thesis in his book states

144. Ibid.

145. The continuum could look like this: Perfection, Excellence, Above Average, Average, Below Average, Poor. The goal is to help perfectionistic leaders reduce their unrealistic standards to expect excellence rather than perfection.

146. Scazzero, *Emotionally Healthy Spirituality*.

that it is impossible to be spiritually mature without also being emotionally mature. In the next chapter I will explore *Orthodynamis*, including pure power and influence motives informed by virtue ethics, and Wesley's (and Edwards') concept of Christian affections.

Reflection Questions and Exercises

(Please pray for the leading of the Holy Spirit before you answer the reflection questions and complete the exercises)

1. How well do you balance loving God, others, and self?
2. Reflect on the following sentence: "Purity of intention is a work of sanctifying grace and is imparted by the Holy Spirit."
3. Take the attachment style screen: http://www.yourpersonality.net/rel-structures/. To what extent are you surprised about the results?
4. To what extent do you fear dependence or independence and/or change or routine?
5. Reflect on how well you have differentiated from your parents, since our relationship to our parents influence power and authority dynamics: To what extent are you separate from your parents?
6. To what extent do you manage anxiety and stress?
7. Write down three action steps towards developing interdependence:
    a. _____
    b. _____
    c. _____
8. Securely attached and differentiated people do not feel inferior to others nor do they feel superior. Reflect on when you felt inferior or superior to colleagues and followers.
9. Rate how well you are using Godwin's interpersonal muscles:

Interpersonal Muscles	Rate from 1–5 (1=poor, 5=excellent)
Awareness	
Humility	
Responsibility	
Reliability	
Empathy	

Chapter 5

Orthodynamis

Right Power Motives and Christian Affections

WHAT ARE OUR MOTIVES in pursuing leadership? Many define leadership as having influence and authority over followers. What are biblical values that can inform our leadership? In this chapter I will explore "right power and influence" motives that serve as core values for leaders and for organizations (see chapter 6). *Orthodynamis* as the second component in the model, includes right power and influence motives that should inform formational leadership. These power motives are based on three key Christian affections; humility, gratitude, and compassion.

In this chapter I will discuss Wesley's religious (Christian) affections with the focus on three key religious affections, humility, gratitude, and love as expressed in compassionate feelings and acts. These three Christian affections provide the basis for ethical leadership behaviors and biblical core values that will be examined in chapter 6. Before I discuss Wesley's Christian affections, I will first provide a brief summary of virtue ethics that underlies Wesley's ethical understanding, namely Aristotlean virtues ethics and biblical ethics. Then I will outline Christian affections and how they apply to power and influence from a behavioral science perspective. This chapter will also provide an integrated view of pure power motives and leadership based on emotional maturity. Finally, I will outline Wesley's means of grace that can strengthen Christian affections and I will list important implications for leadership development.

Virtue Ethics: The Contribution of Aristotle and Biblical Ethics

Generally speaking, there are three broad ethical approaches, the deontological approach most often associated with Immanuel Kant's categorical imperative, with its focus on objective and universal morality, and the teleological approach, which includes Utilitarianism usually associated with John Stuart Mill with its focus on placing ethical value on the outcome or consequence of the act.[1] The third approach refers to virtue ethics, which focuses on the development of a moral character. Virtue ethics is predominantly associated with Aristotle.[2] Before I explore how Wesley integrated virtue ethics with Christian affections, I will first briefly examine Aristotle's *Eudemean Ethics*.[3]

The ethical life according to Aristotle includes not only knowing about what is good, but choosing the good.[4] This also requires that these ethical actions are guided by wisdom.[5] Like most classical Greek thinkers, Aristotle emphasized *eudaimonia* or happiness. Wright asserts that the goal of *eudaimonia* is closer to the idea of having a life that is "flourishing."[6] When I think of a life that is flourishing I am reminded of John 10:10 (". . . I am come that they might have life, and that they might have it more abundantly," KJV) and of how some biblical scholars define biblical abundance, namely as "the real possibility of health for your total being (body, mind, emotions, relationships) [and] that "your material needs [are] being met."[7] It is important to note that this definition is holistic and includes that God meets our needs, but not always our wants. The abundant life concept also adds to our definitions of spiritual maturity *and* emotional maturity.

In addition, *eudaimonia* needs to be derived from inward perfection or excellence, which includes maturity.[8] Inward perfection according to Aristotle "involves being in the process of moving from potential to actual", which includes having a *telos* or purpose.[9] The purpose of Christians according to Wesley is being "created for love and to love."[10]

---

1. Grenz, *Moral Quest*, 30, 35.
2. Leclerc, "Being Whole."
3. Zeller, *Outlines of the History*, 188.
4. Grenz, *Moral Quest*, 73.
5. Zeller, *Outlines of the History*, 190.
6. Wright, *After You Believe*, 33.
7. Hayford, *Spirit Filled Life Bible*, 1593.
8. Zeller, *Outlines of the History*, 189.
9. Oord, "Attaining Perfection," 67.
10. Ibid., 72.

In addition, this inward perfection or excellence also refers to character, which Aristotle differentiates into four types: the vicious, incontinent, continent and virtuous character.[11] The person with a vicious character routinely chooses the bad without feeling remorse. People with incontinent character know what ought to be done and choose the right action, but fail to be consistent in carrying out the right action. The person with continent character routinely performs in the right action, but his or her motive is to avoid punishment or out of duty. Only persons with a virtuous character know the good and choose the right action "for the sake of virtue itself; not out of internal pressure of guilt, nor external pressure of a fear of punishment, or even a promise of reward."[12] Thus, the person with a virtuous character has an *internal motivation* to do what is right versus the person with a continent character who merely has external motives (avoid punishment, obtaining a reward, etc.). Virtuous character resembles Christian maturity as defined in previous chapters (*Orthokardia*). Having an internal or intrinsic ethical motivation points to the highest moral reasoning abilities according to Kohlberg's moral reasoning theory, which is the post-conventional moral developmental stage.[13] However, Kohlberg's model only emphasizes moral reasoning and fails to provide the link between moral reasoning and right conduct, which usually includes having pure motives and a virtuous character.[14]

The question can be posed as to when an ethical action is considered truly moral in its quality. A true moral act is based on "the correct mean between excess and defect," which refers to Aristotle's golden mean concept.[15] Thus, virtue lies between the vice of deficiency and the vice of excess.[16] Aristotle emphasized four primary virtues:

> Courage, justice, prudence, and temperance. These, Aristotle proposed, were the "hinges" upon which the great door to human fulfillment and flourishing would swing open. That is why those four are often called the "cardinal virtues": *cardo* in Latin means "hinge."[17]

---

11. Leclerc, "Being Whole," 55.
12. Ibid., 55.
13. Newman and Newman, *Theories of Human*, 104.
14. Kretzschmar, "Formation," 26.
15. Zeller, *Outlines of the History*, 190.
16. Grenz, *Moral Quest*, 74.
17. Wright, *After You Believe*, 34.

The person who desires to develop a virtuous character needs to "habituate" virtuous acts "until they become natural or actualized in his or her being."[18] Here we can see the similarity between Aristotle's virtue ethics and Wesley's concept of religious or Christian affections. Wesley was indirectly influenced by Aristotle via Aquinas's Christianized version of Aristotle's thought.[19] His concept of Christian affections as an expression of a virtuous character was derived from Aristotle's ethical approach.

The biblical ethical tradition also contributed to Wesleyan ethics. For example, Wesley's Sermons 21 to 33 were based on the "Sermon on the Mount" (Matthew 5:1—7:27).[20] The major themes of the Old Testament ethical tradition includes obedience as covenant people, which included the separation from the "defiled," holiness that included one's blameless walk, and social solidarity.[21] A major emphasis in the Hebrew Scriptures centers on three great social justice themes illustrated by three Hebrew words: *mishpat* (justice), *hesed* (compassion), and *shalom* (wholeness, unity).[22] The books of Amos and Micah, among other prophets in the Old Testament, focus on "blatant [social] injustices," "the abuse of power," meaning "power that was being used to manipulate, to control, to destroy."[23] In chapter 6, I will address the social justice themes in Wesley's theology and spirituality.

The New Testament ethical themes include "an ethic of the kingdom," "an ethic of the family of God," "an ethic of imitation" when it comes to Jesus's life.[24] The ethic of the early church with the emphasis on the life of Paul focuses on "salvation: the basis of the moral life," "Christlikeness: the goal of the moral life," "spiritual conflict: the context of the moral life," "love: the manner of the moral life," "self-discipline: the means to the moral life," and "the Holy Spirit: agent of the moral life."[25] Regarding to the ethical theme of imitation, Wright notes that

> Jesus was urging and modeling—the character of patience, humility, and above all generous, self-giving love. And the message of Mark at this point seems to be that you don't get that character just by trying. You get it by following Jesus.[26]

18. Leclerc, "Being Whole," 56.
19. Ibid., 54.
20. Wesley, *Works*, vol. 5.
21. Grenz, *Moral Quest*, 99, 102.
22. Foster, *Streams of Living*, 167–71.
23. Ibid., 145–46.
24. Grenz, *Moral Quest*, 110–14.
25. Ibid., 118–26.
26. Wright, *After You Believe*, 48.

This means we become more like Jesus by following his example. We follow Jesus by reading his Word regularly and by being open to the Holy Spirit and other believers for correction and discipline. For example, the Beatitudes in Matthew 5:1–12 provide an important ethical foundation for the moral life based on the New Testament:

> Blessed are the *poor in spirit*, for theirs is the kingdom of heaven. ⁴ Blessed are those *who mourn*, for they will be comforted. ⁵ Blessed are the *meek*, for they will inherit the earth. ⁶ Blessed are those who *hunger and thirst for righteousness*, for they will be filled. ⁷ Blessed are the *merciful*, for they will be shown mercy. ⁸ Blessed are the *pure in heart*, for they will see God. ⁹ Blessed are the *peacemakers*, for they will be called children of God. ¹⁰ Blessed are those who are persecuted because of righteousness, for theirs is the kingdom of heaven.
>
> ¹¹ Blessed are you when people insult you, persecute you and falsely say all kinds of evil against you because of me. ¹² Rejoice and be glad, because great is your reward in heaven, for in the same way they persecuted the prophets who were before you. (vv. 3–12, NIV, my emphasis)

The disciples in these Beatitudes are called blessed because they have responded to Jesus's call to follow him.[27] The goal of the Beatitudes was to "bring *all* who hear it to decision and salvation."[28] However, Wright integrates the Beatitudes with virtue ethics, which is more relevant for Wesleyan spirituality and ethics:

> Here is the goal, the telos: not "happiness" in the sense of Aristotle's *eudaimonia*, but "blessedness" in the Hebrew sense of *ashre* or *baruch* (Greek *makarios*). . . . And the key point about "bless," "blessing," and "blessed"—one of the things that marks Jesus out over against Aristotle in terms of the source and driving energy of the "virtues"—is that this includes "happiness," but it includes it as the result of something else—namely, the loving action of the creator God. . . . "Blessedness," however, is what happens when the creator God is at work both in someone's life and through that person's life[29]

The sayings "blessed are the merciful" and "blessed are the pure in heart" are especially relevant for Christian leadership. Bonhoeffer interprets "merciful" as having "an irresistible love for the down-trodden, the sick, the

---

27. Bonhoeffer, *Cost of Discipleship*, 107.
28. Ibid.
29. Wright, *After You Believe*, 103–4.

wretched, . . . the outcast," which reminds one of Matthew 25:34–36 when Jesus praises the "blessed" disciples who fed the hungry, gave a drink to the thirsty, clothed the naked, looked after the sick, and visited the prisoners.[30] He further comments on "merciful" that if someone "falls into disgrace, the merciful will sacrifice their own honour to shield him, and take his shame upon him."[31] This is the sacrificial attitude Christian leaders should hold. The "pure in heart" refers to those who have surrendered their "hearts completely to Jesus," those who have a "child-like simplicity like Adam," and those whose "hearts are free from all defiling phantasies and are not distracted by conflicting desires and intentions."[32] The last reference resembles virtue ethics and Wesley's views on sanctification as purity of intention as discussed before. Wright also bridges the Beatitudes with virtues that disciples are called to develop:

> These qualities—purity of heart, mercy, and so on—are not, so to speak, "things you have to do" to earn a "reward," a "payment." Nor are they merely the "rules of conduct" laid down for new converts to follow—rules that some today might perceive as somewhat arbitrary. They are, in themselves, the signs of life, the language of life, the life of new creation, the life of new covenant, the life which Jesus came to bring . . . they are part of that radical Christian *modification of the ancient Greek notion of virtue, the modification that quickly settled into the overall pattern of faith, hope, and love.*[33]

Matthew 5:33–37 is also very relevant for Christian leadership, which refers to truthfulness ("All you need to say is simply 'Yes' or 'No'; anything beyond this comes from the evil one," NIV). As I mentioned before, pride prevents the leader from recognizing truth. This passage here provides the ethical mandate for Christian leaders to live a truthful life: "The commandment of complete truthfulness is really only another name for the totality of discipleship."[34] This means that true disciples have nothing to hide from God and "their life is revealed before him" and "sin has been uncovered and forgiven by Jesus."[35] This requires for us to practice the presence of God by using the means of grace below. Truthfulness also alludes to virtues. Virtues according to Wright refer to the "habits of the heart" that "generate and

---

30. Bonhoeffer, *Cost of Discipleship*, 111.
31. Ibid.
32. Ibid., 112.
33. Wright, *After You Believe*, 106 (my emphasis).
34. Bonhoeffer, *Cost of Discipleship*, 138.
35. Ibid.

sustain this new way of being human that the specifically Christian "virtue" is designed to produce."[36] Wright emphasizes three virtues here, faith, hope, and love (*agape*) based on 1 Corinthians 13:13:

> All three, themselves gifts from God, point away from ourselves and outward: *faith*, toward God and his action in Jesus Christ; *hope*, toward God's future; *love*, toward both God and our neighbor.[37]

Wright refers to love as "the language they speak in God's world" and that love "is not a 'duty.' . . . It is our destiny." This is similar to the concept of love in Wesleyan spirituality, namely love being our *telos* since love is equal to perfection or Christian maturity.[38] He defines faith as "the settled, unwavering trust in the one true God whom we have come to know in Jesus Christ," and hope, according to Wright, refers to "the settled, unwavering confidence that this God will not leave us or forsake us, but will always have more in store for us than we could ask or think."[39] It is important to keep in mind that these three virtues are gifts from God.[40] However, Wesleyan spirituality views them as co-operant.

The fruit of the Spirit in Galatians 5:22–23: "But the fruit of the Spirit is love, joy, peace, forbearance, kindness, goodness, faithfulness, gentleness and self-control" (NIV) can also be fostered in believers. The fruit of the Spirit does not grow automatically, but as gifts from God and as "habits of heart and mind," they only develop in a person who makes a conscious decision to cultivate them, which resembles Wesleyan spirituality.[41] Thus, the fruit of the Spirit is both "infused" and "acquired."[42] Paul's mandate to walk with the Spirit (Gal 5:25) also illustrates our conscious choice to acquire the fruit of the Spirit.[43] The word "clothe" or "put on" in Colossians 3:12 ("Therefore, as God's chosen people, . . . *clothe* yourselves with compassion, kindness, humility, gentleness and patience," NIV, my emphasis) also alludes to "making conscious and repeated decisions to put on the clothes appropriate for the new life [one is] going to follow."[44] In concluding this section on

---

36. Wright, *After You Believe*, 129.
37. Ibid., 205.
38. Ibid., 188.
39. Ibid., 203.
40. Ibid., 205.
41. Ibid., 195, 197.
42. Ibid., 197.
43. Ibid., 196.
44. Ibid., 147.

biblical ethics, the virtues of faith, hope, and love motivate Christian leaders to focus on God and others:

> to insist that the three primary virtues are faith, hope, and above all love is to insist that to grow in these virtues is precisely to grow in looking away from oneself and toward God on the one hand and one's neighbor on the other. The more you cultivate these virtues, the less you will be thinking about yourself at all.[45]

By focusing on God and others, narcissistic and obsessive-compulsive leaders become more virtuous leaders. What virtues or Christian affections are most helpful for Christian leadership? We will answer this question, but first we will explore the concept of religious/Christian affections.

Religious/Christian Affections

Orthodynamis includes the Wesleyan concept of religious affections. There are several Christian affections that Wesley described: Thankfulness (or gratitude), faith (in a sense of trust), hope, love, humility, peace of God, fear of God, which refers to a "humbling perception of God," and joy.[46] Clapper discusses the importance of spiritual experiences in Christianity. He asserts that, "theology must understand the causes, nature, and the importance of felt experience within the religious life."[47] He outlines the religious affections according to Wesley and contrasts them with Jonathan Edwards's understanding of religious affections. For Wesley the affections "are not simply feelings . . . they are indispensable motivating inclinations behind human action" which integrate "rational and emotional dimensions of human life into holistic inclinations toward action."[48] Similarly, the Christian philosopher and ethicist Robert Roberts (2007) conceptualizes spiritual emotions as "concern-based construals," meaning they "are affected by what the subject cares about, what is important to him or her; and many emotions tend to move [the person] to action . . ."[49] Furthermore, Christian affections are not "self-causative," but are triggered by one's experience with God, meaning one has the liberty to "enact any particular inclination."[50] This requires an active cooperation with God. Clapper observes that for Wesley, Christian

---

45. Ibid., 204.
46. Clapper, "John Wesley," 122–24.
47. Ibid., 1.
48. Maddox, "Reconnecting the Means," 40.
49. Roberts, *Spiritual Emotions*, 11.
50. Maddox, "Reconnecting the Means," 40.

affections "are not the random sensations which can come and go without our control but are voluntary, ordered, and reasonable."[51] Neither are these affections "inherent" and "independent," but focus on the "things of God."[52] Thus, Christian affections are better described as "enduring dispositions" or "tempers."[53] Land summarizes Christian affections as "objective, relational, and dispositional."[54] They require that God is the *object* (*objective*), since "if God is not the object, they are not Christian affections."[55] They are *relational* because they are experienced in relationship with God and others, and Christian affections are *dispositional* because they become more like virtues or personality traits if perfected. The last aspect resembles Aristotle's virtue ethics and is very important for the formation of Christian leaders. Christian leaders can develop ethical personality traits, such as being loving, compassionate, forgiving, etc. The focus is on others, since the telos of Christian affections is "outside of the self," meaning "to love God and one's neighbor, to take joy in the happiness of others, . . . all imply dispositions to behave in certain ways."[56] This distinguishes the moral secular leader from the Christian leader who cooperates with God towards Christian perfection.

Jonathan Edwards's treatise on religious affections was a major influence on Wesley, especially on religious affections.[57] Wesley came in contact with Edwards's writings in 1738 and abridged and published his *Treatise Concerning Religious Affections.*[58] Both, Edwards and Wesley agreed on the central importance of religious experience, but Wesley disagreed strongly with Edwards's Calvinistic doctrine. He especially disagreed with Edwards's denial of human freedom ("made nonsense of the moral life") as well as with classic Calvinistic doctrinal positions, such as "irresistible grace," "unconditional election," and the "perseverance of the saints."[59] Wesley agreed with Edwards on the sovereignty of God, but emphasized prevenient grace and the Holy Spirit's "perfecting possibilities."[60]

---

51. Clapper, "John Wesley," 80.

52. Clapper, *Renewal of the Heart*, 75.

53. Collins, "John Wesley's Topography," 171; Maddox, "Reconnecting the Means," 41.

54. Land, *Pentecostal Spirituality*, 134.

55. Clapper, "John Wesley," 111.

56. Ibid., 113.

57. Ibid., 188.

58. Ibid., 186, 189.

59. Ibid., 188, 194.

60. Ibid., 189.

Jonathan Edwards was born in East Windsor, Connecticut, in 1703 the same year John Wesley was born.[61] He was educated at Yale University and was fascinated with the natural sciences, philosophy, and theology. His epistemology, having been influenced by Locke and Newton, was "nothing more than philosophical empiricism."[62] Yet, his emphasis on feelings, "sense of the heart," was the center of his psychology and theology.[63] However, he warned against superficial emotionality that is disconnected from God by devoting the largest part of his *Treatise Concerning Religious Affections* on distinguishing holy affections from those that are not.[64] Therefore, religious affections have a rational component:

> Put differently, an affection is not a passion. Whereas a passion overwhelms a person to the exclusion of understanding, affections involve ideas and perceptions. An affection is a *response* of the person, accompanied by understanding.[65]

Thus, Edwards claimed that affections need to be exercised with understanding, meaning affections are integrated with one's rational faculties.[66] Wesley generally shared this understanding of affections. However, Wesley often mentioned the witness of the Spirit, which refers to the "spiritual senses" that point to "experience as direct inward awareness."[67] In sermon 10, on the "witness of the Spirit" (Rom 8:16), Wesley alludes to the assurance of faith:

> But what is that testimony of God's Spirit, which is superadded to, and conjoined with, this? How does he "bear witness with our spirit that we are the children of God?" It is hard to find words in the language of men to explain "the deep things of God." Indeed, there are none that will adequately express what the children of God experience. But perhaps one might say, (desiring any who are taught of God to correct, to soften, or strengthen the expression,) The testimony of the Spirit is an inward impression on the soul, whereby the Spirit of God directly witnesses to my spirit, that I am a child of God; that Jesus Christ hath loved me, and given himself for me; and that all my sins are blotted out, and I, even I, am reconciled to God. . . . Now we cannot love God, till we know he loves us. "We love him, because he first loved us."

61. Ibid., 184.
62. Ibid., 186.
63. Ibid., 186.
64. Ibid., 199.
65. Ross, "Jonathan Edwards," 18.
66. Clapper, "John Wesley," 198.
67. Maddox, "Enriching Role," 118.

> And we cannot known his pardoning love to us, till his Spirit witnesses it to our spirit. Since, therefore, this testimony of his Spirit must precede the love of God and all holiness, of consequence it must precede our inward consciousness thereof, or the testimony of our spirit concerning them.[68]

Wesley refers to the presence of the Holy Spirit that conveys to the believer that he or she is saved.[69] This means that Wesley acknowledged emotional experiences when it comes to being aware or as inwardly conscious of the presence of the Holy Spirit. It is important to note that people rarely achieve balance and many Christians either focus on extreme rationality or on superficial emotionality. As discussed in the previous chapter, it is biblical to experience emotions. However, Edwards and Wesley remind us that one's rational faculties need to be integrated with one's emotional experiences. The Wesleyan Pentecostal theologian Steven Land illustrates this point by saying, "there is no mere balancing of head and heart, of thought and feeling; rather there is integration, an affective understanding which is essential to Christian existence."[70] Furthermore, he asserts that deep Christian emotions resemble the fruit of the Holy Spirit.[71] He views three Christian affections, gratitude, compassion, and courage, as having their source in God's righteousness (gratitude), love (compassion), and power (courage) that can be emotionally expressed during worship (gratitude), prayer (compassion), and witness (courage).[72] Thus, these affections have their origin in God and can be expressed emotionally. However, compassion can also be experienced and expressed during acts of mercy, which will be addressed in the next section. Another "safeguard against enthusiasm" according to Edwards and Wesley is humility, which serves as "a quality of all other affections."[73]

The three affections, humility, gratitude and compassion[74] are the key foci of this book and will be discussed next. I chose them because they are

---

68. Wesley, *Works*, 5:179.

69. Regarding the connection of the assurance of faith with the Holy Spirit, Wesley followed Luther and Calvin according to Maddox (*Responsible Grace*, 314).

70. Land, *Pentecostal Spirituality*, 133.

71. Ibid.,134.

72. Ibid., 139.

73. Clapper, "John Wesley," 202.

74. Since affections are treated as dispositions, habits of the heart, and virtues, other views have been expressed over the last two millennia. For example, Augustine reinterpreted the four virtues of the Platonic tradition as an expression for the love for God: temperance, fortitude, justice, and prudence (Grenz, *Moral Quest*, 139). Vest (*Desiring Life*, 61, 89), following the Benedictine spiritual tradition, mentions the same virtues, but emphasizes humility based on the Rule of Benedict. Thomas Aquinas added to the

very relevant for Christian leadership and constitute the opposites of vices that narcissistic and obsessive-compulsive leaders often struggle with. The opposite of narcissistic pride is *humility*, the opposite of narcissistic entitlement and obsessive-compulsive greed is *gratitude*, and the opposite of anger, impatience, and aggression many narcissistic and obsessive-compulsive leaders experience and demonstrate refers to *compassion*.

Three Key Affections: Humility, Gratitude, and Compassion

Wesley viewed humility as a direct result of God's sanctification in the life of a Christian and as the "surest proof of the increase of love."[75] It is the most important Christian affection and can be said to provide a foundation for the remaining Christian affections. It is also an expression of the love of God according to Wesley:

> And this is the true, genuine, Christian humility, which flows from a sense of the love of God, reconciled to us in Christ Jesus. Poverty of spirit, in this meaning of the word, begins where a sense of guilt and of the wrath of God ends; and is a continual sense of our total dependence on him, for every good thought, or word, or work; of our utter inability to all good, unless he "water us every moment" and an abhorrence of the praise of men, knowing that all praise is due unto God only. (Sermon 21)[76]

As an indication of sanctification, Wesley asserts that humility aids in accurate self-perception, which is important for healthy relationships:

> Circumcision of heart implies humility, faith, hope, and charity. Humility, *a right judgment of ourselves*, cleanses our minds from those high conceits of our own perfections, from that undue opinion of our own abilities and attainments, which are the genuine fruit of a corrupted nature. This entirely cuts off that vain thought, "I am rich, and wise, and have need of nothing;" and convinces us that we are by nature "wretched, and poor, and miserable, and blind and naked." (Sermon 17)[77]

---

four classical Greek virtues three theological virtues: faith, hope, and love (Grenz, *Moral Quest*, 150). Martin Luther developed an "ethic of grace" thereby de-emphasizing virtuous character, but stressed "a new nature given by God through faith" (ibid., 156–58).

75. Wesley, *Plain Account*, 99.
76. Wesley, *Works*, 5:322.
77. Ibid., 5:270 (my emphasis).

Wesley emphasized humility in relating to others and for correcting fellow believers. Since Wesley stressed mutual accountability in small groups for the development of a virtuous character, correcting others needed to take place with a humble attitude:

> Meantime the greatest care must be taken that you speak in the spirit of *humility*. Beware that you do not think of yourself more highly than you ought to think. If you think too highly of yourself; you can scarce avoid despising your brother. And if you show, or even feel, the least contempt of those whom you reprove, it will blast your whole work, and occasion you to lose all your labor. In order to prevent the very appearance of pride, it will be often needful to be explicit on the head; to disclaim all preferring yourself before him; and at the very time you reprove that which is evil, to own and bless God for that which is good in him. (Sermon 65)[78]

However, humility also prepares believers to receive correction in a non-defensive way. In the absence of humility, those being corrected are tempted to refuse correction and cease to be teachable according to Wesley:

> If you are hurt in your humility, it will appear by this token: You are not so teachable as you were, not so advisable; you are not so easy to be convinced, not so easy to be persuaded; you have a much better opinion of your own judgment and are more attached to your own will. (Sermon 87)[79]

There are several perceptions of the nature of humility. Humility according to Aristotle is a vice of deficiency, and "highmindedness" is considered a virtue of moderation.[80] However, Wesley conceptualized humility as "the centre of all virtues" and saw it as a "kind of self-annihilation."[81] This means humility does not mean thinking negatively of oneself but refers to thinking less of oneself. Similarly, a similar Christian view of humility was developed by a British minister in the seventeenth century and one of Wesley's early mentors, Jeremy Taylor:

> First, do not think better of yourself because of any outward circumstance that happens to you. . . . Second, humility does not consist of criticizing yourself, or wearing ragged clothes, or walking around submissively wherever you go. Humility

---

78. Ibid., 6:322.
79. Ibid., 6:20.
80. Grenz, *Moral Quest*, 75.
81. Wesley, *Plain Account*, 100.

consists in a realistic opinion of yourself, namely, that you are an unworthy person. Third, when you hold this opinion of yourself, be content that others think the same of you . . .[82]

While this view still appears a little harsh for twenty-first-century Christians, one needs to keep in mind that this view is much more positive than a classical Greek view of humility. The main point is that humility refers to having a realistic view of self (cf. Rom 12:3), which means taking into consideration one's strengths and weaknesses. Roberts holds a similar view and defines humility as a "transcendent form of self-confidence."[83] Humility according to Roberts includes assertiveness, self-confidence, and a realistic view of one's abilities.[84] Humility, according to Roberts, is:

> the ability, without prejudice to one's self-comfort, to admit one's inferiority [or remark one's superiority], in this or that respect, to another. As such, humility is a psychological principle of independence from others and a necessary ground of genuine fellowship with them . . .[85]

Thus, Christian humility is the prerequisite for genuine fellowship and emotional intimacy. It reflects true interdependence between two parties and contributes to healthy vulnerability and accountability. When both parties practice humility they consider themselves equal, which reduces the need for competitive pride:[86]

> Humility is the disposition to view oneself as *basically equal* with any other human being even there are objective differences in physical beauty, wealth, social skills, intelligence, or other resources.[87]

It resembles emotional maturity because of its interdependent nature. When two people view each other as equal, they are more likely to support each other and have a cooperative relationship. Humility is therefore not only the most important and central affection, but also constitutes the foundation for the two remaining affections. Christian leaders can be secure in themselves ("loving themselves") and can be grateful for Christ for the gifts they have received from him. In turn, they love others the same way by being compassionate.

82. Taylor, "Grace of Humility," 244–45.
83. Roberts, *Spiritual Emotions*, 81.
84. Ibid.
85. Ibid., 83.
86. Ibid., 85.
87. Emmons, "Personality and Forgiveness," 164 (my emphasis).

Two other Christian affections, namely gratitude and compassion, are also relevant for Christian leadership. These two affections have a direct relationship to the use of prosocial power when it comes to Christian leadership, since power needs to be associated with mature Christian character.[88]

Gratitude is Christian affection that believers can develop during the process of sanctification. It involves the emotional experience as well as the virtue of being grateful.[89] Jonathan Edwards distinguished between natural and spiritual gratitude.[90] The former refers to being grateful to God for benefits received whereas the latter is being grateful to God for his goodness regardless of received benefits. Wesley viewed gratitude as the foundation for the love of others (Sermon 114):

> True religion is right tempers towards God and man. It is, in two words, gratitude and benevolence; gratitude to our Creator and supreme Benefactor, and benevolence to our fellow-creatures. In other words, it is the loving God with all our heart, and our neighbor as ourselves. . . . *Gratitude towards our Creator cannot but produce benevolence to our fellow-creatures.*[91]

Thus, one's gratitude toward God in turn produces love towards others, which is the essence of sanctification. Gratitude further illustrates our dependence on God and our interdependence to one another:

> Gratitude . . . as a virtue . . . belongs to a view of the world in which human beings are by nature and design dependent creatures . . . human beings depend on God for our creation, preservation, and all the blessings of this life, and we are also made to be dependent on one another . . .[92]

Gratitude again points to emotional maturity. Gratitude decreases anger and resentment according to Nouwen, Christensen, and Laird: "Gratitude makes the interruption into an invitation, and the occasion of complaint into a moment for contemplation."[93] Emotionally mature leaders need to experience and develop gratitude, which will also help them focus on the needs of others, such as their subordinates, stakeholders, and society at large. Emotion theorists place gratitude within empathic emotions, since receiving and giving gifts and benefits require the capacity for empathy, the

---

88. Kretzschmar, "Authentic Christian Leadership," 54.
89. Roberts, *Spiritual Emotions*, 131.
90. Emmons and Crumpler, "Gratitude," 60.
91. Wesley, *Works*, 7:290–91 (my emphasis).
92. Roberts, *Spiritual Emotions*, 139.
93. Nouwen et al., *Spiritual Formation*, 66.

ability to put oneself in somebody's else's shoes.[94] In addition, gratitude is related to prosocial behavior and it predicts social integration leading to generativity, which involves a desire to give back to society.[95] This has important implications for Christian leadership. A Christian leader who experiences gratitude toward God and others is motivated to increase the well-being in others and in society at large. This motivation should be the driving force behind leadership power and influence. A desire to help others includes compassion for others, which I will discuss next.

The moral emotion of compassion is especially relevant for leadership in general and Christian leadership in particular. It is derived from the Hebrew word, *chesed*, which can also be translated as "mercy, grace, loyalty, lovingkindness, and compassion."[96] Maddox asserts that "certain key virtues" need to be strengthened by "works of mercy" of which compassion is an example.[97] Compassion encourages leaders to identify with the needs of others and resembles empathy. However, empathy is value neutral and needs to be developed further into the moral emotion of compassion in order to affect righteous outcomes. Empathy is the prerequisite of compassion and involves a "cognitive awareness of another person's internal states" and a "vicarious affective response to another person, which emphasizes putting oneself in the position of another."[98] It is "a manifestation of God's (prevenient) grace" and is "a manifestation of hope in God."[99] Empathy is strengthened through *acts of mercy*, such as visiting the sick according to Wesley.[100] While Wesley did not use the word empathy, it can be implied by his use of words, such as "sympathy" and "tenderness of the spirit."[101] Thus, visiting the sick (and other acts of mercy) can be considered *means of grace* based on its effects on the development of empathy.[102] This is an important aspect for the circular formational leadership model, since right leadership practices that resemble acts of mercy (*orthopraxis*) reinforce the development of a pure heart (*orthokardia*), which further strengthens Christian affections, such as compassion among others (*orthodynamis*).

Empathy can develop into compassion if the believer makes a conscious decision to cooperate with God's sanctifying grace and the Holy

---

94. Emmons and Crumpler, "Gratitude," 63.
95. Froh et al., "Being Grateful,"153.
96. Oord, *Nature of Love*, 130.
97. Maddox, "Formation for Christian,"122.
98. Lazarus, *Emotion and Adaptation*, 288.
99. Armistead, "Empathy," 64.
100. Shrier and Shrier, "Wesley's Sanctification," 232.
101. Ibid., 233.
102. Ibid., 235.

Spirit, which produces the will to develop more compassion.[103] According to emotion theorists, compassion is an emotion that involves "feeling personal distress at the suffering of another and wanting to ameliorate it" and "being moved by another's suffering and wanting to help."[104] Arthur Schopenhauer, a German philosopher and contemporary of Immanuel Kant, offered an alternative ethical approach, argues that there are essentially "three fundamental incentives" or motives:

   a. Egoism: this desires one's own weal [or well-being] (is boundless)
   b. Malice: this desires another's woe (goes to the limits of extreme cruelty)
   c. Compassion: this desires another's weal (goes to the length of nobleness and magnanimity).[105]

Compassion prevents us from acting egotistically and maliciously. Egoism and malice resemble the motives of toxic leaders, which include narcissistic and psychopathic leaders. Furthermore, Schopenhauer considered justice and philanthropy as "cardinal virtues" that are rooted in compassion.[106] Justice, especially social justice, which I will address in chapter 6.

Compassion as a form of love and Christian affection goes beyond the emotional aspect. If strong and persistent enough to be considered as a character trait, compassion involves a strong action component.[107] This is important because emotions are considered states and are by nature not enduring. However, if compassion is *both* a state *and* a trait it can be enduring and can produce consistent ethical choices and behaviors. As I stated above, empathy and compassion also have a biological basis and are housed in the orbitofrontal cortex (OFC).[108] The OFC is less well developed in people with insecure attachment patterns. In addition, mirror neurons are also responsible for "feeling with another person," which act "rapidly and automatically" and are produce a "gut-level empathy."[109] From a Wesleyan perspective, the biological nature of empathy/compassion could be seen as the result of prevenient grace. However, compassion can be strengthened in cooperation with the Holy Spirit:

---

103. Ibid., 237.
104. Lazarus, *Emotion and Adaptation*, 289.
105. Schopenhauer, *On the Basis*, 145.
106. Ibid., 148.
107. Roberts, *Spiritual Emotions*, 180.
108. Goleman, *Social Intelligence*, 64.
109. Ibid., 70, 85.

> The initial breath of the Spirit in us, the initial impulse to be empathic, and our empathic response reveal Wesley's sanctification narrative to be consistent with *holistic dualism*. If our mirror neuron systems function correctly we will experience the suffering of another person. It is the initial working of the Holy Spirit within us, however, that empowers us to respond to that person with a Christian love that places the needs of the other person before our own. Once we are empowered, we must still choose to act on the initial experience and the Holy Spirit's empowerment.[110]

Thus, compassion can be strengthened through the Holy Spirit and by engaging in acts of mercy, such as by visiting the sick. Acts of mercy occur within a community and community in itself can contribute to the development of compassion. McNeil, Morrison, and Nouwen write that "in the Christian community, we can fully recognize the condition of our society without panicking."[111] This means we can practice compassion in our Christian community and encourage one another to grow in compassion despite its uncomfortableness because "wherever true Christian community is formed, compassion *happens* in the world."[112] Our tendency to be comfortable and complacent prevents us from growing in compassion. We develop compassion once we are committed to sacrifice. McNeil, Morrison, and Nouwen comment on the relationship of overcoming one's comfortableness or "false comfort" with compassion:

> Voluntary displacement [which means overcoming one's comfortableness and commitment to sacrifice] leads to compassion; by bringing us closer to our brokenness it opens our eyes to our fellow human beings, who seek our consolation and comfort.[113]

Thus, by being aware of our own brokenness and by our willingness and commitment to sacrifice we become more compassionate. In summary, humility, gratitude, and compassion are all connected. Our dependence on God produces gratitude and "gratitude involves self-confidence [i.e., humility] that is also necessary for compassion."[114] How do these three affections/virtues relate to power and leadership? In order to answer this question, we need to first explore the concept of power and influence from a social science and leadership perspective.

110. Shrier and Shrier, "Wesley's Sanctification," 238.
111. McNeil et al., *Compassion*, 56.
112. Ibid., 57.
113. Ibid., 64,74.
114. Roberts, *Spiritual Emotions*, 191.

Power, influence, and Leadership

Orthodynamis includes the concept of power motive well known in the secular leadership literature.[115] Power and leadership are closely related depending on one's definition of leadership. McClelland conceptualizes leadership as an influence relationship between a leader and his or her followers.[116] Power can be defined as "the ability to change the behavior of others," as opposed to the concept of authority, which is "the *right* to try to change or direct others."[117] Kets de Vries views power as being "rooted in the heart of human nature and behavior, involving fundamental feelings about superiority and inferiority, autonomy and dependence, even love and hate."[118] Thus, power can be considered to be fundamental to the fallen human condition. When it comes to morality, power is essentially value neutral and can therefore be used for both good and evil. Raven links social power with influence and defines social influence as "a change in a person's cognitions, attitude, or behavior which has its origin in another person or group."[119] Social power is therefore viewed as one's potential influence. French and Raven discuss five sources of social power: reward power (the "ability to reward"), coercive power (the "ability to manipulate the attainment of valences"), legitimate power (based on a "legitimate right to influence"), expert power (based on "the extent of knowledge" that is attributed to a leader), and referent power (based on "a feeling of oneness" with the leader).[120] Raven added informational power, which he defined as a potential influence "result[ing] [in] a basic change in cognitive elements . . . [based on] information communicated by the agent." [121]

Kelman articulates three classical influence processes; compliance (expecting rewards or approval or avoiding specific punishments), identification (based on a desire to have a satisfying relationship to another person), and internalization (meaning the adoption of values that are congruent with one's own").[122] These influence processes correspond with three power

---

115. French and Raven, "Bases of Social"; Raven, "Comparative Analysis"; Raven, "Bases of Power"; McClelland, *Power*.

116. McClelland, *Power*.

117. Vecchio, "Power, Politics,"71.

118. Kets de Vries, "On Becoming," 123.

119. Raven, "Comparative Analysis," 173.

120. French and Raven, "Bases of Social," 155–63.

121. Raven, "Comparative Analysis," 173.

122. Kelman, "Compliance, Identification," 53. *Internalization* here means embracing these values and changing our behavior because we want to render our behavior congruent with our espoused values. They serve as internal motivators for engaging in

types: means-control, attractiveness, and credibility. Raven compares Kelman's power typology with French and Raven's power typology: means control corresponds with reward and coercive power, attractiveness with referent power, and credibility matches expert and informational power.[123] Raven could not match legitimate power with Kelman's power types since Kelman views legitimacy as "cutting across [his] three processes of influence, so that it may be associated with any of the three sources of power."[124] Regarding the relationship between the sources of power and Kelman's influence processes, Raven and Kelman argue that (means control) reward and coercive power lead to compliance, (attractiveness) and referent power lead to identification, and (credibility) and expert and informational power lead to internalization (see Table 1).[125]

Table 1: Power Sources, Power Types, and Influence Processes

French and Raven's and Raven's Power Sources	Kelman's Power Types	Kelman's Influence Processes
Reward and Coercive Power	Means Control	Compliance
Referent Power	Attractiveness	Identification
Expert and Informational Power	Credibility	Internalization

The question arises how motives affect the sources of power. Raven argues that there are several motives that affect the choice of a particular power source:

> (1) attaining extrinsic goals (e.g., increase productivity), (2) satisfying internal needs (i.e., "power, status, security, self-esteem"), (3) role requirements/higher authority, (4) motivation to benefit or harm, and (5) desired status in the eyes of self, target, third party.[126]

Regarding satisfying an internal need, and maybe regarding desired status and power as well, Raven cited some evidence that influencing agents who lack self-confidence will more likely "use 'harder' forms of influence, such as coercion, even when information might be effective."[127] These internal motives and needs resemble those of toxic leaders.

---

behaviors that are congruent with these values.
  123. Raven, "Comparative Analysis."
  124. Kelman, "Further Thoughts," 161.
  125. Raven, "Comparative Analysis"; Kelman, "Further Thoughts."
  126. Raven, "Bases of Power," 240.
  127. Ibid., 269.

McClelland conceptualizes the power need by outlining four different stages, which also correspond to the four stages of ego development following Freud and Erikson:[128] Stage I (the intake modality) is characterized by obtaining strength from the outside (i.e., mother, etc.), stage II (the autonomy modality) refers to the need to control oneself, stage III (the assertion modality) involves the need to control and impact others, and stage IV (the mutuality modality) represents the need to use power for others. Stage IV can be said to be the most mature stage, since people who reach stage IV "are more responsible in organizations, less ego-involved, more willing to seek expert help when appropriate, more open with intimates," yet "without feeling that [they are] 'losing' [themselves] in the process." However, a better conceptualization of maturity is being flexible "to use whatever mode is appropriate to the situation."[129] Maturity also serves to differentiate between negative and positive sides of power. The negative and positive sides of power correspond to personalized and socialized forms of power. McClelland defines personalized power as being "characterized by the dominance-submission mode: If I win, you lose."[130] Personalized (P) power is more primitive and "leads to simple and direct means of feeling powerful—drinking heavily, acquiring 'prestige supplies,' and being aggressive," which is often associated with narcissism.[131] On the other hand, socialized (S) power is characterized by:

> a concern for group goals, for finding those goals that will move men, for helping the group to formulate them, for taking the initiative in providing means of achieving them, and for giving group members the feeling of competence they need to work hard for them. In fantasy it leads to a concern with exercising influence *for* others . . .[132]

Thus, S power is more emotionally mature than P power based on its emphasis on altruism. It also resembles interdependence. By applying S power in leadership, we have to wrestle with a paradox: In order to be an effective leader, he or she "must turn all of his [or her] followers into leaders," which requires that the leader is secure in him- and herself.[133]

The relationship between power and effective leadership, such as transformational and authentic leadership, depends on motives and values.

128. McClelland, *Power*, 23–24.
129. Ibid., 24.
130. Ibid., 263.
131. Ibid.
132. Ibid
133. Ibid., 262.

Bass and Steidlmeier assert that transformational leadership is based on altruistic values, as opposed to self-centered values that underlie pseudo-transformational leadership.[134] Thus, authentic transformational leaders behave morally, whereas pseudo-transformational leaders behave immorally. Regarding the power motive, transformational leaders can be said to utilize McClelland's socialized power, whereas pseudo-transformational leaders use personalized power. Authentic leadership emphasizes a shift from "I" to "We," which is the most important step for leaders to become authentic.[135] This shift alludes to a socialized power: "Only when leaders stop focusing on their personal ego needs are they able to develop other leaders."[136] Collins's *Good to Great* leadership style, called "Level 5 Executive[s]" appear to display socialized power by "channel[ing] their ego needs away from themselves and into the larger goal of building a great company."[137] These leaders were found to be humble and driven to make their organizations great.

Regarding power motives in Christian leadership, Nouwen observes that power is very tempting for leaders:

> What makes the temptation of power so seemingly irresistible? Maybe it is that power offers an easy substitute for the hard task of love. It seems easier to be God than to love God, easier to control people than to love people, easier to own life than to love life.[138]

Thus, seeking power competes with our motive for attachment and love. Christian leaders and leaders in general tend to be intimacy avoidant and may utilize power over people as a defense. Nouwen addresses this tendency here:

> The temptation of power is greatest when intimacy is a threat. Much Christian leadership is exercised by people who do not know how to develop healthy, intimate relationships and have opted for power and control instead. Many Christian empire-builders have been people unable to give and receive love.[139]

This again refers to healthy attachment in Christian leaders combined with higher levels of differentiation. However, as I stated above, power in itself is not evil as higher moral forms of power illustrate (cf. socialized power orientation).

134. Bass and Steidlmeier, "Ethics, Character."
135. George and Sims, *True North*, 44.
136. Ibid., 45.
137. Collins, *Good to Great*, 21.
138. Nouwen, *In the Name*, 76.
139. Ibid., 79.

Hagberg and Guelich discuss six stages of power from a Christian perspective: powerlessness, power by association, power by achievement, power by reflection, power by purpose, and power by wisdom.[140] Power by achievement (stage 3) resembles McClelland's personalized power orientation by its focus on "power over resources and decisions."[141] Whereas McClelland's socialized power motive is apparent in stages 4 to 6. For example, power by reflection (stage 4) focuses on influence and Christian leaders who are in this stage are "competent in collaboration," are "skilled at mentoring" and show "true leadership (honesty, fairness [or display justice], sound judgement, and follow-through."[142] Power by purpose (stage 5) focuses on "power [as] inner vision" with its emphasis on humility, self-acceptance, "giving away power," and on the leader's life being "transforming around our life purpose, which we have received from God."[143] Finally, power by wisdom (stage 6) consists of "selflessness," being "comfortable with paradox," "conscience of the community," and "compassion for the world."[144] Christian leaders who lead from this stage "are mentors, role models, and supporters of others who want to pursue their deepest heart's desires."[145] It is interesting to note that the two Christian affections discussed above, humility and compassion, are included in stages 5 and 6. The following table summarizes the correspondence between the two models:

Table 2: Power Motives and Christian Power Stages

McClelland's Power Motives	Hagberg and Guelich's Stages of Power
Personalized Power Orientation (P-Power)	Power by Achievement ("power over") (stage 3)
Socialized Power Orientation (S-Power)	Power by Reflection ("collaboration, mentoring, true leadership") (stage 4)
	Power by Purpose ("humility, self-acceptance, giving away power") (stage 5)
	Power by Wisdom ("selflessness, conscience of the community, compassion for the world") (stage 6)

How can organizations develop compassion and social justice? Bass and Steidlmeier and Sashkin and Sashkin assert that transformational

---

140. Hagberg and Guelich, *Critical Journey*, 217–28.
141. Ibid., 220.
142. Ibid., 222.
143. Ibid., 226.
144. Ibid., 228.
145. Ibid., 228.

leaders display the "virtue" of credibility.[146] Sashkin and Sashkin equate credibility with consistency between what a leader says and does.[147] O'Keefe views credibility as comprised of two aspects: expertness and trustworthiness.[148] He associated the connection between credibility and expertness and trustworthiness (being unselfish and having personal integrity) with reliable communication:

> Perhaps it is not surprising that both competence [expertness] and trustworthiness emerge as basic dimensions of credibility, since as a rule only the conjunction of competence and trustworthiness makes for reliable communications.[149]

Reliable communication from a leader promotes security and reduces uncertainty in followers. When it comes to linking credibility to the sources of power, expert and informational power constitute credibility and foster internalization in followers.[150] Thus, the primary influence process in transformational (and formational leadership) is fostering internalization, which can be accomplished by exerting expert and informational power. Authentic leadership emphasizes compassion for others (one of the five characteristics) and George argues that when leaders develop compassion they grow in authenticity.[151] In addition, Christian leadership is based on "God factor" power, which refers to the "sacred weight" of Christian leaders as they "represent God." [152] "God factor" power can be considered as spiritual expert power. It is the power and influence Christian followers ascribe to Christian leaders based on what followers expect Christian leaders to embody (spiritual maturity, anointing, knowledge of the Bible, discernment, etc.). It is therefore particularly devastating when Christian leaders display toxic leadership because these leaders are understood to represent God and his kingdom on earth (see Table 3).

---

146. Bass and Steidlmeier, "Ethics, Character"; Sashkin and Sashkin, *Leadership That Matters*.
147. Sashkin and Sashkin, *Leadership That Matters*, 44.
148. O'Keefe, *Persuasion*, 132.
149. Ibid., 133.
150. Raven, "Comparative Analysis"; Kelman, "Further Thoughts."
151. George, *Authentic Leadership*, 40.
152. Scazzero, *Emotionally Healthy Leader*, 246.

Table 3: Power Sources, Power Types, Influence Processes, and Leadership Styles

Power Sources French and Raven, Raven, and Scazzero	Power Types Kelman	Influence Processes Kelman	Leadership Styles or Approaches (cf. Sashkin and Sashkin)
Reward and Coercive Power	Means Control	Compliance	Transactional
Referent Power	Attractiveness	Identification	Charismatic
Expert, Informational Power, and "God Factor" Power	Credibility	Internalization	Transformational [Authentic and Formational]

Sashkin and Sashkin also view the "internalization of shared values held by leaders . . ." as the primary means to influence followers.[153] This means that values can be a power source in themselves. Burns assigns a central role to values in binding leaders to followers. These values need to be motivating for followers by appealing to follower's sense of morality and spirituality.[154] Thus, Burns calls these values "transformational values" affecting "deep change."[155] Furthermore, transformational values strengthen leadership, empower followers, and serve as "power resources" to transform society including organizations towards higher levels of morality.[156] Christian affections, such as humility, gratitude, and compassion can serve as transformational values that followers can internalize. These three affections/values need to be modeled by formational leaders in order for internalization to occur. These three affections are interconnected with humility being the foundational affection. Thus, *orthodynamis* is essentially informed by a socialized power motive (cf. McClelland) and includes the advanced Christian power stages 4–6 (cf. Hagberg and Guelich). It is expressed through these three Christian affections:

---

153. Sashkin and Sashkin, *Leadership That Matters*, 77.
154. Burns, *Transforming Leadership*, 212.
155. Ibid., 198.
156. Ibid., 213.

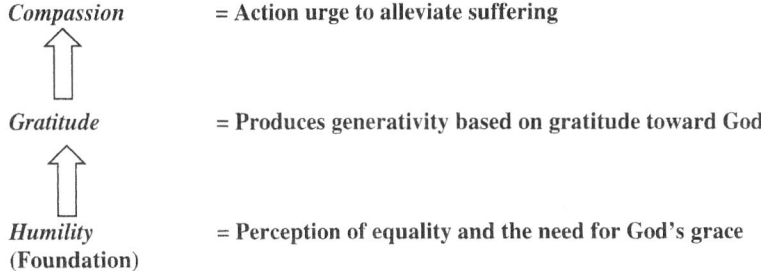

Figure 6: Relationships between Humility, Gratitude, and Compassion

How do the means of grace according to Wesley inform Christian leadership development? I will argue below that the means of grace outline spiritual mechanisms for change in the Christian leader.

Means of Grace

Protestantism has become a more individualistic faith tradition over the last few hundred years. In Catholicism, believers are encouraged to confess one's sin to a priest. However, James 5:16 says "*confess* your sins to *each other* and *pray for each other* so that you may be healed" (NIV, my emphasis), which means that, as was the case in the early church. Thus, it is more difficult for Christians to grow spiritually without the input from a Christian community. Wesley's focus on Christian community and accountability was an important correction to Protestant individualism. While Pietism influenced Methodism, it was still individualistic in its focus.[157] Wesley viewed holiness as a common goal that needed to be shared with the Christian community.[158] When it comes to the means of grace, Wesley followed Calvin's "position of a 'spiritual' mediation of grace through the act of communing."[159] Wesley viewed the Holy Spirit's presence as the efficient cause or power for conveying God's grace to believers. Wesley's Eastern therapeutic understanding of salvation as discussed in chapter 3, is again apparent here: "Moreover, since deification is a process of healing rather than juridical change in status, the full benefit of the sacraments (and other means of grace) is realized gradually and cumulatively."[160] Wesley differentiated between ordinary and

---

157. Runyon, *New Creation*, 102.
158. Ibid., 103.
159. Maddox, *Responsible Grace*, 193.
160. Ibid., 197.

extraordinary means of grace[161] or, as Collins called them, instituted and prudential means of grace.[162] Ordinary or instituted means of grace refers to baptism and the Lord's Supper whereas public worship, accountability groups and works of mercy refer to extraordinary or prudential means of grace. In order for believers to grow in their spiritual walk holistically, Leclerc suggests addressing several domains of one's spirituality.[163] Foster lists three domains: The inward, outward, and corporate domain. The inward domain especially focuses on exploring the "inner caverns of the spiritual realm."[164] This domain includes the following disciplines: meditation, prayer, fasting, and study of scripture reading.[165] The outward domain stresses the interpersonal implication that includes: simplicity, solitude, submission, and service.[166] Finally, the corporate domain helps believers practice accountability as a member of a faith community and includes the following practices: confession, worship, guidance, celebration.[167] Spiritual practices from all three domains should be emphasized in churches.

Regarding baptism, Wesley affirmed infant baptism as the "beginning of the 'process' of salvation," but he did not believe that baptism completes the salvation process.[168] Baptism removes the penalty of original sin, which Wesley associated with prevenient grace.[169] He likened baptism, similar to Calvin, to the Jewish practice of circumcision as a "sign of the covenant."[170] Wesley's association of new birth with baptism originates from two religious influences, his "sacramental" view came from Anglicanism and his "evangelical" view arose from his reformist motives.[171] His "evangelical" view made him insist on looking for outward signs of the new birth in believers, which were faith, love, and hope.[172] In summary, Wesley affirmed the role of baptism in the process of salvation and viewed it as a starting point.

Regarding the Lord's Supper, Wesley assumed a "receptionist" view, meaning he believed that God's grace and real presence is being conveyed

---

161. Ibid., 193.
162. Collins, *Theology of Wesley*, 257, 266.
163. Leclerc, "Finding the Means," 78.
164. Foster, *Celebration of Discipline*, 1.
165. Ibid., 15–62.
166. Ibid., 79–126.
167. Ibid., 143–90.
168. Runyon, *New Creation*, 140.
169. Collins, *Theology of Wesley*, 264.
170. Runyon, *New Creation*, 140.
171. Collins, *Theology of Wesley*, 265.
172. Ibid., 265.

to the person who receives the elements rather than Jesus Christ being embodied in the elements.[173] Wesley's view is similar to Zwingli's Memorial view.[174] It is also similar to Calvin's view in that the efficacy of the sacrament is mediated by the Holy Spirit.[175] However, unlike Calvin's view,[176] Wesley viewed the Lord's Supper as a means of bringing Christ to the recipient: "*the Spirit brings Christ to us*, expressing the grace and love of God toward us through the means of bread and wine."[177] Finally, Wesley regarded the Lord's Supper as a means for "transforming our sin-distorted lives," which again points to his therapeutic view of salvation.[178] The Lord's Supper occurs within a liturgical framework, which includes a "guided reflection on and confession of our sins."[179] This last aspect points to the extraordinary means of grace, which I will be discuss next.

Extraordinary means of grace refer to accountability groups, private exercises, works of mercy, etc. The rationale for extraordinary means of grace is based on the fact that the "Christian life requires self-knowledge" and the "means of grace provides practices which facilitate critical self-awareness."[180] Knight further expands on this concept by asserting that:

> The means of grace in the Methodist movement counter presumptive claims through encouraging accountable discipleship, self-examination, and repentance within a community of forgiveness and love.[181]

This means that the Christian affections of humility and love can be fostered in a supportive community.[182] In addition, in supportive communities "a living faith, an expectant hope, a humble love for God and one's neighbor" can be developed.[183] Thus, Wesleyan mutual spiritual guidance or direction was conducted in groups, such as in "classes, bands, societies, families,

---

173. Maddox, *Responsible Grace*, 204; Collins, *Theology of Wesley*, 262.

174. Collins, *Theology of Wesley*, 260.

175. Ibid., 262.

176. Calvin believed that believers are "lifted up by the Spirit to feed on the body of Christ that is in heaven," according to Collins (*Theology of Wesley*, 262).

177. Runyon, *New Creation*, 130.

178. Maddox, *Responsible Grace*, 205.

179. Ibid.

180. Knight, "Presence of God," 131.

181. Ibid.

182. Ibid.

183. Ibid., 139.

and 'twin soul' and faith mentoring pairs."[184] These groups shared several characteristics:

1. They were a "means by which Christians could strengthen one another's faith."

2. They provided the structure for "watch[ing] over one another in love" and for being "accountable to one another concerning their discipleship."

3. Members were "mutually responsible for one another" and "helped each other work out their salvation."

4. Members "accepted Wesley as a spiritual director" and, as the movement grew in size, others who served as spiritual directors.[185]

Regarding individual groups, classes contained twelve persons that met on a weekly basis.[186] During class meeting "Methodist doctrines, sermons, and practices were explained" and the class was a place for "love and mutual support."[187] Mutual accountability was practiced in class meetings, but it emphasized accountability to the leader who served the role as a pastor or spiritual director.[188] Classes were designed for those newer in the Methodist faith and Wesley therefore saw a need to create smaller groups for those who desired a more "intimate and intensive" group experience.[189]

These smaller groups, called "bands," consisted of five to six persons of the same gender with the purpose of sharing their spiritual journeys that included spiritual successes and failures.[190] Before a person was allowed to join a band he or she needed to be examined "by means of eleven questions" ("Have you the forgiveness of sins and peace with God . . . ?" "Has no sin, inward or outward, dominion over you?" etc.).[191] Each band meeting was started with five questions that pertained to possible spiritual failures, temptations experienced and delivered from, new revelations from God to the band member about his or her motives, lifestyle, and attitudes, and spiritual problems. Band members needed to follow three rules: to "carefully" avoid

---

184. Tracy, "Spiritual Direction," 118.
185. Knight, "Presence of God," 142.
186. Tracy, "Spiritual Direction," 120.
187. Ibid., 120.
188. Knight, "Presence of God," 144.
189. Ibid., 147.
190. Tracy, "Spiritual Direction," 121.
191. Ibid., 121.

evil, to "zealously" do good works, and to "constantly" "observe the ordinance of God."[192]

Of particular importance for formational leadership is Wesley's "final [group] substructure" called the select society, which was designed for "those who were actively pressing after the experience of entire sanctification [and] to provide more serious mutual support and accountability for their quest."[193] These groups consisted of leaders who were "most faithful and dedicated" with the purpose of increasing love for each other, helping them "advance in perfection," and "improving every leadership talent."[194] Wesley insisted on enhanced confidentiality in these groups, since he utilized these for mutual accountability.[195] Knight asserts that the select society "was the culmination of trends which began with classes and extended through the bands" and the intensified discipline became "a way of life" in the select society.[196] The select society meetings were less structured, but had more "mutuality in spirituality in spiritual direction."[197] The select society was the "fullest social realization of the Christian life" expressed through a "unity of love" and an "increased sensitivity to the presence of God."[198] These groups provide a model for leadership development that can be practiced in the twenty-first century. These groups could provide the means for fostering humility, gratitude, and compassion in Christian leaders. Christian narcissistic and perfectionistic leaders would benefit from feedback from other leaders in the group. Other group members can provide constructive feedback to toxic leaders, which can provide them with interpersonal insights. Toxic leaders are more likely to express their thoughts and feelings during group once they trust other group members.

Finally "twin souls" and "faith mentoring" are two additional ways for creating mutual love and accountability.[199] Two people can provide spiritual guidance and accountability for each other, which could also be utilized for leadership development purposes. Faith mentoring is similar to classical spiritual direction, but is more informal. It involves for a person who is more mature in the faith to guide someone new in the faith or someone who desires faith mentoring.

192. Knight, "Presence of, God" 148.
193. Maddox, *Responsible Grace*, 213.
194. Tracy, "Spiritual Direction," 122.
195. Maddox, *Responsible Grace*, 213.
196. Knight, "Presence of God," 149.
197. Ibid., 149.
198. Ibid., 148, 149.
199. Tracy, 123.

When it comes to private exercises, the Wesleyan tradition emphasized spiritual disciplines, such as prayer and fasting among others.[200] Prayer is the essential discipline and the most important means to draw near to God according to Wesley.[201] Wesley viewed prayer as a "way of life" and as an "integration of activity and receptiveness."[202] This receptivity refers to believers becoming more aware of God's presence in their lives.[203] Thompson asserts that the baptism in the Holy Spirit along with speaking in tongues is another means of grace to experience God's presence and assists the Wesleyan Pentecostal believer to receive God's sanctifying grace.[204] The baptism in the Spirit has traditionally been viewed as merely empowerment for service. However, Thompson views glossolalia as both empowerment for service and as a means of grace.

Fasting involved abstaining from "all food, some food, or from pleasant foods."[205]

Wesley noted two reasons for fasting: "sorrow for sin" and helping the believer focus their attention on God by de-emphasizing bodily desires and appetites.[206] When fasting is used with prayer in the context of "mutual accountability and support, in enables Christians to attend to the presence of God, and to the needs of the world."[207]

A work of mercy is also means of grace, which can be defined as an "active expression of love in the world [that] both increases sensitivity to human need and deepens the capacity of love."[208] Works of mercy involve helping the poor to have a better life or attending to any need a fellow human being may have. Wesley preferred works of mercy over works of piety (see private exercises), since these foster our love for others.[209] The works of mercy will be emphasized in chapter 6 when we will focus on social justice and its implications. In the next section I will outline the implications of the above analysis for leadership development.

---

200. Ibid., 127.
201. Tracy, "Spiritual Direction," 127; Knight, "Presence of God," 169.
202. Knight, "Presence of God," 171–72.
203. Ibid., 172.
204. Thompson, "Kingdom Come," 187.
205. Knight, "Presence of God," 176.
206. Ibid., 177.
207. Ibid.
208. Ibid., 163.
209. Collins, *Theology of Wesley*, 267.

Implications for Leadership Development

Orthodynamis is all about the power motives in Christian leaders, which should be based on Christian values and affections. The three religious affections: humility, gratitude and compassion serve as indicators for *orthodynamis*. Humility is the foundation and precondition for taking responsibility, which in turn paves the way for gratitude, empathy and compassion. The Christian leader who practices formational leadership needs to internalize these three affections. A Christian leader should first lead him- or herself before leading others.[210] The formational leader who has gone through his or her personal formation can therefore lead others based on his or her sanctified character, which produces credibility. Credibility is the most important ingredient of effective leadership.[211] As I mentioned above, credibility is the result of two power sources, expert and informational power, which produces internalization of values in followers. Credibility is also included in authentic leadership because self-disciplined leaders, one of the five characteristics of authentic leadership, "remain cool, calm, and consistent" during times of stress, which makes them predictable and gives followers a sense of security.[212]

Christian expert power includes "God-factor" power. This means that the Christian leader should not only be well trained (expert power), but also should be a good communicator and willing to communicate essential information to his or her followers (informational power). In addition, the Christian leader who displays humility, gratitude, and compassion possesses "God-factor" power that produces internalization of these three values/affections. Furthermore, behavioral consistency is another indicator of credibility, which means the leader should do what he or she says.[213] Similarly, 1 Peter 5:3 addressed elders who functioned as leaders in the early church by stating: "Don't shepherd by *ruling over* those entrusted to your care, but *become examples* to the flock" (CEB, my emphasis). This means being role models for followers as opposed to using coercive leadership power. Thus, these three affections constitute influence through values the leader embodies.

---

210. Maxwell, "Reflections on Model," 43.
211. Kouzes and Posner, "Leadership Is," 120.
212. Northouse, *Leadership*, 214.
213. Ibid., 120.

Another implication when it comes to power and influence refers to power sharing:

> *A wise leader strengthens people by giving power away.* Leaders place constituents, not themselves, at the center. Leaders use their power in service of others, not in service of themselves.[214]

This refers to the Christian affection of humility, which requires self-denial and is foundational for formational leadership. A leader serves others when he or she thinks about him- or herself less and who sees him- or herself as equal to others. However, how can a Christian leader improve develop humility, gratitude, and compassion?

Generally speaking, toxic narcissistic and obsessive-compulsive leaders tend to be reluctant to seek help and guidance. Therefore, strong church boards need to be established to hold narcissistic and obsessive-compulsive leaders accountable. The leader may initially be reluctant to engage in the process of guidance, but may gradually work collaboratively with the spiritual director, therapist, or coach if he or she senses that the professional truly respects and cares about him or her. Thus, the working relationship between the leader and coach is crucial and provides a way for transforming the leader, with the help of the Holy Spirit (a co-operant process).

The practice of spiritual disciplines within a Christian community could be another effective means to promote Christian affections in leaders. The spiritual disciplines can also target specific sins that Christian leaders may struggle with ("signature sins"). For example, as I discussed above, of the seven (or eight) deadly sins, Christian leaders may struggle with pride (and vainglory), anger, lust, gluttony, or envy. A Christian coach or spiritual director could guide the Christian leader to visualize and imagine the three corresponding virtues or religious affections, which are humility (pride and vainglory), gratitude (greed), and compassion (anger and envy). Visualization of virtues helps Christian leaders achieve them with the help of the Holy Spirit and motivates them to pursue and develop them. This is similar to leaders who aspire to pursue an organizational vision. To further develop these Christian affections and virtues, Christian leaders could practice two disciplines to foster humility: Solitude and submission. Solitude "puts a stopper on all self-justification" and allows "God to [be] my justifier."[215] Thus, this discipline crucifies the Christian leader's desire or perceived need to be important.[216] Solitude involves being alone with God for one day, a

---

214. Ortberg, "Reflections on Enable," 90.
215. Foster, *Celebration of Discipline*, 101, 107.
216. Ibid.

weekend, or for an entire week. During this time speaking to others should be minimal. Solitude can be a transformational experience for all of us, but especially for toxic Christian leaders:

> Every time we enter into solitude we withdraw from our windy, earthquaking, fiery lives and open ourselves to the great encounter. The first thing we often discover in solitude is our own *restlessness, our drivenness and compulsiveness, our urge to act quickly, make an impact, and to have influence*; and often we find it very hard to withstand the temptation to return as quickly as possible to the worlds of "relevance." . . . Here we touch the greatest gift of solitude. It is the gift of a new self, a new identity . . . we discover our true nature, our true self, our true identity.[217]

Thus, we experience transformation of our personality if we let God, our "creator, redeemer, and sanctifier," touch us during times of solitude.[218] Toxic leaders can especially become more humble during times of solitude because during times of solitude with God there is nobody to impress, nobody to compare oneself to, and nobody to control, etc.

The discipline of submission provides the toxic Christian leader with insight into his or her defensiveness and tendency to rationalize and justify, since "[o]nly submission can free us sufficiently to enable us to distinguish between genuine issues and stubborn self-will."[219] It fosters what Jesus requires of us, namely self-denial, which means "a way of coming to understand that we do not have to have our own way."[220] We submit to God, to Scripture, to our family, our neighbors, the body of Christ, etc.[221] Submission is also accomplished by being willing to join a small group for accountability purposes. However, submission can be more formal as well when a Christian leader seeks direction from a coach, mentor, or spiritual director.

The discipline of simplicity is a good way to develop gratitude. Simplicity means abstaining from modern-day conveniences that we all take for granted. For example, a Christian leader could decide to abstain from using electronic media for one weekend (smartphones, tablets, etc.). He or she would be more appreciative of them when he or she uses them again, which would produce gratitude. Gratitude can also be strengthened by gratitude journaling and the discipline of worship.

---

217. Nouwen, *Clowning in Rome*, 28–29 (my emphasis).
218. Ibid., 28.
219. Foster, *Celebration of Discipline*, 111.
220. Ibid., 113.
221. Ibid., 122–23.

In order to foster compassion, Christian leaders could be encouraged to serve others by working in food banks, prison ministry, or services to the poor to help them acquire better occupational skills, etc. These services may inconvenience Christian leaders, which would potentially create compassion in them as they cooperate with the Holy Spirit. As I stated above, compassion is produced during works of mercy. To cultivate patience, which is often related to the lack of compassion, the leader could practice the "discipline of slowing," which involves "deliberately choosing to place ourselves in positions where we simply have to wait" (slow check-out lines, slow lane on the interstate, etc.).[222] This requires a resolve to sacrifice for others, which is required for social holiness and justice to take root within the leader's heart. I will thoroughly address social holiness and justice in chapter 6.

Regarding specific implications for helping toxic leaders, the following paragraphs will outline some steps. Christian narcissistic leaders are excellent at deceiving themselves (and others) that their grandiose strivings and visions originate in God and belong to "kingdom work." By pointing out to them that their "fantasies of unlimited success" can potentially hurt followers, compromise kingdom values, and ultimately destroy churches and other Christian organizations, will gradually open their eyes. However, too often narcissistic and other toxic leaders are too defensive to receive feedback. Therefore, an assertive leadership board of a Christian organization could gently confront him or her to work collaboratively with the board, which would slowly transform a personalized power orientation into a socialized power orientation with the focus on God's kingdom. Working with a board or under an administrative bishop or other supervisor would strengthen the narcissistic leader's ability to submit and would encourage the discipline of submission, which presupposes self-denial. Self-denial does not entail the loss of the leader's identity nor can self-denial be equated with self-contempt.[223] However, it "declares that [the leader is] of infinite worth and shows [him or her] how to realize it."[224] "When we live outside of self-denial, we demand that things go our way" and "when they do not, we revert to self-pity—'poor me.'"[225] This eloquently describes the internal struggle narcissistic leaders often experience, especially since narcissism is a disorder of self-esteem according to Furnham as stated above. Romans 12:3b is helpful here to illustrate healthy self-esteem: "Don't think you are better than you really are. Be *honest in your evaluation of yourselves*, measuring yourselves

222. Ortberg, *Life You've Always*, 83.
223. Foster, *Celebration of Discipline*, 114.
224. Ibid., 114.
225. Ibid., 114.

by the faith God has given us" (NLT, my emphasis). This means that Christians should hold a realistic view of themselves, neither too high nor too low. The shy narcissistic type tends to shame him- or herself too much and often engages in self-contempt. He or she needs to notice the gifts and talents God has given him or her. The arrogant narcissist overcompensates and projects an unrealistically "perfect" self-esteem and needs to learn to view him- or herself as God sees him or her with God-given talents being able to acknowledge flaws, which is the humility that I discussed in this chapter. Furthermore, Christian narcissistic leaders can benefit from "corrective disillusionment" experiences (constructive feedback from bishop, family illnesses, leave of absence for the purpose of rehabilitation, experiences of failure, etc.) that can correct his or her unrealistic self-evaluations.[226] This entails challenging their unrealistic views of self and "bringing the view of self into greater congruence with actual talents, abilities, and status."[227] Finally, the leader's fantasies can be explored after the leader trusts the coach, etc. to differentiate between personalized and socialized power motives, or in this context, kingdom power motives. A group setting, such as Wesley's select society group model, is especially helpful for exploring unrealistic and grandiose fantasies of narcissistic leaders. This means, similar to group psychotherapy, the group can provide *"reality testing"* to the narcissistic leader, which needs to occur "directly and consistently."[228] However, these confrontations need to be balanced with respect and concern for the toxic leader.[229] The accountability structure of the group is also very conducive to helping an obsessive-compulsive leader become aware of his or her cold interpersonal style and rigidity.

Toxic leaders with obsessive-compulsive traits benefit from knowing that nobody is perfect. Appropriate self-disclosure of the spiritual director, coach, or Christian therapist about his or her fallibility along with the acceptance of it would help the narcissistic (and obsessive compulsive) leader accept his or her own faults.[230] This should occur within a trusting relationship between the leader and the coach/spiritual director, which is most "corrective" when the working relationship is long-term and close.[231]

---

226. Ronningstam, "Narcissistic Personality Disorder," 765.

227. Ibid., 765.

228. Yalom, *Theory and Practice*, 399 (my emphasis).

229. Ibid., 398.

230. Benjamin, *Interpersonal Diagnosis*.

231. Ronningstam, "Narcissistic Personality Disorder," 764. This principle can be applied to treating any personality disorder.

They also need to internalize self-compassion, which will also make them more compassionate towards others.[232]

How do toxic Christian leaders experience their faith? The Swiss Christian psychiatrist Samuel Pfeifer sheds some light on this issue. He asserts that a person with narcissistic personality traits tends to have a more arrogant relationship with God characterized by being anxious about dependency and submission, and by rejecting God's correction.[233] The obsessive-compulsive person tends to have a rigid relationship with God characterized by being anxious about change and breaking rules potentially leading to legalism. He or she also tends to struggle with doubting God.[234] A highly differentiated Christian leader with a secure state of mind is emotionally and spiritually mature and has therefore a secure relationship with God (see chapter 4). He or she is spiritually mature as evidenced by having a pure heart and by practicing the presence of God through the means of grace. In addition, he or she also has responded to God's sanctifying grace and developed Christian affections, especially humility, gratitude, and compassion, which affects how the leader relates to others:

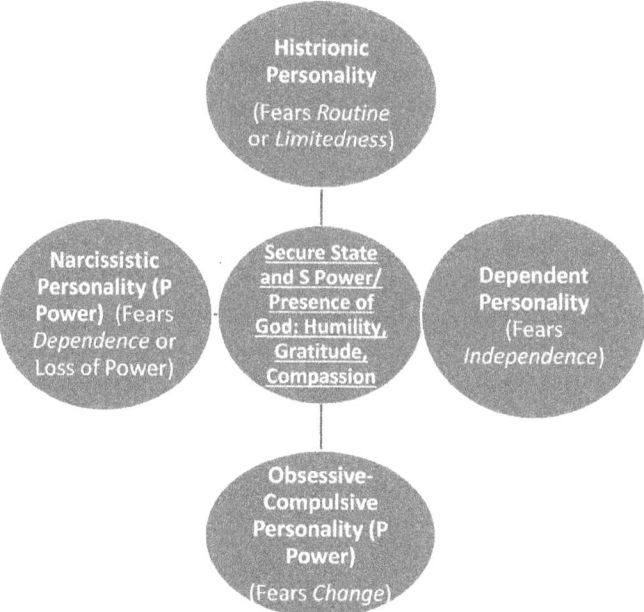

Figure 7: Personality Styles, Power Motives, and Christian Affections

232. Benjamin, *Interpersonal Diagnosis*, 257.
233. Pfeifer, *Sensitive Person*, 268.
234. Ibid.

Conclusion

In this chapter I discussed the ethical context for Wesleyan spirituality, which is derived from the Aristotlean and biblical ethical traditions. Both ethical traditions view virtues or habits of the heart as traits that one needs to develop, which requires a conscious decision. These virtues are both gifts from God and habits that need to be developed. This resembles Wesleyan spirituality in that God desires believers to cooperate with him in producing spiritual maturity. Wesley's spirituality borrowed much from Jonathan Edwards when it comes to the religious or Christian affections. I emphasized three Christian affections in this chapter, namely humility, gratitude, and compassion.

Humility provides the foundation for the other two affections and Wesley viewed humility as the most important affection that helps believers avoid inner deception. It is worth noting that I view Christian affections as both dispositions *and* emotions. This is based on Oord and Elliott who argue that compassion in particular and, it can be argued, gratitude should contain an emotive quality. This resembles Wesleyan Pentecostal affections that are focused on the kingdom of God.[235] It is imperative for narcissistic leaders to replace pride and shame with humility. Further, he or she could become more grateful, which would help him or her eliminate entitlement. Finally, the narcissistic leader could develop compassion to counteract envy and anger. The toxic leader with a perfectionistic personality style will especially benefit from developing Christ-centered emotions, since he or she tends to focus too much on rationality and reason. In addition, he or she could develop compassion for self and others to remove shame. Gratitude could help a perfectionistic leader reduce his or her unrealistic expectations of him- or herself or of others. Humility could help such a leader view him- or herself as "good enough," which would eliminate the perfectionistic strivings.

Furthermore, these three affections are helpful for correcting impure power and influence motives. Humility, gratitude, and compassion constitute essential ingredients for formational leadership. Humility prevents the abuse of power and gratitude fosters the intention to empower one's subordinates. Compassion includes care and concern for others, which means Christian leaders who practice formational leadership display authentic care and compassion for their employees similar to the concept of being godly "shepherds." According to large study, the majority of employees who participated preferred a caring leader and viewed this as being more important

---

235. Land, *Pentecostal Spirituality*, 174.

than making more money.[236] Compassion and caring are components of social intelligence, which is essential to formational leadership.

Regarding power and influence, the most important power sources are expert, "God-factor," and informational power in that they produce credibility in the leader. The most mature power motive is socialized (S) power which provides the formational leader with a willingness to share power, cooperate with others, and practice interdependence. Humility, gratitude, and compassion can assist in developing a socialized power orientation.

The means of grace provide ways for formational leaders to develop Christian affections. A peer-led support group, such as Wesley's select society group, can be a helpful tool for mutual accountability, which can be used for leadership development. The practice of the spiritual disciplines is another essential means for character formation in general and for developing Christian affections in particular. Works of mercy are also means of grace to enhance compassion primarily. In the following chapter we will answer the question on how relevant Wesley's emphasis on social ethics and social justice are for formational leadership.

Reflection Questions and Exercises

(Please pray for the leading of the Holy Spirit before you answer the reflection questions and complete the exercises)

1. What feelings and thoughts come to your mind about Bonhoeffer's statement that "complete truthfulness is really only another name for the totality of discipleship" and that we have nothing to hide from God.

2. Do you agree or disagree with the statement that Christian humility is the prerequisite for genuine fellowship and emotional intimacy. What are your God-given strengths and talents and what are your weaknesses?

3. Journal about things and people you are grateful for.

4. Write a letter from the perspective of someone who hurt you in the past in order to strengthen your empathy skills (also will help you with forgiving the person).

5. How has your tendency to be comfortable and complacent prevented you from displaying compassion towards others?

---

236. Goleman, *Social Intelligence*, 280.

6. Which of your traits and skills constitute your expert, informational, and "God" power?

7. Practice some of the following disciplines for 1–14 days: fasting, solitude, simplicity, service (food bank, etc.), "discipline of slowing" (Ortberg), and Christian meditation by focusing on a brief passage of Scripture.

8. Practice mutual accountability by joining a discipleship group, etc. and/or meet with a spiritual mentor/director for at least 6 months (once a month).

9. How do you delegate power and authority?

Chapter 6

Orthopraxis

Right and Just Leadership Practices

IN THIS FINAL CHAPTER I will discuss Wesley's social ethics and its implications for formational leadership. As I stated in chapter 1, *orthopraxis*, as the third component in the model, refers to "right" and just leadership behaviors informed by Wesley's social holiness and justice values. Toxic leaders affect their organizations in detrimental ways. For example, narcissistic leaders can be verbally abusive to followers when they feel ignored or disrespected. Obsessive-compulsive leaders tend to rigidly enforce rules and often struggle with delegating authority. They also tend to micromanage their followers, which is often experienced as being verbally abusive and/or shaming. These two toxic leader types may also fail to enforce justice in their organizations, which affects the organizational culture. In particular, narcissistic and perfectionistic organizational cultures may often exclude minorities and the poor for different reasons. Narcissistic organizational cultures may view the inclusion of minorities and concern for the poor as a distraction and waste of financial resources and time. Perfectionistic cultures may be reluctant to include different ethnicities because they are less willing to change their way of doing things. Therefore, the three key Christian affections (humility, gratitude, and compassion) discussed in chapter 5 need to serve as organizational core values that influence right leadership practices and behaviors.

This chapter will provide an overview of Wesleyan social ethics. In addition, Wesley's spirituality needs to engage with contemporary postmodern thought and culture that can provide important contributions and correctives. Wesley's works of mercy and his passion for social activism provide a foundation for organizational culture building, which is one of the more important leadership tasks and practices. First we will explore postmodern thought and its relevance for Wesley's spirituality and social ethics.

Wesleyan Spirituality and Postmodern Thought and Culture

Postmodernity is a more recent philosophical and cultural trend that is difficult to define and refers to a time that "is becoming fluid and flexible, pluriform, and contingent, fast and ephemeral."[1] Two (anti-) modern movements, romanticism and existentialism, "paved the way" for postmodernism.[2] Unlike its predecessor, modernism, it rejects moral absolutes, individualism, patriarchy, consumerism and nationalism and has been critical of materialism. There are different responses to postmodernism. Some welcome postmodernism as seen in an increased interest in spirituality, which is viewed as an essential part of personal and social identity. Postmodernism has "clear affinities with Hinduism and Buddhism" as well as New Age religions that emphasize that one is divine and god.[3] Others view postmodernism quite negatively for departing from foundationalism[4] and from departing from objective truth and special revelation as revealed in Scripture.[5] In addition, postmodernism embraces moral relativism, which many Christians criticize. This means postmodern truth and morals cease to be objective, but have become local and subjective. However, there are some evangelical theologians that view postmodernism more positively.[6]

Indeed, postmodernism has promising contributions for evangelical Christianity in general and for Wesleyan spirituality in particular. The late Stanley Grenz encouraged evangelicals to engage postmodernism by providing a "theology that is truly evangelical" that includes viewing the gospel "through the lens of convertive piety."[7] While Grenz was not a Wesleyan theologian, he alluded to the potential contributions Wesleyan theology could make to postmodernity. According to Knight, Wesley's theology is particularly helpful for engaging postmodern thought.[8] Wesley's

---

1. Schweitzer, *Postmodern Life*, 4.
2. Veith, *Postmodern Times*, 35.
3. Ibid., 199.
4. Geivett, "Is God," 50.
5. Smith, "Christian Postmodernism," 65.
6. Grenz, *Primer on Postmodernism*; Grenz, *Renewing the Center*; Franke, "Christian Faith."
7. Grenz, *Renewing the Center*, 191.
8. Knight, "Love and Freedom," 66.

focus on community is congruent with the postmodern emphasis on social context. In addition, Wesley's theology focuses on experience and authentic Christian living, which goes beyond foundationalism and is therefore in accord with postmodernity.[9] Furthermore, Wesley's spirituality in general and his social activism in particular are very relevant in our postmodern culture. Wesley's social ethics provides voices for the poor and oppressed (social holiness) that, if coupled with true character transformation through sanctification (personal holiness), conveys authenticity.

In particular, Grenz outlines how the gospel of Jesus Christ can be lived out in our postmodern culture: "The postmodern situation requires that we embody the gospel in a manner that is *post-individualistic, post-rationalistic, post-dualistic,* and *post-noeticentric.*"[10] The following few paragraphs will briefly discuss the meaning of each aspect as well as how each relates to Wesleyan spirituality.

The gospel message according to Wesley was post-individualistic and always included a social emphasis, as discussed in the previous section. The postmodern emphasis on connectedness and interdependence is consistent with a biblical anthropology.[11] John Wesley's biblical theology included social holiness, Christian community, and the means of grace, which emphasized mutual accountability. This means that Wesley's spirituality promotes biblical interdependence and de-emphasizes religious individualism. Grenz observes that "the postmodern world encourages us to recognize the importance of the community of faith," which means that Wesley can be said to have been ahead of his time in promoting a gospel that was biblical and postmodern.[12]

A post-rationalistic gospel refers to religious experiences that are "transformative."[13] Modernity overemphasized reason, which postmodernity has been correcting. The image of *"second naivete"* borrowed from the perspective of human development is helpful here since it connotes an "uncritical acceptance for the stories and symbols" similar to how young children perceive the world.[14] John Wesley's spirituality, along with Jonathan Edwards', emphasizes the role of religious experiences, especially the Christian affections (see chapter 5). Wesley's focus on experiential Christianity, along with contemporary Pentecostal and charismatic theologies, speaks to postmodernists and constitutes the means for transformation in believers.

---

9. Ibid., 66.
10. Grenz, *Primer on Postmodernism*, 167.
11. Schweitzer, *Postmodern Life*, 95.
12. Grenz, *Primer on Postmodernism*, 169.
13. Ibid., 170.
14. Schweitzer, *Postmodern Life*, 93.

A post-dualistic gospel embraces "biblical holism."[15] The Enlightenment split reality into "mind" and "matter," meaning it viewed humans as a "soul" ("thinking substance") and "body" ("physical substance").[16] Grenz argues for an anthropology that takes the Bible seriously: ". . . our identity includes being in relationship to nature, being in relationship with others, being in relationship with God, and, as a consequence, being in true relationship with ourselves."[17] A Wesleyan spirituality provides a truly biblical anthropology that emphasizes our interdependence with others and nature, our dependence on God, and the way we treat ourselves (see chapter 3). Wesley's emphasis on sanctification/perfection focuses on loving God, others, and self (see chapter 4). Furthermore, Runyon and Lodahl assert that Wesleyan theology addresses ecological ethics, since the political image mandates responsible stewardship of environmental resources, including the animal kingdom.[18] In particular, Lodahl refers to sanctification that needs to affect a responsible treatment of nature:

> Whatever Wesley may have meant when he wrote about being restored "into the whole image of God," it surely does include the human role of representing the Creator, in conscious and intentional ways, within creation. In other words, it includes what he meant by the political image. It falls to us human beings to exercise this sort of power—and to be increasingly conscious that we do so.[19]

Finally, a postmodern gospel needs to be post-noeticentric, meaning living as a Christian surpasses merely knowing about the faith, but embracing the fact that the "purpose of correct doctrine is to serve the attainment of *wisdom*."[20] In order for the gospel to be post-noeticentric it needs to integrate activism with quietism.[21] Grenz informs us that "we will be able to sustain right action only when it flows from the resources of the Holy Spirit."[22] Wesley's emphasis on social holiness along with personal holiness provides a balance for integrating personal piety ("works of piety") with

---

15. Grenz, *Primer on Postmodernism*, 171.
16. Ibid.
17. Ibid., 172.
18. Runyon, *New Creation*, 202; Lodahl, "Wesley and Nature," 26. The political image according to Lodahl "refers to the human as created and called" to govern the world (cf. Genesis 1:26, "have dominion") ("Wesley and Nature," 23).
19. Lodahl, "Wesley and Nature," 30.
20. Grenz, *Primer on Postmodernism*, 172.
21. Ibid., 173.
22. Ibid.

social responsibility ("works of mercy"), which produces wisdom and common sense. The goal is to achieve a godly character that resembles the image of Christ. Wesleyan spirituality is similar to liberation theologies below in an exploration of his social ethics.

Wesley's Social Ethics and Social Justice

"Learn to do right; *seek justice. Defend the oppressed.* Take up the cause of the fatherless; plead the case of the widow" (Isa 1:17, NIV, my emphasis).

Since the Civil War, American evangelicals have perceived social justice very negatively.[23] The evangelical social activist, Jim Wallis, and his seminary friends discovered a "Bible full of holes" while they were students at Trinity Evangelical Divinity School.[24] They cut out every biblical reference about the poor, injustice, and oppression, etc., from an old Bible. He and his friends further discovered that the second "most prominent theme in the Hebrew Scriptures" was about the poor and God's response to injustice (cf. prophets).[25] After Wallis and his friends cut out Bible verses about the poor and injustice they talked about the many holes they saw, meaning thousands of verses were cut out, and how they had never heard any sermon about the poor or social injustice in their evangelical home churches. This is a shocking oversight, which has contributed to a polarization of American Christianity with "liberal" Christianity on one hand and conservative "evangelical" Christianity on the other. Wallis, while not being a Wesleyan, has concluded that salvation is both personal and social, which means both aspects need to be integrated in order to practice what the Bible actually teaches.[26]

Wesleyan spirituality attends to both aspects as noted above in Wesley's sermons and secondary sources. The focus of this section is on social justice and how Christian organizations can be transformed to foster social justice. "Injustice is the social consequence of sin" according to Knight, and we cannot assume that an evangelical escapist theology can eradicate social injustice in organizations and society.[27] In addition, Wesley did not view Christianity as a means to escape from the problems of this world, but saw true Christianity as "participation in God's own redemptive enterprise," which entailed confronting injustices.[28] This means for us that holiness

23. Thompson, "Kingdom Come," 66.
24. Wallis, *God's Politics*, 212.
25. Ibid., 212.
26. Wallis, *(Un)common Good*, 29.
27. Knight, *Future for Truth*, 161.
28. Runyon, *New Creation*, 169.

needs to be personal *and* social. The example in Acts 6:1–7 illustrates the social concern the early church had for widows. The Hellenistic widows were overlooked regarding the daily food distribution, which was remedied by choosing seven deacons who were entrusted with this ministry. The sanctified believer must be bothered by social injustice and needs to pray for discernment about what steps to take to alleviate social injustices in his or her context. God desires that people are liberated from oppression so that societies become more compassionate and just.[29] It has been argued that John Wesley failed to address socio-economic and political structures in favor of the oppressed and that the Methodist movement slowly departed from the social concern of its founder.[30] While this is true, we also need to keep in mind that Wesley did not believe in democracy, since he was loyal to the King and was against the American Revolution.[31] Therefore, he did not intend to completely change the political and socio-economic structures. Wesley desired to preach and teach personal and social holiness *within* these structures, which can easily be perceived as enabling the oppressive system during his time. In addition, there is no perfection in this life when it comes to personal sin and there is no completely just society on earth.[32] This means for the Wesleyan believer and leader that there is an "already/not yet" tension when it comes to personal holiness and societal justice.[33] As I stated in the introduction to this section, narcissistic and perfectionistic organizational cultures often neglect the inclusion of diverse ethnic groups and people with lower Socioeconomic Status. Hence three social issues are chosen for discussion here. What follows will address Wesley's views on slavery (and racism), poverty, and the role of women in leadership, which correspond to frequent tensions between evangelical churches and groups that have been oppressed in our society, such as minorities and the poor.

Wesley was disgusted by slavery and described it as "execrable sum of all villainies."[34] He accused American colonists of hypocrisy saying that Americans "cry for liberty and at the same time espouse slavery."[35] Wesley was very active in his attempts to influence Great Britain and the American colonies to abolish slavery. He influenced the British politician Wilberforce

29. Knight, *Future for Truth*, 176.
30. Villa-Vicencio, "Towards a Liberating," 96; De Gruchy, "Beyond Intention," 84–85. However, Wesley was a man of his time and could not attend to every facet of life in church and society.
31. Runyon, *New Creation*, 170.
32. Knight, *Future for Truth*, 176.
33. Ibid.
34. Yrigoyen, *John Wesley*, 65.
35. Runyon, *New Creation*, 175.

(and others), who eventually achieved the abolition of slavery, which finally occurred in the entire empire in 1833.[36] It is refreshing to read how Wesley described Africans:

> [Africans] were industrious, quiet, orderly, civil, kind, religious, ready to help those in need, just, honest, and of good disposition. Unless, Wesley added scornfully, "white men have taught them to be otherwise."[37]

In addition, Wesley viewed Africans as superior to some Europeans.[38] This in contrast to how African Americans have been negatively perceived in the US today (inferior, loud, aggressive, lazy, dishonest and as "criminals," etc.), which is a reflection of contemporary prejudice. From the beginning of Wesley's ministry, when he was an Anglican pastor in Georgia in 1736, Wesley was against slavery and engaged in "mild protest against certain wretched conditions."[39] Wesley talked to individual slaves, taught them about the faith, and organized a preaching service for slaves.[40] In essence, Wesley did not differentiate between white and black and he allowed slaves to partake of the Lord's Supper and to be baptized. This was unusual during slavery, which included a strict segregation of whites and blacks. In Wesley's later ministry after 1770, he became more outspoken and, having been influenced by the Quakers, he published *Thoughts upon Slavery* in 1774.[41] This work was intended to correct the prevailing prejudice against Africans, especially the widely held notion that black Africans "were not authentic human beings."[42] Wesley appealed to three groups: the *captains* of slave ships, the *merchants* who sold slaves, and the *plantation owners*.[43] Wesley's main argument against the injustice of slavery was based on the Bible and on natural law that was the moral basis of the Enlightenment.[44] By 1780, Methodists and other denominations declared their opposition of slavery as "contrary to the laws of God, of man, and of nature, and injurious to society."[45]

---

36. Marquardt, *John Wesley's Social*, 68.
37. Yrigoyen, *John Wesley*, 65.
38. Ibid., 66.
39. Marquardt, *John Wesley's Social*, 71.
40. Ibid.
41. Ibid., 73.
42. Ibid.
43. Runyon, *New Creation*, 180.
44. Marquardt, *John Wesley's Social*, 74.
45. Ibid., 72.

How does Wesley's disdain for slavery and prejudice relate to contemporary Christianity and Christian leadership? Unfortunately, racial prejudice is still prevalent in the twenty-first century. Cleveland cites research that American churches are becoming increasingly homogenous regarding ethnicity and culture despite America's growing diversity.[46] The more recent shooting of nine African American congregants by a white male on June 17, 2015, along with the several shootings of black males by white police officers, are evidence for the current racial tension and injustice in the U.S. As a result of these shootings, the Black Lives Matter movement was launched, but white evangelicals are the only religious group that views this movement as unnecessary and "more than six in ten white evangelicals say that police officers treat blacks and whites equally."[47] This is due to ignorance and/or denial of the truth in evangelical churches. Wallis views racism as America's original sin:[48]

> Slavery and the subsequent discrimination against black people in America is of such a magnitude of injustice that one would think national repentance and reparations would be called for. But neither has ever come. Even "apologizing" for this great sin has proved to be quite controversial.[49]

According to this author, the effects of slavery and contemporary prejudice are still prevalent today and need to be addressed by Christian leaders. Martin Luther King Jr. stated that "[s]lavery in America was perpetuated not merely by human badness but also by human blindness," which refers to personal sin, but he also eloquently articulated the process of how racism became a social sin for subsequent generations (i.e., in the form of racial segregation, etc.):[50]

> So men conveniently twisted the insights of religion, science, and philosophy to give sanction to the doctrine of white supremacy. Soon this idea was imbedded in every textbook and

---

46. Cleveland, *Disunity in Christ*, 28.

47. Cleveland, "Black Church."

48. America is not morally worse than any other country. Germany's "original sin" had been the enduring antisemitism culminating in the Holocaust. Other countries also have had original sins, such as China's oppression of the Hmong people group, Czech Republic's disdain for Sinti and Roma, Russia's treatment of the Polish in the past, Iraq's treatment of the Kurds, etc. Discrimination and prejudice is rooted in personal *and* social sin, which need to be eradicated by the Holy Spirit during the process of sanctification.

49. Wallis, *God's Politics*, 308.

50. King, *Strength to Love*, 44.

preached in practically every pulpit. *It became a structured part of the culture.* And men then embraced this philosophy, not as the rationalization of a lie, *but as the expression of a final truth.* They sincerely came to believe that the Negro was inferior by nature and that slavery was ordained by God.[51]

This illustrates America's original sin, which is the perpetuation of overt and covert white supremacy. Overt forms of racism are rare, but covert forms of racism are still very common, which occur in the form of microaggressions[52] which affect all minorities.[53] Microaggressions refer to "modern racism" that has:

> (a) morphed into a highly disguised, invisible, and subtle form that lies outside the level of conscious awareness, (b) hides in the invisible assumptions and beliefs of individuals [i.e., white supremacy, etc.] and (c) is embedded in the policies and structures of our institutions.[54]

Moral leaders can produce just societies and organizations that ensure that these biases and prejudices are confronted and eliminated. Christian leaders need to be aware of them and are responsible for addressing these in their organizations.[55] We all tend to be ethnocentric, thinking that our own ethnicity and cultural heritage is superior to others, which also applies to ethnicities that are minorities. This, again, is a consequence of our sinful nature, which usually morphs into social sin. More specific action steps to reduce biases will be discussed in the section on leadership development. In the next section, we will explore Wesley's concern for the poor along with his economic views.

Biblical Christianity should be a great equalizer when it comes to socio-economic status. There should not be a difference between the poor and the middle class in the Body of Christ, which refers to prejudice and discrimination (cf. Col 3:11). The church should also provide practical help for the poor. The poor were John Wesley's favorite audience.[56] His emphasis on

---

51. Ibid., 45 (my emphasis).

52. Here are examples of microaggressions: http://sph.umn.edu/site/docs/hewg/microaggressions.pdf.

53. Sue, *Microaggressions in Everyday*, 146.

54. Ibid., 142.

55. The Apostle Peter's vision in Acts 10 helped Peter reduce his prejudice of the inclusion of Gentile believers (or, in Luke, "God worshippers"). It is an excellent example of the biblical mandate for cross-cultural unity. Peter concludes with the following: "I now realize how true it is that God does *not* show favoritism but accepts from *every nation* the one who fears him and does what is right" (Acts 10:34–35, NIV, my emphasis).

56. Jennings, *Good News*, 50.

social holiness compelled him to focus on practical help for the poor, which included providing essential needs. For example, Wesley urged Methodist societies to share belongings with the poor, which followed the account in Acts 4.[57] However, this proposal was not supported by Wesley's advisors. John Wesley's concern for the poor was clearly evident during his time at Oxford University when he organized the Holy Club that focused on meeting the needs of the poor.[58] The members of the Holy Club were encouraged to render both financial assistance for the poor and visiting the sick and people in prison. In 1740, Wesley and his followers began a systematic relief initiative for the poor.[59] Caring for the poor and sick also included taking care of their medical needs by dispensing herbal remedies, which contributed to some funds that enabled Wesley to publish *Primitive Physic*.[60] Wesley followed the Anglican clergy tradition and therefore viewed the practice of lay medicine as part of pastoral care.[61] In 1746, Wesley also provided systematic financial relief efforts for the poor when he created a loan fund for struggling Methodists.[62] Wesley's loan fund occurred 150 years before philanthropists created a similar system. In 1773, three years before Adam Smith published *The Wealth of Nations*, John Wesley had published a tract called *Thoughts on the Present Scarcity of Provisions*, which was a protest against the victimization of the poor during Britain's transition to an early industrial economy.[63] Wesley's zeal for the poor and oppressed along with the Methodists significantly influenced individuals and the political sphere of eighteenth-century Great Britain by effecting the modification of laws (e.g., the abolition of the death penalty for minor offenses, the abolition of child labor, and prison reform).[64]

As I mentioned in chapter 4, Oord, based on Wesley's sermon "On Zeal," observed that works of mercy included helping the poor as the third most important Christian activity (after loving God and the development of Christian affections) and ranked "alongside private and public prayer or the sacraments themselves."[65] In addition, John Wesley based his concern for the poor on Matthew 25, and perceived visiting the sick, poor and prison-

57. Runyon, *New Creation*, 185.
58. De Gruchy, "Beyond Intention," 77.
59. Ibid., 78.
60. Ibid.
61. Madden, "Medicine and Moral," 743.
62. De Gruchy, "Beyond Intention," 79.
63. Runyon, *New Creation*, 186.
64. De Gruchy, "Beyond Intention," 80.
65. Oord, "Love, Wesleyan Theology," 152; Jennings, *Good News*, 54.

ers as an important biblical mandate to be followed consistently by stating that one must do it if one believes in the Bible.[66] Hence, he emphasized the importance of the means of grace, which God uses to transform the individual believer. Regarding visiting and helping the poor, this work of mercy produces more than empathy and compassion for the poor. By having contact with the poor, false stereotypes and prejudices that many people held about the poor were dispelled.[67] For example, many thought that the poor were lazy, which provided a justification for the prevailing indifference during Wesley's time. However, Wesley provided rational "recognizable causes" of poverty (low minimum wage, unemployment, scarcity, high prices, monopolies, etc.).[68] By continued contact with and ministry to the poor, Christians learn about these rational and structural causes of poverty.

Another rational cause of poverty refers to the unjust distribution of wealth. The well-known saying about money Wesley uttered, "gain all you can; save all you can; give all you can," serves as a good organizing and balancing principle for a godly economy.[69] The last part ("give all you can") constitutes the mandate for people "whose income exceeded the necessities of life" to attend to the needs of the poor.[70] The essential idea that lies underneath this saying is that God owns it all and Christians are merely stewards. Stewardship for Wesley meant giving to the poor, which fostered solidarity with the poor.[71] Wesley strongly critiqued luxury during his time, since he viewed it as an important cause of poverty and "social discrimination" based on a large number of underpaid poor people employed by the rich that provided the means for the rich to sustain and even expand their luxurious lifestyle.[72] Similarly, in the twentieth century, Martin Luther King Jr., pretending to be the apostle Paul, drafted a letter to American Christians, which critiqued American capitalism without suggesting communism: "The misuse of capitalism may also lead to tragic exploitation. . . . I am told that one tenth of 1 percent of the population controls more than 40 percent of the wealth."[73] He urged American Christians to "use your powerful economic resources to eliminate poverty from the earth."[74] This observation

---

66. Jennings, *Good News*, 54.
67. Ibid., 55.
68. Marquardt, *John Wesley's Social*, 31, 44.
69. Ibid., 35.
70. Ibid., 36.
71. Jennings, *Good News*, 103.
72. Marquardt, *John Wesley's Social*, 45.
73. King, *Strength to Love*, 139.
74. Ibid., 139.

was made during the 1960s, but Jim Wallis states the latest statistics in the twenty-first century show that "the top 1 percent controls more wealth than the next 95 percent."[75] In addition, since 1979 the family income of the top 5 percent has increased by 72.7 percent, whereas "the real family income for the bottom 20 percent has dropped 7.4 percent."[76] The incidence of poverty in the U.S. is currently at the highest rate (15.1 percent) since 1993.[77] Sadly, women, children, and racial minority groups are over-represented among the poor. A forced governmental action is not desired, as is the case in socialism or communism, but government ought to promote "the common good" for its society.[78] In particular, government according the apostle Paul,[79] needs to "protect its people from the chaos of evil" and to promote the common good, which entails protecting the interest of the poor and contributing to their well-being.[80] This can be accomplished by just rules and regulations that "protect the people and the economy" in order to prevent financial meltdowns in the future, such as the one in 2008 that harmed millions of Americans and other people across the world.[81] In addition, the poor need to have a social safety net that ensures their basic needs for food and shelter, which should include health care. Just laws necessitate a bipartisan involvement and new partnerships between the "public sector, private sector, and nonprofit civil society (including faith communities)" in order to work together on creating a just society.[82]

When it comes to the private sector, the above statistics should motivate the top 5 percent and other affluent Americans to give more resources to the poor in the U.S. Christian leaders with narcissistic and perfectionistic personality traits may neglect these truths due to their limited capacity for empathy and compassion and emotional awareness. Unfortunately, just as it was during Wesley's time, there are negative stereotypes about the poor in the U.S. today that the poor are lazy, taking advantage of the system, etc., that justify the indifference and refusal to help them. Alternatively, people may defer to government to take care of the poor, which is insufficient. How can Christian organizations be transformed to cultures of social holiness and justice?

---

75. Wallis, *(Un)common Good*, 210.

76. Ibid., 210.

77. Newton, "Social Class," 169.

78. Wallis, *(Un)common Good*, 225.

79 Romans 13:4 (NIV, my emphasis): "For the one in authority is God's servant *for your good*. But if you do wrong, be afraid, for rulers do *not bear the sword* for no reason."

80. Ibid., 227, 228.

81. Ibid., 234.

82. Ibid., 236. The focus of this chapter is on what Christian organizations can do to promote the good for their employees and for the society.

Organizational Cultures Based on Social Holiness and Justice

As I stated above, in narcissistic organizational cultures Janis's groupthink tends to be more prevalent,[83] since followers of narcissistic leaders uncritically accept their decisions, and because leaders are "seen as infallible."[84] This also impacts the organization's willingness to be inclusive when it comes to ethnic, gender, or economic diversity. The perfectionistic organizational culture often monitors internal operations, dictates dress codes, and demands frequent staff meetings.[85] This can also restrict organizational diversity based on the rigid leadership approach of perfectionistic leaders. Christian organizational cultures that tend to be narcissistic or perfectionistic need to embrace Wesleyan values. What are the elements of organizational cultures and how can these be transformed?

Schein defines organizational culture as: "A pattern of shared basic assumptions that the [organization] group learned . . ."[86] It includes three levels: "basic underlying assumptions" (beliefs, perceptions, thoughts, feelings), "espoused values," and "artifacts" ("organizational structures and processes"), with assumptions being the deepest level.[87] Wesley's views regarding human nature, sin, and salvation were explored in chapter 3 and can be considered as basic assumptions. Organizational cultures are generated from the founder's assumptions and beliefs.[88] It is important to explore Wesley's specific underlying assumptions and values as they relate to the culture of the early Wesleyan movement.

Wesley's leadership approach and his values serve as a model for how Christian organizational cultures should function. Wesley valued diversity and "was always reaching out to those who were different."[89] Wesley's leadership incorporated diverse people from the community and "leaders were male and female, ordained and lay, of noble birth and modest origin, black and white."[90] Wesleyan and early Methodist leadership was characterized by pragmatism and by an "egalitarian spirit."[91] The Wesleyan movement

---

83. Janis, *Victims of Groupthink*.
84. Brown, "Narcissism, Identity," 254.
85. Kets de Vries, *Leadership Mystique*, 125.
86. Schein, *Organizational Culture*, 12.
87. Ibid., 17.
88. Ibid., 211.
89. Weems, *Leadership*, 96.
90. Ibid., 60.
91. Ibid., 62.

was based on an "inclusive theology" and was a "grassroots movement with concerns for the poor and marginalized of society."[92]

For example, Wesley encouraged female leadership. Based on observing his mother's dedication to the "work for God," Crawford asserts that he was in favor of female leadership.[93] Runyon and Crawford both assume that Wesley's acceptance of female leadership stemmed from watching his mother function as a lay spiritual leader.[94] During Wesley's early ministry in Georgia, he had appointed women as deacons.[95] In addition, women later served as leaders of classes and bands, initially for women only. But later, based on "unusual ability to provide spiritual guidance and nurture to men and women" that some female leaders displayed, female leadership gradually became accepted.[96] Even to the point that "women outnumbered men 47 to 19" in the Foundry Society. Wesley even authorized female class leaders to preach and acknowledged the call and the gifts female leaders evidenced, which eventually led him to conclude that "God had blessed the work of women leaders and their effectiveness could not be doubted."[97] As a result, many well-known female leaders came out of the Wesleyan movement and later Methodism, such as Mary Bosanquet, wife of Wesley's successor John Fletcher, Lady Huntington, Catherine Booth, and Phoebe Palmer to name a few.[98] Unfortunately, female leadership in the Methodist church declined after Wesley's death as men reasserted patriarchal control over women.[99]

Wesleyan leadership also included lay leaders from all classes and ethnicities.[100] African Americans were appointed as lay preachers who "contributed significantly to the Wesleyan movement."[101] Unfortunately, the early inclusion of the poor and minorities gradually ended because they were no longer welcomed. This led African American church leaders to establish their own churches, such as the African Methodist Episcopal Church, among others.[102] Thus, early Wesleyan leadership was characterized by equality and mutual influence among its members, which is one of the

---

92. Crawford, "Womanist Christology," 214.
93. Ibid., 218.
94. Runyon, *New Creation*, 195; Crawford, "Womanist Christology," 218.
95. Runyon, *New Creation*, 195.
96. Ibid.
97. Ibid., 197.
98. Ibid., 198, 200.
99. Ibid., 200.
100. Weems, *Leadership*, 63, 65.
101. Ibid., 65.
102. Ibid., 50.

indicators of leadership that includes social justice.[103] In addition, Wesley's leadership fostered unity among his members by integrating various "incompatible commitments," such as "personal holiness and social holiness, doctrinal responsibility and doctrinal freedom, law and gospel, worship and service, piety and action."[104] Significantly, Wesleyan leadership focuses on "unity in Christ" without sacrificing "distinctiveness and self-identity."[105] This emphasis reflects a high level of emotional maturity and differentiation in Wesley and his early leaders. Tragically, this focus on unity in diversity faded away after Wesley died.

Similar to Wesley's vision for the church, Martin Luther King, Jr., had a vision of the "beloved community" comprised of different ethnicities that emphasize love and justice.[106] There should not be any outsiders in the kingdom of God, since all people are created in God's image.[107] This vision also includes the poor, handicapped, the elderly, and other subgroups that are marginalized in today's U.S. society. However, the current reality of cultural idolatry prevents the successful inclusion of minority members in American evangelical churches.[108] It takes leadership to cast the vision of this beloved diverse church community.

Scazzero defines success for a church or any other Christian organization as "radically doing God's will," which includes the following: leaders being transformed "deep beneath the surface," "bridging racial, cultural, economic, and gender barriers," and "serving our community and the world," which includes helping the poor.[109] All three of these success criteria look very Wesleyan because of their resemblance with personal and social holiness. But how can an organizational culture based on social justice be developed? Before I will outline some action steps, I will first review three major leadership paradigms, primal leadership and socially intelligent leadership, Sashkin and Saskin's version of transformational leadership, and George's authentic leadership.[110]

Formational leadership, as an eclectic leadership development model, can incorporate concepts from transformational, authentic, and primal

103. Ibid., 68.
104. Ibid., 82.
105. Ibid., 101.
106. Wallis, *(Un)common Good*, 120, 121.
107. Ibid., 124.
108. Cleveland, *Disunity in Christ*, 147.
109. Scazzero, *Emotionally Healthy Leader*, 188, 191, 192, 193.
110. Goleman et al., *Primal Leadership*; Goleman, *Social Intelligence*; Goleman and Boyatzis, "Social Intelligence"; Sashkin and Saskin, *Leadership That Matters*; George, *Authentic Leadership*.

leadership theories (*orthopraxis*). Formational leadership presupposes that a spiritually and emotionally mature leader (*orthokardia*) develops Christian affections in cooperation with the Holy Spirit—especially humility, gratitude, and compassion—and operates from a socialized power orientation (*orthodynamis*). Thus, *orthokardia* and *orthodynamis* both enable the Christian leader to perform effective and empowering leadership behaviors that transformational, authentic, and primal leadership theories prescribe.

Goleman, Boyatzis, and McKee's primal leadership model includes the concepts of emotional and social intelligence and consists of two major competency domains: personal competence (equals emotional intelligence: self-awareness and self-management) and social competence (equals social intelligence: social awareness and relationship management, but without concern for others/compassion).[111] We can see the similarities of primal leadership with the concepts of differentiation/interdependence and secure attachment patterns, which resembles emotional maturity, as we saw earlier. Similarly, Goleman and Boyatzis's socially intelligent leadership model includes empathy and compassion/caring, which also points to emotional maturity and the Christian affection of compassion within the formational leader.[112] Socially intelligent leadership also includes effective stress management skills similar to the abilities of leaders who are highly differentiated and who operate from a secure state of mind regarding one's attachment style.

The four C's of transformational leadership behavior are the following: communication (effective communication with followers), credibility (being authentic and having integrity), caring (demonstrating concern and respect for followers), and creating empowerment opportunities (empowering and encouraging that fosters growth).[113] These transformational leadership behaviors are shared by many effective leaders and are not unique. As I stated above, formational leadership presupposes that a Christian leader develops spiritual and emotional maturity, which enables him or her to demonstrate the four Cs.

Authentic leadership includes five leadership characteristics or dimensions. The first one refers to understanding one's purpose and includes "understanding yourself, your passions, and your underlying motivations."[114] This dimension alludes to a socialized power orientation and Christian affections, such as humility, gratitude, and compassion that serve as motivations. "Practicing Solid Values" is the second characteristic and refers to being cred-

---

111. Goleman et al., *Primal Leadership*, 39.
112. Goleman and Boyatzis, "Social Intelligence."
113. Sashkin and Sashkin, *Leadership That Matters*, 43–48.
114. George, *Authentic Leadership*, 19.

ible by practicing the values the leader "preaches."[115] "Leading with Heart" is the third dimension which includes compassion for followers.[116] Compassion is being developed by getting to know those the leader works with and by understanding the backgrounds of people. This aspect is similar to the fourth dimension "Establishing Enduring Relationships" with followers, which is "at the heart of leadership."[117] This is accomplished by operating from a secure state of mind and by having achieved a higher level of differentiation. Finally, "Demonstrating Self-Discipline" is the fifth characteristic of George's authentic leadership approach.[118] George asserts that in order to be authentic, "leaders must behave with consistency and self-discipline, not letting stress get in the way of their judgment."[119] This last dimension alludes to credibility and emotional maturity that will inoculate the leader from overwhelming stress and anxiety. More recently, the authentic leadership model was further developed and it was discovered that three factors serve as prerequisites for authentic leadership, which are self-awareness, ethics, and self-regulation.[120] Self-awareness and self-regulation refer to emotional maturity whereas ethics points to moral motives and virtues and a socialized power orientation. These three aspects tend to be absent in toxic leaders.

Now let us return to transformational leadership in order to integrate formational leadership with the concept of organizational culture. One of the three characteristics of transformational leadership approach, principled leadership, is based on Schein's organizational culture concept. Principled leadership focuses on developing the organizational culture.[121] In particular, there are three ways a leader can develop an organizational culture; first, by defining "an explicit *organizational philosophy*" which includes "a clear, brief statement of values and beliefs"; second, by determining "*policies, develop[ing] programs* and institut[ing] *procedures* that put the philosophy into action"; and third, by leaders modeling values and beliefs.[122] The last one is most important because it facilitates the social learning process in followers. Schein calls modeling cultural values and beliefs a "primary embedding mechanism" and he includes six:

1. What leaders pay attention to, measure, and control on a regular basis.

115. Ibid., 20, 38.
116. Ibid., 22, 39.
117. Ibid., 23–24.
118. Ibid., 24.
119. Ibid., 41.
120. Beddoes-Jones and Swailes, "Authentic Leadership," 96.
121. Rosenbach and Sashkin, *Leadership Profile*, 9.
122. Sashkin and Sashkin, *Leadership That Matters*, 122.

2. How leaders react to critical incidents and organizational crises.
3. Observed criteria by which leaders allocate scarce resources.
4. Deliberate role modeling, teaching, and coaching.
5. Observed criteria by which leaders allocate rewards and status.
6. Observed criteria by which leaders recruit, select, promote, retire, and ex-communicate organizational members.[123]

Mechanisms 1, 4, 5, and 6 are especially relevant for Christian leadership. Number 1 is one of the most effective ways a leader can develop cultural values as long as it is done systematically and consistently.[124] A Christian leader who wants to instill the value of humility, gratitude, and compassion would want to point out behaviors in followers that demonstrate one or more of these affections. This also includes regular communication of the core values of the organization. Regarding item number 4 (teaching and coaching), a Christian leader could provide regular leadership development and could teach about the importance of personal holiness, emotional and spiritual maturity, diversity and how to reduce biases and prejudices. In addition, a Christian leader could convey information about the nature of love for God, others, and self, and about the three Christian affections. It also entails utilizing informational, expert, and "God factor" power to convey humility, gratitude, and compassion, which then can be more readily internalized by followers.

Item number 5 (allocate rewards and status) resembles transactional leadership, but can also be integrated with formational leadership. A formational leader can reward followers who embody values that are consistent with social justice (humility, compassion, love for diversity, etc.). This process constitutes the internalization of moral values, which is contrasted with narcissistic organizational cultures where followers "idolize" leaders and followers are rewarded for being loyal to leaders (cf. identification).[125] It can also be contrasted with obsessive-compulsive organizational cultures that are "rigid, inward-directed, and insular" and leaders who reward followers based on submission and their ability to closely follow rules.[126] In reference to item 6 (recruit, select, promote, retire, and excommunicate organizational members), formational leaders who want to develop a culture of diversity need to recruit and select a diverse leadership team. If the value of diversity is merely communicated, but no efforts are being made to recruit and select a diverse

---

123. Schein, *Organizational Culture*, 231.
124. Ibid., 231.
125. Kets de Vries, *Leadership Mystique*, 110.
126. Ibid., 112.

leadership, team followers will find the organizational culture contradictory and the leader will lose credibility. Cleveland suggests that, in addition to including a culturally diverse leadership team, Christian organizations need to foster a culture of equal status that includes an awareness of "privilege and power differentials."[127] This means the organizational culture that emphasizes humility and equality will help a diverse leadership team and diverse congregants to feel valued and accepted. Authentic leadership views the inclusion of diversity at the top as "critical to success."[128] In particular an effective leadership team includes not just diversity regarding race and gender, but also regarding background and experience.[129] George credited a diverse leadership team for Medtronic's success in becoming a "truly global organization."[130]

Specific leadership activities that foster unity include: "modifying the organizational purpose to include unity goals, teaching/preaching regularly on the topic of unity, allocating significant organizational resources toward the goal of unity . . ."[131] In general, regarding the inclusion of a diverse leadership team and/or diverse work force, organizations go through three stages: from being "parochial and monocultural" to "ethnocentric and nondiscriminatory" to "synergistic and multicultural."[132] The first stage is characterized by deliberately ignoring cultural diversity, whereas in stage 2, diversity is included and partly tolerated, but white male standards are still used to evaluate staff. Organizations in stage 3 "value diversity [and] view it as an asset rather than a problem."[133] A leader who wants to foster truly formational organizational culture will follow Wesleyan social justice values, which will move the organizational culture toward a stage 3 organization.

In summary, Wesleyan organizational cultures should reflect social holiness and justice. In particular, the three key Christian affections, among others, could serve as organizational values. For example, an organizational

---

127. Cleveland, *Disunity in Christ*, 166. Kretzschmar ("Cultural Pathways," 572) defines (national culture) "as an integral system which exemplifies the values, beliefs, customs and institutions of a particular community, or group of communities." She (ibid., 576) argues for flexibility, mutual respect and appropriate application. This fact necessitates diversity training for the majority (U.S.) culture *and* for minority cultures. See also the discussion on the cultural values model in Hofstede et al., *Cultures and Organizations*.

128. George, *Authentic Leadership*, 97.

129. Ibid., 97.

130. Ibid., 98. Medtronic is the world's leading medical technology company in St. Paul, Minnesota. Bill George who conducted research on authentic leadership was Medtronic's chief executive from 1991–2001 and chairman of the board from 1996 to 2002.

131. Cleveland, *Disunity in Christ*, 174.

132. Sue, *Multicultural Social* Work, 236.

133. Ibid., 236.

culture of pride and traditional white male superiority should be transformed to a culture of *humility* and equal status, a culture of entitlement and white privilege should be transformed to *gratitude* and inclusion, and a culture of abusive and rigid control should be transformed to *compassion* and servanthood. What are the implications of these insights for leadership development?

Implications for Leadership Development

As mentioned above, ethnocentrism is part of our sinful nature and refers to the belief that our culture and ethnicity is superior to others. Therefore, diversity training is essential for leading a diverse staff. Research indicates that "diversity initiatives" fail among "Christian groups that idolize their cultural identities."[134] This "cultural idolatry" poses a problem for developing cross-cultural relationships in the Body of Christ.[135] In addition, unbiblical American exceptionalism constitutes ethnocentric nationalism that affects how Americans relate to other nations and people from other countries.[136] Wallis states that the problem with American exceptionalism lies in its "low view of sin," meaning that people who espouse this ideology tend to excuse sinful behavior.[137] In contrast, Christianity should emphasize one's citizenship of heaven (Phil 3:20) and its focus on "a universal and international community centered in Jesus Christ, who breaks down the principal human barriers—race, class, and gender."[138] Therefore, the following action steps will enable Christian leaders to modify their attitudes and perceptions in order to promote inclusive organizational cultures.[139]

The Christian social psychologist Cleveland draws on Gordon Allport's *Contact Theory*, which consists of fostering meaningful cross-cultural contact between various ethnic groups.[140] The Acts of the Apostles (especially Acts 6:1–7; 10:1–48; and 15:1–29) and the book of Galatians, especially Galatians 3:28, provide the biblical rationale for meaningful cross-cultural contact in the Body of Christ: "There is neither *Jew nor Gentile, neither slave nor free, nor is there male and female,* for *you are all one* in Christ Jesus" (NIV, my emphasis). These cross-cultural contacts provide opportunities to reduce erroneous

---

134. Cleveland, *Disunity in Christ*, 147.

135. Ibid., 144–45.

136. Wallis, *(Un)common Good*, 114.

137. Ibid., 119.

138. Ibid., 114.

139. While these action steps are useful for several ethnicities regarding the development of multicultural competence, the focus of these action steps is on what members of the white majority culture can do.

140. Cleveland, *Disunity in Christ*, 153.

perceptions and prejudices in participants and help white Christians "treat culturally different Christians in a loving, inclusive and gracious way."[141] However, these contacts need to be well thought through and intentional in order to accomplish a reduction of negative biases.[142] Cross-cultural interactions need to include four elements: leadership (which was addressed above), working towards a superordinate goal, promoting equal status, and "engaging in personal interactions."[143] Superordinate goals, based on Sherif's Robbers Cave study, provide means to lay aside previously held biases and helps participants to "create a common ingroup identity."[144] The common "ingroup" identity should be based on belonging to the Body of Christ, as opposed to identities based on nationality, culture, ethnicity and race, etc.[145] Weems states that "diverse people of faith must hold something in common that is stronger than all their differences," which is our faith in Jesus Christ.[146]

Cooperation contributes to interdependence in the Body of Christ. Tasks that focus on superordinate goals include working together to help the poor in the community and creating committees in churches that are comprised of individuals with different ethnicities, etc. In order to foster a common group identity, cooperative projects need to be longer term to ensure lasting friendships are being developed and that "each group make unique and necessary contributions to the common goal."[147] This means minority members need to have equal input and take equal responsibility in accomplishing tasks needed for project completion.

Equal status is the third element needed for cross-cultural contact, which entails Caucasian Christians acknowledging the white privilege and power differential.[148] Equal status can be fostered when minority members no longer feel marginalized, which includes that members from the majority culture *identify* with minority members (cf. Rom 12:15: "rejoice with others who rejoice and mourn with others . . ."), pay *attention* to minority members (being sincerely interested in them), assign *importance* to them (truly caring about minority members), *appreciate* them (feeling valued by majority members), which results in minorities feeling integrated by perceiving that

---

141. Ibid., 154–55.
142. Ibid., 155.
143. Ibid., 158.
144. Ibid., 159.
145. Ibid., 178.
146. Weems, *Leadership*, 99.
147. Cleveland, *Disunity in Christ*, 163.
148. Ibid., 166.

majority members *depend* on them to achieve interdependence.[149] When one or more of these ingredients are missing minority members feel marginalized.

Finally, leaders from the majority culture should engage in personal interactions with minority members, which means fostering natural relationships in an "ongoing setting in which . . . friendships" can be developed.[150] These elements serves as action steps that can be applied toward promoting unity based on various variables of differences, such as culture, age, gender, income, etc.

More specific actions steps include reducing biases towards the poor which entails reflecting on one's own life story regarding class and Socio-economic Status (SES), volunteering at local organizations that work with the poor and lower SES individuals, attending workshops on social class issues, and completing a class privilege inventory[151], which helps Christian leaders become aware of invisible class privileges.[152] This awareness can aid Christian leaders in their development of empathy and gratitude.

In summary, this chapter emphasized individual and group action steps for Christian leaders to reduce negative stereotypes about different ethnicities and members of lower socioeconomic classes. These action steps can be well integrated with the three key Christian affections of humility (equal status), gratitude (viewing diversity as an asset), and compassion, which is based on acquired empathy toward people who are less privileged.

The question can be posed as to why Christian leaders should embrace diversity and recruit a diverse work force or pastor a diverse congregation. As I mentioned above, compassion increases when Christian leaders are inconvenienced or sacrifice their own needs. However, Christian leaders need to be make a conscious choice to grow in compassion and in the other two Christian affections and virtues, but it is also helpful to explore some biblical and scientific rationales. The parable of the Good Samaritan in Luke 10:25–37 provides a biblical mandate among other passages for helping and ministering to one's neighbor. The Samaritans were ethnically diverse and Jews were prejudiced against them based on their ethnicity and religious syncretism. Jesus emphasized that everyone, regardless of ethnicity, culture and economic status, is our neighbor and needs to be treated with compassion. The divine Trinity and Jesus's sacrificial death also provides another theological rationale for cross-cultural inclusion, "[to] partake in the sacrificial love of the Trinity is to participate in sacrificial love with all others

---

149. Ibid., 169.
150. Ibid., 172.
151. Class Acts, "Invisibily."
152. Newton, "Social Class," 177.

not just the ones who are part of [the Christian leader's] own homogenous Christian group."[153] Christ's sacrificial work eliminates the distinctions between different ethnic and economic groups.[154] Furthermore, Christian narcissistic and perfectionistic leaders could be persuaded with scientific research findings that diverse groups "are better groups" because they tend to be more creative and effective than non-diverse groups.[155] This is because these groups provide a variety of ideas, opinions, and resources.[156] This would also reduce the "groupthink" fallacy narcissistic organizations often experience. Groupthink prevents unity in the Body of Christ by focusing on minor doctrinal differences.[157] Christian narcissistic and perfectionistic leaders need to be led by the Holy Spirit, informed by Scripture, and convinced by science and experience to diversify their organizations.

Conclusion

In this final chapter I emphasized the congruence between Wesleyan spirituality and postmodernity; they have common foci on community, social justice, and authenticity. This chapter further included a discussion of Wesley's views regarding diversity, in particular his views on slavery, racial prejudice, poverty and female leadership. Wesley's spirituality thus includes an emphasis on social justice. This chapter also discussed how Christian organizational culture, and its leaders, should reflect Wesleyan assumptions and values; leadership practices need to be based on social holiness and justice.

This chapter ended by outlining some implications for leadership development that included action steps for individuals and groups to reduce negative biases about diversity and ways to establish healthy and authentic relationships with culturally and economically different individuals. As I discussed above, contemporary American evangelicals have struggled to embrace social justice since the Civil War. Wesley integrated personal and social holiness, but many denominations have focused on one or the other, and struggled to keep them in balance. Unfortunately, promoting harmony and unity among ethnically and economically diverse organizational members is an ambitious task. This requires that Christian leaders develop a willingness to be inconvenienced and a resolve to sacrifice so they can work on embracing diversity. Organizational values that reflect diversity along with

153. Cleveland, *Disunity in Christ*, 35.
154. Ibid., 36.
155. Ibid., 39.
156. Ibid.
157. Ibid., 41.

their components of humility (equal status), gratitude (valuing diversity), and compassion (focus on helping one another to succeed regardless of perceived differences) could be instilled in Christian leaders.

For example, unlike Wesley, later Methodist leaders failed to keep the focus on unity, which resulted in the establishment of African American churches such as the African Methodist Episcopal Church, and in the founding of the Church of the Nazarene, which focused on the needs of the poor.[158] Four years before Wesley's death in 1787, Wesley preached on God's vineyard in Isaiah 5:4,[159] in which Wesley criticized his own Methodist movement by pointing out that the wild grapes the movement displayed were "ingratitude, lack of discipline, self-advancement, and lack of attention to the poor"[160]:

> But, instead of this, it brought forth *wild grapes*,—fruit of a quite contrary nature. It brought forth error in ten thousand shapes, *turning many of the simple out of the way*. It brought forth enthusiasm, imaginary inspiration, ascribing to the all-wise God all the wild, absurd, self-inconsistent dreams of a heated imagination. It brought forth *pride*, robbing the Giver of every good gift of the honor due to his name. It brought forth *prejudice, evil surmising, censoriousness, judging and condemning one another;— all totally subversive of that brotherly love* which is the very badge of the Christian profession; without which whosoever liveth is counted dead before God. It brought forth *anger, hatred, malice, revenge, and every evil word and work*;—all direful fruits, not of the Holy Spirit, but of the bottomless pit! (Sermon 107)[161]

This blunt sermon excerpt serves to remind and admonish Christian leaders who want to follow Wesley's spirituality to focus on the essentials of Wesley's contribution to Western Christianity, namely a synthesis of personal and social holiness. Kretzschmar comments on how social action promotes Christian character:

> Spiritual formation thus gives depth of insight, character, and courage to those engaged in social action. This circular process of deepened vision and engagement with context redeems the leader's intellectual capacity, their attitudes, convictions, motivation, volition (will), affections, and actions.[162]

---

158. Weems, *Leadership*, 50–51.

159. "What more could have been done for my vineyard than I have done for it? When I looked for good grapes, why did it yield only bad?" (NIV).

160. Green and Willimon, *Wesley Study Bible*, 860.

161. Wesley, *Works*, 7:V/23 (my emphasis).

162. Kretzschmar, "Authentic Christian Leadership," 346.

Thus, based on above sections, the Christian leader increases his or her Christian affections in response to God's grace and intentional practice of practicing right leadership informed by social justice values, which results in a higher level of purity in the leader's heart as evidenced in increased love for God and others. This formational process is self-perpetuating:

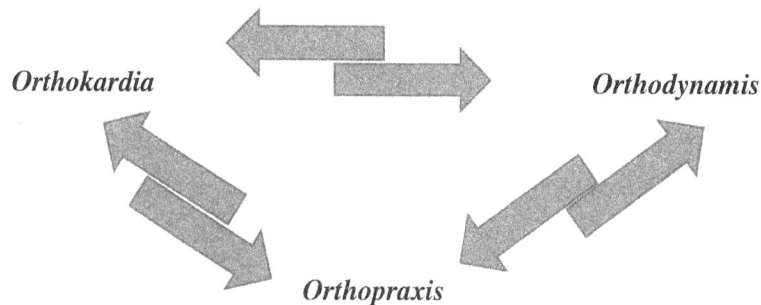

Figure 8: Relationships between Orthokardia, Orthodynamis, and Orthopraxis

By improving his or her virtuous character, the leader also becomes more spiritually mature. This needs to be associated with increased levels of emotional maturity achieved by the interpersonal and communal process of change, which will results in more effective leadership capabilities.

Reflection Questions and Exercises

(Please pray for the leading of the Holy Spirit before you answer the reflection questions and complete the exercises)

1. Draft your personal core values (e.g., integrity, respect, etc.), mission, and vision statement as a leader.

2. For at least one month, journal daily about empathy (compassion) for a people group you hold prejudices against.

3. How have you been aware of "modern racism" (*microaggressions*) in your faith community and/or organization you are a leader of, and in your local community?

4. Reflect on your views regarding female leaders who are called to serve as a Christian leader in churches and in other Christian organizations? Where do these views originate from?

5. Attend ethnic events that are different from your own ethnicity. Afterwards, get to know and talk to a member of the ethnic community (e.g., African, African American, Arab/Muslim, Native American, Hispanic American, etc.).

6. Serve the poor at food banks, etc. and be mindful of how this can positively affect your ability to be empathic and compassionate toward the poor.

7. Take and have your followers complete the Formational Organizational Culture Questionnaire (see appendix).

Chapter 7

Final Conclusion

IN THIS BOOK I have provided a prophetic vision of Christian leadership formation inspired by Wesleyan theology and spirituality. In chapter 1, I provided the background, rationale and aims of this study. Chapter 2 outlined the problem of toxic leadership, as found in both secular and Christian leadership. Narcissistic and perfectionistic leaders engage in sinful thought patterns and behavior, such as pride, vainglory, anger, and greed. Toxic leadership was defined as the abuse of leadership power that *directly* results in interpersonal emotional, physical, and sexual harm in followers. Toxic leaders frequently cause harm in followers by manipulation, verbally aggressive abuse, micromanagement, neglecting emotional needs, etc. I posed the question as to why Christian leaders fail to be aware of their toxic leadership behaviors. The discussion on the development personality disorders provided some answers to this question, namely that the toxic leader's defenses block awareness and prevent ethical leadership behaviors. The narcissistic leader struggles with empathy, denies, rationalizes, and compartmentalizes, whereas the perfectionistic leader is less aware of feelings and has limited compassion for self and others. In chapter 3, I provided the theological framework of this study by exploring Wesley's views on anthropology, hamartiology, and soteriology. These three theological concepts are relevant for ethical Christian leadership. Anthropology establishes a biblical view of human nature. Wesley viewed humans as being created in the image of God consisting of the natural, political, and moral image. All three need to be transformed in order for ethical leadership to occur. Hamartiology describes the spiritual reason for toxic leadership (original and personal sin) and soteriology outlines the spiritual solution, namely God's justification and sanctification. These three theological concepts correspond to developmental and personality psychology (anthropology), psychopathology (hamartiology), and the therapeutic foci and interventions that this book includes (soteriology). Hence, these three theological concepts were integrated with developmental and personality psychology, psychopathology, and therapeutic psychology (counseling, etc.). In chapter 4, I discussed *orthokardia*, which includes the concepts of spiritual maturity and emotional maturity. Spiritual maturity essentially resembles Wesley's views on sanctification, which he defined as loving God with all one's mind and soul, etc. and loving others as one loves one's self. This chapter also emphasized the cooperative nature of grace and in particular that of sanctifying grace. The second component of *orthokardia* also includes emotional maturity, which was defined as interdependence through the process of differentiation. For this purpose, this fourth chapter discussed two psychological theories that emphasize healthy emotional development. Attachment theory emphasized secure attachment, which can occur during childhood or later in life (earned attachment). Bowen's theory emphasized emotional maturity, which is defined as differentiation. Differentiation means the leader is a separate self and interdependent from others. In addition, it means that the leader can take responsibility for him- or herself and is capable of remaining neutral when others act irresponsibly. This includes that he or she is able to remain calm when being in the presence of colleagues and followers who display anxiety and other negative emotions. I also outlined how Christian leaders can work on developing spiritual and emotional maturity, which is achieved by means of practicing the spiritual disciplines in the context of a Christian community. In chapter 5, I discussed *orthodynamis*, which includes right power and influence motives that should inform formational leadership. These power motives are based on three key Christian affections (humility, gratitude, and compassion). Aristotle's and biblical virtue ethics were explored and its similarities with Wesleyan ethics outlined. The concept of religious or Christian affections was discussed and I compared Jonathan Edwards's views on religious affections with the views Wesley held. I stressed three key Christian affections in this chapter: humility, gratitude, and compassion, which are character traits toxic leaders usually lack. This chapter then focused on Wesley's means of grace to help the Christian leader develop and nurture Christian affections. I also explained the importance of Christian community as a context for the means of grace to take place. Finally, I outlined the implications for leadership development in the context of accountability relationships within a Christian community. In particular, toxic leaders could be included in small groups comprised of Christian leaders modeled after Wesley select society. These group could be led by trained coaches, spiritual directors, or Christian mental health professionals who can provide guidance and direction, which can further enforce accountability. In chapter 6, I emphasized *orthopraxis*, which refers to right and just leadership behaviors informed by Wesley's social holiness and justice values. Social holiness and justice was applied to Wesley's views on slavery and racism, his views on the poor and poverty, and his views on female leadership. Wesley viewed slavery and racism as wicked and evil, which was an uncommon view during his time. He also provided practical help for the poor and noted systemic reasons for poverty that reduced the prevalent prejudice toward the poor during the eighteenth century. Furthermore, Wesley did not differentiate between male and female leaders and viewed female leaders as equal. Overall, Wesley emphasized the inclusion of diverse ethnicities, people from a lower socio-economic status, and both genders and thereby promoted unity in diversity. This chapter also stressed leadership behaviors that promote the formation of organizational cultures that focus on social holiness and justice. In particular, primal leadership, transformational leadership, and authentic leadership approaches were discussed and integrated with formational leadership. Organizational cultures that focus on social justice value diversity, humility (valuing equality), gratitude (valuing inclusion) and compassion (valuing the less privileged).

In this study I have successfully argued that spiritual and emotional maturity in leaders, which I called formational leadership, will counteract toxic leadership. Formational leadership is a leadership development model that includes aspects of mostly transformational, authentic, and primal leadership. The formational process in the Christian leader is accomplished by developing spiritual maturity through God's sanctifying grace in cooperation with the leader. In addition, the leader becomes emotionally mature by acquiring interdependence through the process of differentiation. Furthermore, Christian leaders who are spiritually and emotionally mature (*orthokardia*) are open to developing three key Christian affections (humility, gratitude, and compassion) that produce pure power motives (*orthodynamis*). These three affections will produce just leadership behaviors that foster social holiness and justice in Christian organizations (*orthopraxis*). Professional coaches, spiritual directors, and Christian mental health professionals can help Christian leaders in this formational change process. The major change agent is the Holy Spirit, to whom the Christian leader needs to respond throughout the process of change (sanctification). Preferably, this formational leadership process should occur within a Christian community that is supportive and yet can hold the Christian leader accountable.

Since narcissistic and perfectionistic individuals tend to seek positions of power, they often occupy leadership positions in Christian organizations including churches. They frequently manipulate their followers to overemphasize ministry thereby causing a work-life imbalance, often tend to be verbally abusive, often tend to micromanage followers, and frequently impose or reinforce legalistic theologies that can cause spiritual abuse. These toxic leaders need to be transformed by the Holy Spirit so that Christian leaders and organizations can be "Salt and Light" in secular societies. This will enable Christian organizations to fulfill Jesus's mandate to love God, self, others, and creation and to make disciples of all nations. Future research could empirically test this leadership model by operationalizing the three leadership components and by developing an instrument to test its validity.

Leader Personality Style Questionnaire
(Adapted from DSM-5)

Leader Personality Style Gamma

1. In my leadership I tend to be very outgoing.
2. During team meetings I am often the center of attention.
3. I often find myself talking with members of the opposite gender.
4. Leading others includes showing my feelings.
5. My appearance is very important.
6. Work task and team meetings often can get very boring and I am often looking for projects that are more exciting.
7. I enjoy the fact that due to my leadership role I often meet new people.
8. It is very easy for me to connect to colleagues, followers, and people on my team.

Leader Personality Style Beta

1. I tend to be a more passive and laid back leader.
2. Colleagues and followers can easily influence me to change my mind.
3. I prefer to make important leadership decisions together with others.
4. I tend to avoid conflicts and disagreements because I fear rejection or anger.
5. When I feel I won't do projects well I tend to delegate them to others.
6. I try hard to please my followers and superiors.

7. The worst thing in having a leadership position is being alone and needing to be independent.
8. I find it hard to say no to followers and colleagues, even when saying yes harms me.

Leader Personality Style Delta

1. My followers and colleagues think of me as a reserved and serious person.
2. In my work it is very important that I plan and organize everything.
3. Good leadership involves avoiding mistakes and having a routine.
4. When I am at work I always see to it that my work is finished—there is no play and fun at work.
5. My followers and colleagues tell me that I tend to be very inflexible and rigid.
6. In my leadership I struggle with delegating tasks and responsibility to others.
7. I tend to keep a close eye on my budget so my department/ organization is prepared if a financial need comes up.
8. Organizational rules are absolutely necessary because they are a good guide to follow.

Leader Personality Style Alpha

1. My success or failure as a leader has a direct bearing on my self-image and sense of personal worth.
2. I often like to be recognized as a good leader.
3. Exceptional leaders understand my leadership the best.
4. I often find myself encouraging my followers to appreciate the things I do.
5. I often think that I deserve special attention from my superiors.
6. I tend to focus too much on my own needs according to my superiors and followers.

7. I often struggle with envying other leaders or people who are more successful than me.
8. My followers tend to perceive me as very confident.

Scoring

Gamma=Histrionic
Beta=Dependent
Delta=Obsessive-Compulsive
Alpha=Narcissistic
2-3 Mild Traits
4+ Pronounced Traits

Formational Organizational Culture Questionnaire

1. I feel appreciated for my gifts, talents, and job performance.
2. People in my organization appear to be grateful.
3. The leadership conveys to followers that they appreciate them and that they are seen as assets.
4. People are supportive and empathic in my organization.
5. I feel heard and understood by my supervisor.
6. My colleagues told me that they feel appreciated by their leadership.
7. My supervisor is a warm and compassionate person.
8. My supervisor does not convey to my colleagues that he/she is better than us.
9. My colleagues and I feel that we are equal.
10. I feel a spirit of collaboration in my team as opposed to competition.
11. My supervisor emphasizes collaboration not competition.
12. My colleagues are warm and compassionate to me.
13. The organizational core values emphasize collaboration and team work.
14. We help one another in my organization in times of stress.
15. I trust my supervisor.
16. I trust my colleagues.
17. I feel ignored by supervisor (reverse).
18. My colleagues do not appreciate me (reverse).
19. My supervisor expresses his or her appreciation.
20. My colleagues act superior to me (reverse).

21. I am motivated by my supervisor to become more grateful.
22. My colleagues tend to be humble.
23. Some of my colleagues model gratitude well.
24. Humility is an important value in my organization.

Scoring

Endorsed items (deduct reverse items):

1, 2, 3, 6, 18 (reverse), 19, 21, 23 =   Gratitude   (#) =

4, 5, 7, 12, 14, 15, 16, 17 (reverse) =   Compassion   (#) =

8, 9, 10, 11, 13, 20 (reverse), 22, 24 =   Humility   (#) =

Bibliography

Ainsworth, Mary D., Mary C. Blehar, Everett Waters, and Sally Wall. *Patterns of Attachment: Psychological Study of the Strange Situation.* Hillsdale, NJ: Erlbaum, 1978.
American Psychiatric Association (APA). *Diagnostic and Statistical Manual of Mental Disorders: DSM-IIIR.* 3rd ed. rev. Washington, DC: APA, 1987.
———. *Diagnostic and Statistical Manual of Mental Disorders: DSM-5.* 5th ed. Washington, DC: APA, 2013.
Armistead, M. Kathryn. "Empathy: A Bridge between Wesleyan Theology and Self-Psychology." In *Wesleyan Theology and Social Sciences: The Dance of Practical Divinity and Discovery*, edited by M. Kathryn Armistad et al., 53–67. Newcastle upon Tyne: Cambridge Scholars, 2010.
Barna, George. "Nothing Is More Important than Leadership." In *Leaders on Leadership: Wisdom, Advice and Encouragement on the Art of Leading God's People*, edited by George Barna, 17–30. Ventura, CA: Regal, 1997.
———. *The Second Coming of the Church.* Nashville: Word, 1998.
Bartholomew, Kim, Marylin J. Kwong, and Stephen D. Hart. "Attachment." In *Handbook of Personality Disorders*, edited by W. John Livesley, 196–230. New York: Guilford, 2001.
Bass, Bernard M. *Leadership and Performance beyond Expectations.* New York: Free Press, 1985.
———. *Transformational Leadership: Industry, Military, and Educational Impact.* Mahwah, NJ: Erlbaum, 1998.
Bass, Bernard M., and Bruce J. Avolio. *Improving Organizational Effectiveness through Transformational Leadership.* Thousand Oakes, CA: Sage, 1994.
———. "Transformational Leadership: A Response to Critiques." In *Leadership Theory and Research: Perspectives and Directives*, edited by Martin M. Chemers and Roya Ayman, 49–80. San Diego: Academic, 1993.
Bass, Bernard M., and Paul Steidlmeier. "Ethics, Character, and Authentic Transformational Leadership Behavior." *Leadership Quarterly* 10/2 (1999) 181–217.
Bauerlein, Valerie, and Dawn Chase. "Jury Finds McDonnell Guilty of Corruption." *Wall Street Journal*, Septempber 4, 2014.
Beck, Richard. "Love in the Laboratory: Moving from Theology to Research." *Journal of Psychology and Christianity* 31/2 (2012) 167–74.
Beddoes-Jones, Fiona, and Stephen Swailes. "Authentic Leadership: Development of a Three-Pillar Model." *Strategic HR Review* 14/3 (2015) 94–99.

Benjamin, Lorna. S. *Interpersonal Diagnosis and Treatment of Personality Disorders*. 2nd ed. New York: Guilford, 1996.

———. "An Interpersonal Theory of Personality Disorders." In *Major Theories of Personality Disorders*, edited by John F. Clarkin and Mark F. Lenzenweger, 141–220. New York: Guilford, 1996.

———. "Structural Analysis of Social Behavior." *Psychological Review* 81 (1974) 392–425.

Bennis, Warren G., and Burt Nanus. *Leaders: The Strategies for Taking Charge*. New York: Harper and Row, 1985.

Bentley, Wessel. "The Formation of Christian Leaders: a Wesleyan Approach." *Koers* 75/3 (2010) 551–65.

Berry, B.O. 2010. "Spiritual Abuse in the Christian Community." DMin diss., Asbury Theological Seminary, 2010.

Bonhoeffer, Dietrich. *The Cost of Discipleship*. New York: Simon and Schuster, 1959.

———. *Life Together: The Classic Exploration of Faith in Community*. San Francisco: Harper, 1954.

Bowlby, John. *Attachment and Loss*. Vol. 1: *Attachment*. New York: Basic Books, 1969.

———. "Attachment and Loss: Retrospect and Prospect." *American Journal of Orthopsychiatry* 52/4 (1982) 664–78.

Blanchard, Ken, and Phil Hodges. *The Servant Leader: Transforming your Heart, Head, Hands & Habits*. Nashville: Countryman, 2003.

Brown, Andrew D. "Narcissism, Identity, and Legitimacy." *Academy of Management Review* 22/3 (1997) 643–86.

Brown, Daniel P., and David S. Elliott. *Attachment Disturbances in Adults: Treatment for Comprehensive Repair*. New York: Norton, 2016.

Burns, James M. *Leadership*. New York: Harper and Row, 1978.

———. *Transforming Leadership: A New Pursuit of Happiness*. New York: Grove, 2003.

Burns, Bob, Tabita D. Chapman, and Donald C. Guthrie. *Resilient Ministry: What Pastors Told Us about Surviving and Thriving*. Downers Grove, IL: InterVarsity, 2013.

Carter, Charles W. "Hamartiology: Evil, the Marrer of God's Creative Purpose and Work." In *A Contemporary Wesleyan Theology: Biblical, Systematic, and Practical*, edited by Charles W. Carter, 2:233–82. Salem: Schmul, 1992.

Carter, John D., and Bruce Narramore. *The Integration of Psychology and Theology*. Grand Rapids: Baker, 1979.

Chittister, Joan. *The Rule of Benedict: A Spirituality for the 21st Century*. New York: Crossroad, 2010.

Clapper, Gregory S. *As If the Heart Mattered: A Wesleyan Spirituality*. Nashville: Upper Room, 1997.

———. "John Wesley on Religious Affections: His Views on Experience and Emotion and Their Role in the Christian Life and Theology." PhD diss., Emory University, 1985.

———. "Orthokardia: The Practical Theology of John Wesley's Heart Religion." *Quarterly Review* 10/1 (1990) 49–66.

———. *The Renewal of the Heart Is the Mission of the Church: Wesley's Heart Religion in the Twenty-First Century*. Eugene, OR: Cascade, 2010.

Class Acts. "The Invisibily of Upper Class Privilege." Boston: Women's Theological Center, 1997. http://www.thewtc.org/invisibility_of_Class_Privilege.pdf.

Cleveland, Christina. *Disunity in Christ: Uncovering the Hidden Forces that Keep Us Apart*. Downers Grove, IL: InterVarsity, 2013.

———. "The Black Church: A Necessary Refuge." *Christianity Today*, September 2015, 27.

Clinton, J. Robert, and Richard W. Clinton. "The Life Cycle of a Leader." In *Leaders on Leadership: Wisdom, Advice and Encouragement on the Art of Leading God's People*, edited by George Barna, 149–82. Ventura, CA: Regal, 1997.

Coe, John H., and Todd W. Hall. *Psychology in the Spirit: Contours of a Transformational Psychology*. Downer Grove, IL: InterVarsity, 2010.

Collins, Francis S. *The Language of God: A Scientist Presents Evidence for Belief*. New York: Free Press, 2006.

Collins, Jim. *Good to Great: Why Some Companies Make the Leap . . . and Others Don't*. New York: HarperBusiness, 2001.

Collins, Kenneth J. "John Wesley's Topography of the Heart: Dispositions, Tempers, and Affections." *Methodist History* 36/3 (1998) 162–75.

———. *The Theology of John Wesley: Holy Love and the Shape of Grace*. Nashville: Abingdon, 2007.

———. "Wesley's Life and Ministry." In *The Cambridge Companion of John Wesley*, edited by Randy L. Maddox and Jason E. Vickers, 43–59. Cambridge: Cambridge University Press, 2010.

Conger, Jay A. "Charismatic and Transformational Leadership in Organizations: An Insider's Perspective on These Developing Streams of Research." *Leadership Quarterly* 10/2 (1999) 145–79. "

———. "The Dark Side of Leadership." In *Leading Organizations: Perspectives for a New Era*, edited by Gill Robinson Hickman, 250–60. Thousand Oakes, CA: Sage, 1998.

Conger, Jay A., and Rabindra N. Kanungo. *Charismatic Leadership in Organizations*. Thousand Oakes: Sage, 1998.

———. "Toward a Behavioral Theory of Charismatic Leadership in Organizational Settings." *Academy of Management Review* 12 (1987) 637–47.

Costa, Paul, Jr., and Robert R. McCrae. *Revised NEO Personality Inventory Manual*. Odessa, FL: Psychological Assessment Resources, 1992.

Crawford, Elaine A. "A Womanist Christology and the Wesleyan Tradition." *Black Theology: An International Journal* 2/2 (2006) 213–20.

De Gruchy, Aubin. "Beyond Intention – John Wesley's Intentional and Unintentional Socio-Economic Influences on 18th Century England." *Journal of Theology for Southern Africa* 68 (1989) 75–85.

De Waal, Esther. *Seeking God: The Way of Benedict*. Collegeville, MN: Liturgical, 2001.

Downs, Alan. *Beyond the Looking Glass: Overcoming the Seductive Culture of Corporate Narcissism*. New York: Amacom, 1997.

Elliott, Matthew. "The Emotional Core of Love: The Centrality of Emotion in Christian Psychology and Ethics." *Journal of Psychology and Christianity* 31/2 (2012) 105–17.

Emmons, Robert. A. "Personality and Forgiveness." In *Forgiveness: Theory, Research, and Practice*, edited by Michael E. McCullough et al., 156–75. New York: Guilford, 2000.

Emmons, Robert. A., and Cheryl A. Crumpler. "Gratitude as a Human Strength: Appraising the Evidence." *Journal of Social and Clinical Psychology* 19/1 (2000) 56–69.

Erickson, Millard J. *Christian Theology*. Grand Rapids: Baker, 1985.

Fairbairn, William R. *An Object Relations Theory of the Personality.* New York: Basic Books, 1954.
Ford, Leighton. "Helping Leaders Grow." In *Leaders on Leadership: Wisdom, Advice and Encouragement on the Art of Leading God's People*, edited by George Barna, 123–48. Ventura, CA: Regal, 1997.
Foster, Richard J. *Celebration of Discipline: The Path to Spiritual Growth.* Rev. ed. San Francisco: Harper, 1988.
———. *Streams of Living Water: Celebrating the Great Traditions of the Christian Faith.* San Francisco: Harper, 1998.
Franke, John R. "Christian Faith and Postmodern Theory: Theology and the Nonfoundationalist Turn." In *Christianity and the Postmodern Turn: Six Views*, edited by Myron B. Penner, 105–21. Grand Rapids: Brazos, 2005.
French, John R. P., and Bertram H. Raven. "The Bases of Social Power." In *Studies in Social Power*, edited by Dorwin Cartwright, 150–67. Ann Harbor: University of Michigan, 1959.
Friedman, Edwin H. *A Failure of Nerve: Leadership in the Age of the Quick Fix.* Rev. ed. New York: Church, 2017.
———. *Generation to Generation: Family Process in Church and Synagogue.* New York: Guilford, 1985.
Froh, Jeffrey, et al. "Being Grateful is Beyond Good Manners: Gratitude and Motivation to Contribute to Society among Early Adolescents." *Motivation and Emotion* 34 (2010) 144–57.
Furnham, Adrian. *The Elephant in the Boardroom: The Causes of Leadership Derailment.* New York: Palgrave Macmillan, 2010.
Geivett, R. Douglas. "Is God a Story? Postmodernity and the Task of Theology." In *Christianity and the Postmodern Turn: Six Views*, edited by Myron B. Penner, 37–52. Grand Rapids: Brazos, 2005.
George, Bill. *Authentic Leadership: Rediscovering the Secrets to Creating Lasting Value.* San Francisco: Jossey-Bass, 2003.
George, Bill, and Peter Sims. *True North: Discover your Authentic Leadership.* San Francisco, CA: Jossey-Bass, 2007.
Glad, Betty. "Why Tyrants go Too Far: Malignant Narcissism and Absolute Power." *Political Psychology* 23/1 (2002) 1–37.
Godwin, Alan. *How to Solve your People Problems: Dealing with Your Difficult Relationships.* Eugene, OR: Harvest House, 2008.
Goldman, Alan. "High Toxicity Leadership: Borderline Personality Disorder and the Dysfunctional Organization." *Journal of Managerial Psychology* 21/8 (2008) 733–46.
Goleman, Daniel. *Emotional Intelligence: Why It Can Matter More than IQ.* New York: Bantam, 1994.
———. *Social Intelligence: The New Science of Human Relationships.* New York: Bantam, 2006.
Goleman, Daniel, and Richard Boyatzis. "Social Intelligence and the Biology of Leadership." *Harvard Business Review* (2008) 74–81.
Goleman, Daniel, Richard Boyatzis, and Annie McKee. *Primal Leadership: Realizing the Power of Emotional Intelligence.* Boston, MA: Harvard Business, 2002.
Gonzalez, Justo L. *A History of Christian Thought.* Vol. 2. Nashville: Abingdon, 1971.

Green, Joel B., and William B. Willimon, general editors. *The Wesley Study Bible: Common English Bible*. Nashville: Common English Bible, 2012.
Greenberg, Jay, and Stephen A. Mitchell. *Object Relations in Psychoanalytic Theory*. Cambridge, MA: Harvard University Press, 1983.
Gregory, Jeremy. "The Long Eighteenth Century." In *The Cambridge Companion of John Wesley*, edited by Randy L. Maddox and Jason E. Vickers, 13–39. Cambridge: Cambridge University Press, 2010.
Grenz, Stanley J. *The Moral Quest: Foundations of Christian Ethics*. Downers Grove, IL: InterVarsity, 1997.
———. *A Primer on Postmodernism*. Grand Rapids: Eerdmans, 1996.
———. *Renewing the Center: Evangelical Theology in a Post-Theological Era*. 2nd ed. Grand Rapids: Baker, 2006.
———. *The Social God and the Relational Self: A Trinitarian Theology of the Imago Dei*. Louisville: Westminster, 2001.
Gunter, W. Stephen, at al. *Wesley and the Quadrilateral: Renewing the Conversation*. Nashville, TN: Abingdon, 1997.
Hagberg, Janet O., and Robert A. Guelich. *The Critical Journey: Stages in the Life of Faith*. 2nd ed. Salem, WI: Sheffield, 2005.
Hayford, Jack W.. "The Character of a Leader." In *Leaders on Leadership: Wisdom, Advice and Encouragement on the Art of Leading God's People*, edited by George Barna, 61–79. Ventura, CA: Regal, 1998.
———, general editor. *Spirit Filled Life Bible: A Personal Study Bible Unveiling All God's Fullness in All God's Word*. Nashville: Thomas Nelson, 1991.
Heggen, Carolyn H. *Sexual Abuse in Christian Homes and Churches*. Scottsdale, AZ: Herald, 1991.
Hempton, David N. "Wesley in Context." In *The Cambridge Companion of John Wesley*, edited by Randy L. Maddox and Jason E. Vickers, 60–77. Cambridge: Cambridge University Press, 2010.
Hofstede, Geert, Gert Jan Hofstede, and Michael Minkov. *Cultures and Organizations: Software of the Mind: Intercultural Cooperation and Its Importance for Survival*. 3rd ed. New York: McGraw-Hill, 2010.
Hogan, Robert T., and Jorge E. Fernandez. "Syndromes of Mismanagement." *Journal for Quality and Participation* 25/3 (2002) 28–31.
Holeman, Virginia T. "Wesleyan Holiness and Differentiation of the Self: A Systems Approach." In *Wesleyan Theology and Social Sciences: The Dance of Practical Divinity and Discovery*, edited by M. Kathryn Armistead et al., 83–93. Newcastle upon Tyne: Cambridge Scholars, 2010.
Holeman, Virginia T., and Stephen L. Martyn. *Inside the Leader's Head: Unraveling Personal Obstacles to Ministry*. Nashville: Abingdon, 2008.
Holt, Bradley P. *Thirsty for God: A Brief History of Christian Spirituality*. 2nd ed. Minneapolis: Fortress, 2005.
House, Robert J., and Jane M. Howell. "Personality and Charismatic Leadership." *Leadership Quarterly* 3/2 (1992) 81–108.
Janis, Irving L. *Victims of Groupthink*. Boston: Houghton Mifflin, 1972.
Jennings, Theodore W., Jr. *Good News to the Poor: John Wesley's Evangelical Economics*. Nashville: Abingdon, 1990.
Johnson, Eric L. "Protecting One's Soul: A Christian Inquiry into Defensive Activity." *Journal of Psychology and Theology* 28/3 (2000) 175–89.

Kaplan, Robert E., and Robert B. Kaiser. "Developing Versatile Leadership." *MIT Sloan Management Review* 44/4 (2003) 18–26.

Kelman, Herbert C. "Compliance, Identification, and Internalization: Three Processes of Attitude Change." *Journal of Conflict Resolution* 2/1 (1958) 51–60.

———. "Further Thoughts on the Processes of Compliance, Identification, and Internalization." In *Perspectives on Social Power*, edited by James T. Tedeschi, 125–71. Chicago: Aldine, 1974.

Kernberg, Otto F. *Ideology, Conflict, and Leadership in Groups and Organizations.* New Haven, CT: Yale University Press, 1998.

———. "Pathological Narcissism and Narcissistic Personality Disorder." In *Disorders of Narcissism: Diagnostic, Clinical, and Empirical Implications*, edited by Elsa F. Ronningstam, 29–51. Washington, DC: American Psychiatric Association, 1998.

———. "Regression in Organizational Leadership." In *The Irrational Executive: Psychoanalytic Explorations in Management*, edited by Manfred F. Kets de Vries, 38–66. New York: International Universities Press, 1984.

———. *Severe Personality Disorders: Psychotherapeutic Strategies.* New Haven, CT: Yale University Press, 1986.

Kerr, Michael E., and Murray Bowen, *Family Evaluation: An Approach Based on Bowen Theory.* New York: Norton, 1988.

Kessler, Volker. "Leadership and Power." *Koers* 75/3 (2010) 527–50.

Kets de Vries, Manfred F. R. "Coaching the Toxic Leader." *Harvard Business Review* (2014) 100–109.

———. *The Leadership Mystique: Leading Behavior in the Human Enterprise.* Harlow, England: Prentice Hall, 2006.

———. "On Becoming a CEO: Transference and the Addictiveness of Power." In *Organizations on the Couch: Clinical Perspectives on Organizational Behavior and Change*, edited by Manfred F. Kets de Vries and Associates, 120–39. San Francisco, CA: Jossey-Bass, 1991.

Kets de Vries, Manfred F. R., and Danny Miller. "Narcissism and Leadership: An Object Relations Perspective." In *Leadership: Understanding the Dynamics of Power and Influence in Organizations*, edited by Robert P. Vecchio, 194–214. Notre Dame, IN: University of Notre Dame Press, 1997.

Kilian, Marcus K., and Stephen Parker. "A Wesleyan Spirituality: Implications for Clinical Practice." In *Spiritual Formation, Counseling, and Psychotherapy*, edited by Mark McMinn and Todd Hall, 201–13. New York: Nova Science, 2003.

King, Martin L., Jr. *Strength to Love.* Philadelphia: Fortress, 1963.

Knight, Henry H., III. *A Future for Truth: Evangelical Theology in a Postmodern World.* Nashville: Abingdon, 1997.

———. "Love and Freedom 'by Grace Alone' in Wesley's Soteriology: A Proposal for Evangelicals." *Journal of the Society for Pentecostal Studies* 24/1 (2002) 57–67.

———. "The Presence of God in the Christian Life: A Contemporary Understanding of John Wesley's Means of Grace." PhD diss., Emory University, 1987.

Kotter, John P., and James L. Heskett. *Corporate Culture and Performance.* New York: Free Press, 1992.

Kouzes, James M., and Barry Z. Posner. *The Leadership Challenge: How to Get Extraordinary Things Done in Organizations.* San Francisco: Jossey-Bass, 1987.

———. "Leadership Is a Relationship." In *Christian Reflections on the Leadership Challenge*, edited by James M. Kouzes and Barry Z. Posner, 119–26. San Francisco: Jossey-Bass, 2004.
Kretzschmar, Louise. "Authentic Christian leadership and Spiritual Formation in Africa." *Journal of Theology for Southern Africa* 113 (2002) 41–60.
———. "Cultural Pathways and Pitfalls in South Africa: a Reflection on Moral Agency and Leadership from a Christian Perspective." *Koers* 75/3 (2010) 567–88.
———. "The Education of Prospective Ministers as an Invitation to Life: Moving from Moral Failure to Moral Excellence through a Process of Moral Formation." *In die Skriflig/In Luce Verbi* 49/1 (2015) 1–10.
———. "Entering through the Narrow Gate and Walking the Hard Road: The Role of Christian Leaders in Exposing Moral Evil in the South African Workplace." *Koers* 79/2 (2014) 1–9.
———. "The Formation of Moral Leaders in South Africa: A Christian Ethical Analysis of Some Essential Elements." *Journal of Theology for Southern Africa* 128 (2007) 18–36.
———. "The Indispensability of Spiritual Formation for Christian Leaders." *Missionalia* 34(2/3) (2006) 338–61.
Kring, Ann M., et al. *Abnormal Psychology*. 12th ed. DSM 5 update. Hoboken, NJ: Wiley and Sons, 2014.
Land, Steven J. *Pentecostal Spirituality: A Passion for the Kingdom*. Sheffield: Sheffield Academic, 1994.
Lazarus, Richard S. *Emotion and Adaptation*. New York: Oxford University, 1991.
Leclerc, Diane. "Being Whole: Holiness and Sanctification as a Wesleyan Paradigm for Spiritual Formation." In *Spiritual Formation: A Wesleyan Paradigm*, edited by Diane Leclerc and Mark A. Maddix, 48–64. Kansas City: Beacon Hill, 2011.
———. "Finding the Means to the End: Christian Discipleship and Formation Practices." In In *Spiritual Formation: A Wesleyan Paradigm*, edited by Diane Leclerc and Mark A. Maddix, 74–86. Kansas City: Beacon Hill, 2011.
Leffel, G. Michael, et al. "Who Cares? Generativity and the Moral Emotions, Part 3: A Social Intuitionist 'Ecology of Virtue.'" *Journal of Psychology and Theology* 36 (2008) 202–21.
Lindström, Harald. *Wesley and Sanctification*. Nappanee, IN: Francis Asbury, 1980.
"List of Religious Leaders Convicted of Crimes." *Wikipedia*. http://en.wikipedia.org/wiki/List_of_religious_leaders_convicted_of_crimes.
Lodahl, Michael. "Wesley and Nature." In *Wesleyan Theology and Social Sciences: The Dance of Practical Divinity and Discovery*, edited by M. Kathryn Armistead et al., 21–32. Newcastle: Cambridge Scholars, 2010.
Loder, James E. *The Logic of the Spirit: Human Development in Theological Perspective*. San Francisco, CA: Jossey-Bass, 1998.
Lubit, Roy. *Coping with Toxic Managers*. New York: Prentice Hall, 2004.
———. "The Long-Term Organizational Impact of Destructively Narcissistic Managers." *Academy of Management Executive* 16/1 (2002) 127–38.
Main Mary, and Judith Solomon. "Procedures for Identifying Infants as Disorganised/Disoriented during the Ainsworth Strange Situation." In *Attachment in the Preschool Years: Theory, Research and Intervention*, edited by Mark T. Greenberg et al., 121–60. Chicago, IL: University of Chicago Press, 1990.

BIBLIOGRAPHY

Maas, Robin, and Gabriel O'Donnell. "An Introduction to Spiritual Theology: The Theory that Undergirds Our Practice." In *Spiritual Traditions for the Contemporary Church*, edited by Robin Maas and Gabriel O'Donnell, 303–19. Nashville: Abingdon, 1990.

Maccoby, Michael. "Narcissistic Leaders: The Incredible Pros, the Inevitable Cons." *Harvard Business Review* 78/1 (2000) 68–77.

———. *The Productive Narcissist: The Promise and Peril of Visionary Leadership*. New York: Broadway, 2003.

Madden, Deidre. "Medicine and Moral Reform: The Place of Practical Piety in John Wesley's Art of Physic." *Church History* 73/4 (2004) 741–58.

Maddix, Mark A. "John Wesley's Formational Experiences: Foundations for his Educational Ministry Perspectives." *Didache* 9/1 (2009) 1–8.

Maddox, Randy L. "The Enriching Role of Experience." In *Wesley and the Quadrilateral*, edited by W. Stephen Gunter et al., 107–127. Nashville, TN: Abingdon, 1997.

———. "Formation for Christian Leadership: Wesleyan Reflections." *American Theological Library Association Summary of Proceedings* 57 (2003) 114–26.

———. "John Wesley and Eastern Orthodoxy: Influences, Convergences, and Differences." *Asbury Theological Journal* 45/2 (1990) 29–53.

———. "Psychology and Wesleyan Theology: Precedents and Prospects for a Renewed Engagement." *Journal of Psychology and Christianity* 23/2 (2004) 101–9.

———. "Reconnecting the Means to the End: A Wesleyan Prescription for the Holiness Movement." *Wesleyan Theological Journal* 33/2 (1998) 29–66.

———. *Responsible Grace: John Wesley's Practical Theology*. Nashville: Kingswood, 1994.

Malphurs, Aubrey. *Being Leaders: The Nature of Authentic Christian Leadership*. Grand Rapids: Baker, 2003.

Marquardt, Manfred. *John Wesley's Social Ethics: Praxis and Principles*. Translated by John E. Steely and W. Stephen Gunter. Nashville: Abingdon, 1992.

Maxwell, John C. "Reflections on Model the Way." In *Christian Reflections on the Leadership Challenge*, edited by James M. Kouzes and Barry Z. Posner, 41–52. San Francisco: Jossey-Bass, 2004.

McClelland, David C. *Power: The Inner Experience*. New York: Irvington, 1975.

McFarlin, Dean B., and Paul D. Sweeney. *House of Mirrors: The Untold Truth about Narcissistic Leaders and How to Survive Them*. London: Kogan Page, 2000.

McGrath, Alister E. *Christian Theology: An Introduction*. 3rd ed. Oxford: Blackwell, 2001.

McIntosh, Gary L., and Samuel D. Rima. *Overcoming the Dark Side of Leadership: How to Become an Effective Leader by Confronting Potential Failures*. Rev. ed. Grand Rapids: Baker, 2007.

McNeil, Donald P., Douglas A. Morrison, and Henri J. M. Nouwen. *Compassion: A Reflection on the Christian Life*. Garden City, NY: Image, 1982.

McWilliams, Nancy. *Psychoanalytic Diagnosis: Understanding Personality Structure in the Clinical Process*. 2nd ed. New York: Guilford, 2011.

Meier, Elke A. "Shedding Light on a Muddled Field: A Christian Ethical Appraisal of Transforming and Transformational Leadership." MTh thesis, University of South Africa, 2014.

Miles, Rebekah L. "The Instrumental Role of Reason." In *Wesley and the Quadrilateral*, edited by W.Stephen Gunter et al., 77–106. Nashville: Abingdon, 1997.

Millon, Theodore. "DSM Narcissistic Personality Disorder." In *Disorders of Narcissism: Diagnostic, Clinical, and Empirical Implications*, edited by Elsa F. Ronningstam, 75–101. Washington, DC: American Psychiatric Association, 1998.

———, et al. *Personality Disorders in Modern Life*. 2nd ed. Hoboken, NJ: Wiley and Sons, 2004.

Moltmann, Jürgen. *The Spirit of Life: A Universal Affirmation*. Translated by Margaret Kohl. Minneapolis: Fortress, 1992.

Mulholland, M. Robert. *Invitation to a Journey: A Road Map for Spiritual Formation*. Downers Grove, IL: InterVarsity, 1993.

Newman, Barbara M., and Philip R. Newman. *Theories of Human Development*. New York: Psychology, 2007.

Newton, Kathryn S. "Social Class and Classism." In *Developing Multicultural Counseling Competence: A Systems Approach*, edited by Danica G. Hays and Bradley T. Erford, 159–88. 2nd ed. Boston: Pearson, 2014.

Nichols, Michael P. *Family Therapy: Concepts and Methods*. 8th ed. Boston: Pearson, 2008.

Northouse, Peter G. *Leadership: Theory and Practice*. 5th ed. Los Angeles: Sage, 2010.

Nouwen, Henri J. M. *Clowning in Rome: Reflections on Solitude, Celibacy, and Contemplation*. New York: Image, 1979.

———. *In the Name of Jesus: Reflections on Christian Leadership*. New York: Crossroad, 1989.

Nouwen, Henri J. M., Michael J. Christensen, and Rebecca J. Laird. *Spiritual Formation: Following the Movements of the Spirit*. New York: HarperCollins, 2010.

O'Boyle, Ernest H., Jr., et al. "A Meta-Analysis of the Dark Triad and Work Behavior: A Social Exchange Perspective." *Journal of Applied Psychology* 97/3 (2012) 557–79.

Oden, Thomas C. *John Wesley's Scriptural Christianity*. Grand Rapids: Zondervan, 1994.

Ogletree, Thomas W. "Agents and Moral Formation." In *The Blackwell Companion to Religious Ethics*, edited by William Schweiker, 36–44. Oxford: Blackwell, 2005.

O'Keefe, Daniel J. *Persuasion: Theory and Research*. Newbury Park, CA: Sage, 1990.

Okholm, Dennis. *Dangerous Passions, Deadly Sins: Learning from the Psychology of Ancient Monks*. Grand Rapids: Brazos, 2014.

———. "To Vent or Not to Vent: What Contemporary Psychology Can Learn from Ascetic Theology about Anger." In *Care for the Soul: Exploring the Intersection of Psychology and Theology*, edited by Mark R. McMinn and Timothy R. Phillips, 164–86. Downers Grove, IL: InterVarsity, 2001.

Oord, Thomas J. "Attaining Perfection: Love for God and Neighbor." In *Spiritual Formation: A Wesleyan Paradigm*, edited by Diane Leclerc, and Mark A. Maddix, 65–73. Kansas City: Beacon Hill, 2011.

———. "Love, Wesleyan Theology, and Psychological Dimensions of Both." *Journal of Psychology and Christianity* 31/2 (2012) 144–56.

———. *The Nature of Love: A Theology*. St. Louis: Chalice, 2010.

Ortberg, John. *The Life You've Always Wanted: Spiritual Disciplines for Ordinary People*. Grand Rapids: Zondervan, 2002.

Ortberg, Nancy. "Reflections on Enable to Act." In *Christian Reflections on the Leadership Challenge*, edited by James M. Kouzes and Barry Z. Posner, 85–98. San Francisco: Jossey-Bass, 2004.

Outler, Albert C. "Pietism and Enlightenment: Alternatives to Tradition." In *Christian Spirituality: Post-Reformation and Modern*, edited by Louis Dupre and Don E. Saliers, 240–56. World Spirituality 18. New York: Crossroad, 1996.

Paulhus, Delroy L., and Kevin M. Williams. "The Dark Triad of Personality: Narcissism, Machiavellianism and Psychopathy." *Journal of Research in Personality* 36 (2002) 556–563.

Peters, Ted. *Sin: Radical Evil in Soul and Society*. Grand Rapids: Eerdmans, 1994.

Pfeifer, Samuel. *Der sensible Mensch: Leben zwischen Begabung und Verletzlichkeit* (*The Sensitive Person: Life between Giftedness and Hurt*). Wuppertal: Brockhaus, 2002.

Post, Jerrold M. "Current Concepts of the Narcissistic Personality: Implications for Political Psychology." *Political Psychology* 14/1 (1993) 99–121.

Raven, Bertram H. "The Comparative Analysis of Power and Power Preference." In *Perspectives on Social Power*, edited by James T. Tedeschi, 172–98. Chicago: Aldine, 1974.

———. "The Bases of Power: Origins and recent developments." *Journal of Social Issues* 49/4 (1993) 227–51.

Reininger, Gustave. "The Christian Contemplative Tradition and Centering Prayer." In *Centering Prayer in Daily Life and Ministry*, edited by Gustave Reininger, 26–46. New York: Continuum, 1998.

Ridgway, James M. "Psychology." In *A Contemporary Wesleyan Theology: Biblical, Systematic, and Practical*, edited by Charles W. Carter, 2:875–950. Salem: Schmul, 1992.

Riemann, Fritz. *Grundformen der Angst: Eine tiefenpsychologische Studie* (*Fundamental Forms of Anxiety: A Psychoanalytic Study*). Munich: Ernst Reinhard, 1996.

Roberts, Robert C. *Spiritual Emotions: A Psychology of Christian Virtues*. Grand Rapids: Eerdmans, 2007.

Ronningstam, Elsa. "Narcissistic Personality Disorder." In *Oxford Textbook of Psychopathology*, edited by Paul H. Blaney and Theodore Millon, 752–71. New York: Oxford University Press, 2009.

Rosenbach, William E., and Marshall Sashkin. *The Leadership Profile: On Becoming a Better Leader*. Seabrook, MD: Ducochon, 2002.

Ross, Melanie. "Jonathan Edwards: Advice to Weary Theologians." *Scottish Journal of Theology* 59/1 (2006) 14–26.

Runyon, Theordore. *The New Creation: John Wesley's Theology Today*. Nashville: Abingdon, 1998.

Sankowsky, Dan. "The Charismatic Leader as a Narcissist: Understanding the Abuse of Power." *Organizational Dynamics* 23/4 (1995) 57–71.

Sashkin, Marshall. "The Visionary Leader: A New Theory of Organizational Leadership." In *Charismatic Leadership: The Elusive Factor in Organizational Effectiveness*, Jay A. Conger and Rabindra N. Kanungo, 120–60. San Francisco: Jossey-Bass, 1988.

Sashkin, Marshall, and William E. Rosenbach. "A New Vision of Leadership." In *Contemporary Issues in Leadership*, edited by William E. Rosenbach and Robert L. Taylor, 19–41. 5th ed. Boulder, CO: Westview, 2001.

Sashkin, Marshall, and Molly G. Sashkin. *Leadership That Matters: The Critical Factors for Making a Difference in People's Lives and Organizations' Success*. San Francisco: Berrett-Koehler, 2003.

Scazzero, Peter. *The Emotionally Healthy Leader: How Transforming Your Inner Life Will Deeply Transform Your Church, Team, and the World.* Grand Rapids: Zondervan, 2015.

———. *Emotionally Healthy Spirituality: Unleash a Revolution in Your Life in Christ.* Nashville: Thomas Nelson, 2006.

Schein, Edgar H. *Organizational Culture and Leadership.* 2nd ed. San Francisco: Jossey-Bass, 1992.

Schell, Bernadette H. *Management in the Mirror: Stress and Emotional Dysfunction in Lives at the Top.* Westport, CT: Quorum, 1999.

Schopenhauer, Arthur. *On the Basis of Morality.* Translated by E. F. J. Payne. Providence, RI: Oxford, 1995.

Schweitzer, Friedrich L. *The Postmodern Life Cycle: Challenges for Church and Theology.* St. Louis: Chalice, 2004.

Schore, Alan. *Affect Regulation and the Repair of the Self.* New York: Norton, 2003.

Shaver, Phillip R., and Mario Mikulincer. "Adult Attachment and Emotion Regulation." *Handbook of Emotion Regulation,* edited by James J. Gross, 237–50. 2nd ed. New York: Guilford, 2014.

Sheafer, Heather M. *The Narcissist Next Door: An Intimate Look at Narcissistic Culture.* Kindle ebook ed. N.p.: Page Turner, 2014.

Shrier, Paul, and Cahleen Shrier. "Wesley's Sanctification Narrative: A Tool for Understanding the Holy Spirit's Work in a More Physical Soul." *Pneuma* 31 (2009) 225–41.

Siegel, Daniel J. *The Developing Mind: How Relationships and the Brain Interact to Shape Who We Are.* 2nd ed. New York: Guilford, 2012.

Smith, R. Scott. "Christian Postmodernism and the Linguistic Turn." In *Christianity and the Postmodern Turn: Six Views,* edited by Myron B. Penner, 53–70. Grand Rapids: Brazos, 2005.

Steinke, Peter L. *How Your Church Family Works: Understanding Congregations as Emotional Systems.* New York: Alban Institute, 1993.

Stone, Michael H. "Normal Narcissism." In *Disorders of Narcissism: Diagnostic, Clinical, and Empirical Implications,* edited by Elsa F. Ronningstam, 7–28. Washington, DC: American Psychiatric Association, 1998.

Sue, Derald W. *Microaggressions in Everyday Life: Race, Gender, and Sexual Orientation.* Hoboken, NJ: Wiley and Sons, 2010.

———. *Multicultural Social Work Practice.* Hoboken, NJ: Wiley and Sons, 2006.

Sullivan, Harry S. *The Interpersonal Theory of Psychiatry.* New York: Norton, 1953.

Synan, Vinson *The Holinesss-Pentecostal Movement in the United States.* Grand Rapids: Eerdmans, 1971.

Taylor, Jeremy. "The Grace of Humility." In *Devotional Classics: Selected Readings for Individuals and Groups,* edited by Richard J. Foster and James B. Smith, 244–50. New York: Harper Collins, 1993.

Thompson, Curt. *Anatomy of the Soul: Surprising Connections between Neuroscience and Spiritual Practices That Can Transform your Life and Relationships.* Carroltown, TX: Tyndale, 2010.

Thompson, Matthew K. "Kingdom Come: Revisioning Pentecostal Eschatology." PhD diss., Luther Seminary, 2007.

Thompson, R. Duane. "Social Involvement: The Responsibility of God's People." In *A Contemporary Wesleyan Theology*, edited by Charles W. Carter, 2:689–732. Salem: Schmul, 1992.

Thunberg, Lars. "Eastern Christianity." In *Christian Spirituality: Origins to the Twelfth Century*, edited by Bernard McGinn et al., 1:291–312. New York: Crossroad, 1986.

Toegel, Ginka, and Jean-Louis Barsaux. "How to Become a Better Leader." *MIT Sloan Management Review* 53/3 (2012) 50–60.

Tracy, Wesley D. "Spiritual Direction in the Wesleyan–Holiness Tradition." In *Spiritual Direction and the Care of Souls: A Guide to Christian Approaches and Practices*, edited by Gary W. Moon and David G. Benner, 115–36. Downers Grove, IL: IVP Academic, 2004.

Twenge, Jean M., and W. Keith Campbell. *The Narcissism Epidemic: Living in the Age of Entitlement*. New York: Atria, 2009.

Vecchio, Robert P. "Power, Politics, and Influence." In *Leadership: Understanding the Dynamics of Power and Influence in Organizations*, edited by Robert P. Vecchio, 69–99. Notre Dame, IN: University of Notre Dame, 1997.

Veith, Gene E. *Postmodern Times—A Christian Guide to Contemporary Thought and Culture*. Wheaton, IL: Crossway, 1994.

Vest, Norvene. *Desiring Life: Benedict on Wisdom and the Good Life*. Cambridge, MA: Cowley, 2000.

Vickers, Jason E. "'And We the Life of God Shall Know': Incarnation and the Trinity in Charles Wesley's Hymns." *Anglican Theological Review* 90/2 (2008) 329–44.

———. "Wesley's Theological Emphases." In *The Cambridge Companion of John Wesley*, edited by Randy L. Maddox and Jason E. Vickers, 190–206. Cambridge: Cambridge University Press, 2010.

Villa-Vicencio, Charles. "Towards a Liberating Wesleyan Social Ethic for South Africa Today." *Journal of Theology for Southern Africa* 68 (1989) 92–102.

Wallin, David J. *Attachment in Psychotherapy*. New York: Guilford, 2007.

Wallis, Jim. *God's Politics: Why the Right Gets It Wrong and the Left Doesn't Get It*. San Francisco: Harper, 2005.

———. *The (Un)common Good: How the Gospel Brings Hope to a World Divided*. Grand Rapids: Brazos, 2013.

Walton, Robert C. *Chronological and Background Charts of Church History*. Grand Rapids: Zondervan, 1986.

Weems, Lovett H. *Leadership in the Wesleyan Spirit*. Nashville: Abingdon, 1999.

Wesley, John. *A Plain Account of Christian Perfection*. London: Epworth, 1952.

———. *The Works of John Wesley*. Vols. 1 and 5–7. 3rd ed. Originally published 1872. CD-ROM. AGES Software, 2000.

Westerfield Tucker, Karen B. "Wesley's Emphases on Worship and the Means of Grace." In *The Cambridge Companion to John Wesley*, edited by Randy L. Maddox, and Jason E. Vickers, 225–241. Cambridge: University, 2010.

White, James E. *The Church in an Age of Crisis: New Realities Facing Christianity*. Grand Rapids: Baker, 2012.

Wright, N. T. *After You Believe: Why Christian Character Matters*. Kindle ebook ed. New York: HarperCollins, 2010.

Yalom, Irvin D. *The Theory and Practice of Group Psychotherapy*. 4th ed. New York: Basic Books, 1995.

Yarhouse, Mark A., and James N. Sells. *Family Therapies: A Comprehensive Christian Appraisal*. Downers Grove, IL: IVP Academic, 2005.
Yrigoyen, Charles, Jr. *John Wesley: Holiness of Heart and Life*. Nashville: Abingdon, 1996.
Zeller, Eduard. *Outlines of the History of Greek Philosophy*. Translated by L. R. Palmer. 13th ed. New York: Dover, 1980.

www.ingramcontent.com/pod-product-compliance
Lightning Source LLC
Chambersburg PA
CBHW071231170426
43191CB00032B/1316